POSTMODERN APPROACHES TO THE SHORT STORY

Recent Titles in
Contributions to the Study of World Literature

Victorian Writers and the Image of Empire: The Rose-Colored Vision
Laurence Kitzan

Immigrant Narratives in Contemporary France
Susan Ireland and Patrice J. Proulx, editors

Aristocracies of Fiction: The Idea of Aristocracy in Late-Nineteenth-Century and Early Twentieth-Century Literary Culture
Len Platt

Salman Rushdie's Postcolonial Metaphors: Migration, Translation, Hybridity, Blasphemy, and Globalization
Jaina C. Sanga

Imagining Africa: Landscape in H. Rider Haggard's African Romances
Lindy Stiebel

Seduction and Death in Muriel Spark's Fiction
Fotini E. Apostolou

Unorthodox Views: Reflections on Reality, Truth, and Meaning in Current Social, Cultural, and Critical Discourse
James L. Battersby

Judgment and Justification in the Nineteenth-Century Novel of Adultery
Maria R. Rippon

The Late Modernism of Cormac McCarthy
David Holloway

The Colonial Conan Doyle: British Imperialism, Irish Nationalism, and the Gothic
Catherine Wynne

In My Own Shire: Region and Belonging in British Writing, 1840–1970
Stephen Wade

Multicultural Literature for Children and Young Adults: Reflections on Critical Issues
Mingshui Cai

POSTMODERN APPROACHES TO THE SHORT STORY

Edited by Farhat Iftekharrudin,
Joseph Boyden, Joseph Longo,
and Mary Rohrberger

Under the Auspices of the Society for the Study of the Short Story
Contributions to the Study of World Literature, Number 118

Westport, Connecticut
London

Library of Congress Cataloging-in-Publication Data

Postmodern approaches to the short story / edited by Farhat Iftekharrudin ... [et al.].
p. cm.—(Contributions to the study of world literature, ISSN 0738–9345 ; no. 118)
Includes bibliographic references and index.
ISBN 0–313–32374–7 (alk. paper)
1. Short story. I. Iftekharrudin, Farhat. II. Series.

PN3373 .P695 2003
809.3′1—dc21 2002072546

British Library Cataloguing in Publication Data is available.

Library of Congress Catalog Card number: 2002072546
ISBN: 0–313–32374–7
ISSN: 0738–9345

First published in 2003

Praeger Publishers, 88 Post Road West, Westport, CT 06881
An imprint of Greenwood Publishing Group, Inc.
www.praeger.com

Printed in the United States of America

The paper used in this book complies with the
Permanent Paper Standard issued by the National
Information Standards Organization (Z39.48–1984).

10 9 8 7 6 5 4 3 2 1

Contents

Preface

Psycholinguists have noted that a human child's first complex utterances are in story form. Extrapolating from this thesis, these scientists propose that we regard the short story, not the word, phrase, or sentence, as the most basic unit of human expression. Parallel to this finding and as far as scholars have been able to determine, the roots of the short story go back very far indeed. They are in Greek, Norse, Native American, African, and Celtic mythologies (to name a few). They are in the matter of Britain, France, and Rome; they are in the Biblical parables of the Old and New Testaments. It is even probable that they are within the oral traditions of prehistoric human interactions that took place around the first campfires of the first human communities.

However, these early narratives were likely different from the short stories we write today. In fact, most literary historians and short-story theorists date the short story as genre from the early nineteenth century when the impact of the prose narrative creations of Nathaniel Hawthorne and Edgar Allan Poe (in the United States), and Nikolai Gogol (in Russia) compelled literary theorists to find a name for a unique method of storytelling. In 1842, Poe's review of Hawthorne's *Twice Told Tales* described the kinds of stories that Hawthorne included in that collection, stories that had been previously published in different journals, thus, twice-told.

Poe's chapter remains a critical touchstone for many scholars engaged in short-story theory. Besides insisting that the short story be short enough to be read in one sitting, Poe emphasized that a primary characteristic of the short story, then called "tale," must be its unity of effect. In other words, all the elements within the composition of the tale ought to elicit from the reader one coherent response. Additionally, Poe remarked on submerged metaphors, which a reader, reading with a "kindred art" must find and understand before the meaning of the story would be understood. From its beginnings, then, the short story appropriated the tools and condensed imagery of poetry to create a compact, multivalent prose composition.

Arguably, the prototypical short story is "My Kinsman, Major Molineux," published by Hawthorne in 1832. Poe's and Gogol's stories with similar characteristics were not published until the 1840s. Washington Irving's stories that predate Hawthorne's are considerably looser in structure, thus not meeting the standards of condensation of imagery and multivalence. Delightful and popular as they are, Irving's stories are rightfully called tales.

Herman Melville, another American writer and contemporary of Hawthorne and Poe, published in 1856 *The Piazza Tales* in which he included stories that moved toward a more realistic dimension and thus marked a move away from the obsessed, even mythical characters of Hawthorne, Poe, and Gogol. "Benito Cereno" and "Bartleby, the Scrivener" are probably the best of these stories; at least, they are the most anthologized. Although highly symbolic and even mythic in their proportions, both stories contain a realistic depiction of scene and character and speak directly to the culture of the time.

But Melville did more than introduce realism in some of his stories. Just as important, he made use of subtle variations in point of view. "Benito Cereno" is probably the best example of a shifting viewpoint. In that story Melville uses a third-person narrator who is limited in omniscience at different points in the story. For example, a reader quickly identifies with the American captain, Amaso Delano, and like Delano misses important passages that complicate the reader's ability to "see" all that is happening on the ship. These subtle variations and shifts in position keep readers guessing about each of the characters and the roles they play, indeed, at times, actively misreading facts set before them.

What these authors seem to have discovered was a powerful new literary form derived from adhering to a dramatic plot development where setting, situation, and character are established through exposition. The plot then introduces complication; the action rises toward a climax or crisis, after which the action appears to descend toward some sort of questionable resolution. Imbedded in the text are patterns of subtle imagery that direct and delineate meaning.

In 1884, forty-two years after the publication of *Twice Told Tales,* seven years after Poe's death, and well after Melville's short stories were published, Brander Matthews, an esteemed literary critic and a creative writer himself, legitimized short-story criticism by announcing the birth of a new genre, the short-story, spelled with a hyphen as opposed to the story that is merely short. It is unfortunate that we did not continue to use the hyphen to distinguish between the short story and the narrative that was merely short. In her book, *Hawthorne and the Modern Short Story,* Mary Rohrberger distinguished between two kinds of short stories: what she called the "simple narrative" and the "short story proper." These two types of story are often identical in the development of plot from introduction to denouement; but the simple narrative lacks the complicated patterned and imagistic substructure of a short story proper. Rather, the simple narrative usually ends on an ironic reversal of some kind. Today, the terms "linear" and "spatial" seem better descriptors for the two types of story.

In the history of the short story, the apparent originators of the form—Hawthorne, Poe, Gogol, and Melville—continued to play important roles as the form of the short story shifted in line with literary and cultural changes. Writers like Mark Twain, Bret Harte, Kate Chopin, Stephen Crane, Henry James, Joseph Conrad, and Edith Wharton, in the United States, explored their worlds in a more realistic light. Conflicts in the writing of these authors usually arose from characters' interactions with the external world and the social forces within them. The narration was often objective, and the short stories of this period are notable for attention to detail and finely crafted plots. Most of the stories are linear; a good many are spatial like some of Conrad's, "Heart of Darkness," for example, and some of James' like "The Tree of Knowledge" and others often anthologized.

Perhaps one reason for the dominance of linear short stories during this time was the increasing number of popular magazines selling to an audience that enjoyed the finely crafted plots and simple ironic reversals that concluded each story. Another reason was surely the emergence of "How to Write the Short Story" books that focused on plot along with a corresponding deadening of interest in what Katherine Mansfield called the "plotty" story and Sherwood Anderson referred to as the "poison plot."

Just as Hawthorne, Poe, Gogol, and Melville had made immense changes in the form of the "tale," another revolutionary group of writers emerged to make similar changes. Russia's Anton Chekhov at the end of the nineteenth century, Ireland's James Joyce and New Zealand's Katherine Mansfield at the beginning of the twentieth century, and a decade or so later Middle America's Sherwood Anderson rejuvenated the form in such a way as to invent what came to be known as the "modern" short story, where plot became form often displayed in layers of symbolic imagery. Thus the total structure of a piece became a powerful conveyance for the rich and intense psychological connection among writer, character, and reader that ended in what seemed to be a shared experience, an experience that Joyce came to call "epiphany." Thus, by beginning stories in medias res, foregoing temporal development and devising associative layers of imagery and metaphor, these modernist authors and those who came after them fostered what seemed to be a new way to access mythic perception.

In a way, the short story returned to its beginnings with Hawthorne, Poe, and Melville, and now scholars could recognize that stories by Hawthorne like "The Hollow of the Three Hills," and "Wives of the Dead," at first thought to be merely sketches and Melville's diptych, "The Paradise of Bachelors and the Tartarus of Maids" (indeed, "The Incantadas") had plot structures similar to modern stories and thus needed to be interpreted in much the same way.

During the third and fourth decades of the twentieth century, the modern short story grew and gained force. Writers all over the Western world—Miguel de Unamuno, Luigi Pirandello, Thomas Mann, D.H. Lawrence, F. Scott Fitzgerald, William Faulkner, John Steinbeck, Isaac Bashevis Singer, Jean-Paul Sartre, Eudora Welty, Ralph Ellison, Shirley Ann Grau—to name just a few, excelled in the form, not only writing single stories published in magazines, journals, and book collections but also in the exploration of short-story cycles such as Joyce's *Dubliners*, Mansfield's *In a German Pension*, Anderson's *Winesburg, Ohio*, Hemingway's *In Our Time*, Faulkner's *Go Down, Moses*, Jean Toomer's *Cane*, and others.

In the 1950s and 1960s, possibly the greatest period of social and scientific upheaval in American history, there came another modal change in the short story. With Franz Kafka, Jorge Luis Borges, and Vladimir Nabokov as precursors and with John Barth, Robert Coover, William Gass, and others following, many short-story writers came to acknowledge that from a scientific point of view there is no guarantee that commonplace "reality" is "real." Consequently, with the loss of belief in the authenticity of the "real" world, a movement called "postmodernism" came to the fore. This is not to say that the "traditional" plot-based story disappeared or that the "modernist" story lost practitioners in great number. Rather, a mixture of the traditional and the modernist were published alongside of what was identified as "postmodern."

The postmodernists wrote stories that often: (1) merged "reality" and "illusion" to the point that distinctions became a matter of interpretation; (2) further blurred the line between "reality" and artifice through "fantasy," games, mimicry, parody; (3) called attention to themselves in an attempt to make authentic the act of knowing; and (4) used apparent disconnection and incongruity as techniques for creating coherence. Plots were either fully realized, represented as a base chain of events not necessarily causal, truncated, as in the modern story, or abandoned altogether (thus antistory).

Metafiction (telling a story about telling a story, etc.) was of special interest to the early postmodernist short-story writers, since the desire to address the text and even the writer within the text was different from what had become the conventional use of "reality" to ground the story. In fact, many writers viewed reality itself as a fiction, a mere construct. The narratives, therefore, made metaphysical sense by calling attention to themselves as artifice in an attempt to view our world through another lens.

Another development associated with postmodernism in the short story, and particularly with Gabriel García Márquez and Isabel Allende, is a movement called magical realism. This kind of story often presents reality as what is absurd, and the absurd, the magical, the transcendent as what is real. In fact, magical realism seems to be in a direct line to the folk traditions and myths of a distant past.

Some short-story theorists believe that another mode developed during the postmodern movement in the latter half of the twentieth century. However, just as many scholars believe that minimalism, as it is called, is not so much a break with modernism as it is a carryover from the Hemingway-type story with its sparseness of detail and objective stance. Writers considered minimalists are said to include Raymond Carver, Anne Beattie, Lorrie Moore, Richard Ford, Mary Robison, Rick Bass, and others. Some short-story scholars refer to minimalism as "dirty realism," since subject matter is usually limited to people of the lower- or lower-middle socioeconomic class where standards of living contribute to an overabundance of trailer parks, unkempt neighborhoods, polyester clothes, as well as leisure activities that stereotypically denote the under- or unemployed: frequent drinking, gaming, fighting, boredom, and so forth.

Postmodernism, as a mode of the contemporary short story, has been clearly established and recognized by short-story theorists, but postmodern "theory" (deconstruction, structuralism, reader response, semiotics, etc.), as pervasive as it has been among academics in the last half of the century, has not yet been applied to the short-story genre in any coherent way, likely because postmodern theorists make no distinctions among literary genres, treating short stories, novels, poems, and other storytelling media alike as narrative forms.

What we do have are various "postmodern theoretical approaches" being applied to the interpretation of short stories. By incorporating postmodern theoretical issues and themes, such as gender and sexual roles, cultural, postcolonial, linguistic, psychological, historical studies, and so forth into their interpretations of the short story, scholars and critics have enlarged the areas of their interests and their vocabularies.

This book is a collection of chapters using postmodern theoretical approaches to international short stories, be they in the traditional mode, the modern mode, or the postmodern mode. The chapters are revised versions of a selection of papers presented at the Biennial International Conference on the Short Story held in New Orleans, Louisiana, in July 1998 under the general sponsorship of The Society for the Study of the Short Story.

Acknowledgments

The editors gratefully acknowledge the help of the following individuals in the early and late stages of the preparation of this book: Rebecca Trainor, Aaron Nitzkin, Marcy Haynes, and Nicole Simpson. Many thanks go to Jaie Claudet for collecting and assembling the numerous components of this book, as well as preparing the original manuscript. Thanks also to Nichole Stanford for her tireless proofreading. Of course, without the aid of the editors at Greenwood Press and the authors whose work composes this anthology, this book would not have been possible. Thanks to all of you for contributing to our project.

Part I

Discovering the Shapes of the Short Story

Just as the individual story placement in a collection is vitally important to comprehension of the whole (an idea sharply articulated by Suzanne Ferguson in her study of Katherine Mansfield), so is an initial discussion of shapes of the short story. From Donna Jarrell's exploration of the "novel" embedded in Eudora Welty's "June Recital," to the "prism" effect of the elliptical short-story structure that Andrea O'Reilly Herrera reveals in Sandra Benítez's *A Place Where the Sea Remembers,* we see that postmodern approaches to short stories and short-story cycles illuminate underlying structure in even the most confounding forms.

Elsewhere in this section, David Sheridan's study of "alternate world fiction" of Jorge Luis Borges, Italo Calvino, and Steven Millhauser examines how postmodern literary techniques—elaboration, cataloguing, listing—help to shape these worlds. Sheridan also deals with the question of how to effectively "end" a world an author has created, a theme touched on in Arthur Brown's essay of Henry James' "The Beast in the Jungle." Though more forthrightly realistic than Sheridan's subjects, Brown presents James' notion of an "artistic consciousness" that survives death, "a life of far greater possibilities than those any mortal life could hold." It is this conflict between the immortality shaped by artificial fictional worlds and our conventional mortality that fuels the overall study of the shapes of the short story.

In pondering these shapes, it may be helpful to consider this thought from Brown: "the meaning of life depends on death—not to wrap things up or provide closure, so that we might walk away from life with meaning in hand—but to distinguish life itself from represented or figured or constructed life—in a word, from literature ..."

1

The Challenge of "June Recital": Generic Considerations in the Structure of *The Golden Apples*

Donna Jarrell

> A metronome was an infernal machine, Cassie's mother said when Cassie told on Virgie. 'Mercy, you have to keep moving, with that infernal machine. I want a song to *dip*' (40–41).

The story "June Recital," second of seven in Eudora Welty's 1949 work, *The Golden Apples* (18–85), is difficult to categorize generically. Its place in the collection of linked short stories has posed many questions of interpretation since its first appearance in *Harper's* in 1947. "June Recital" consumes nearly one-third of the 244-page volume and is nearly thirty pages longer than "The Wanderers," its closest challenge. It is not simply proportion or length that creates problems in responses to "June Recital." Approximately midway, it digresses from a story about Loch and Cassie Morrison into an expansive history of Cassie's spinster piano teacher, Miss Eckhart, and her relationship with her student, Virgie Rainey. As Suzanne Hunter Brown discusses in "Discourse Analysis and the Short Story" (217–248), the "reader can ... shift frames" to accommodate such a change in a story's direction (220). In the instance of "June Recital," however, we are left with the challenge of reconciling what Hunter Brown would call "incompatibilities" in "selected frame[s]" (223).

A closer examination of "June Recital" will demonstrate that Welty has essentially embedded a "novel-like" story about Miss Eckhart within a "short story" about Cassie Morrison. I contend that Cassie's epiphany, her initiation, could be effected without this elaborate development of Miss Eckhart, found primarily from pages 42–67. Here, the story deviates from its established generic frame and *dips* into the past. Using Cassie as narrator, it develops Miss Eckhart into what Frank O'Connor has described in his book *The Lonely Voice* as a novel-protagonist, a character placed "in opposition to society … then … mastered by it" (21). Although this novel-like movement may not be essential for the success of "June Recital" as a short story, it establishes Miss Eckhart as an unforgettable character, and places her "story" at the center of the structure of the seven-story sequence. In what Ian Reid termed "intratextual" framing in his essay "Destabilizing Frames for Story" (299–310), this memory of Miss Eckhart's life-fable emphasizes the role of "June Recital" within the collection. It also helps us understand the fates of Cassie Morrison and Virgie Rainey as revealed in "The Wanderers" (Welty 203–244), the final story in *The Golden Apples.*

"June Recital" opens recognizably as a short story: Loch Morrison, sick in bed with malaria, is using his father's telescope to view some surprising activities in the vacant house next door. Upstairs, he sees sixteen-year-old Virgie Rainey and her sailor-lover engage in an afternoon romp; downstairs, he watches a woman he presumes to be the sailor's mother busy herself scattering newspapers. He frames her actions as preparations for a party, but we understand her intention to burn down the house, at once identifying her as a "fallible" narrative center and beginning to recognize a plot beyond Loch's understanding.

At this point, the foundation for the short-story movement in "June Recital" is well laid. The reader has not only had the opportunity to draw on what Ian Reid would refer to as "circumtextual (or paratextual) markers" (301), such as the story's physical placement in a story collection, but also upon his personal "knowledge," or "extratextual frames" (307) to classify genre. Hunter Brown describes the process as "activat[ing] … a framework for meaning" (219). In other words, the reader facilitates comprehension of a text by sorting it into a particular category or schema early in the process.

As the "June Recital" continues, the point of view shifts from Loch to his sister Cassie, who is in her bedroom dyeing a scarf to wear on a hayride to Moon Lake that evening. Prompted by the signature theme of Beethoven's "Für Elise" coming from next door, she thinks about Virgie Rainey, whom she considers her "secret love, as well as her secret hate" (38). Virgie is a gifted musician, "full of the airs of wildness" who "sway[s] and gives way to joys and tempers" (38). This quality, along with her low social status, prevents her from securing approval and acceptance in Morgana.

Cassie also reflects on Miss Eckhart, a German immigrant, and the music teacher she and Virgie shared. Miss Eckhart used to live in the now derelict house, where she held an annual June piano recital. The reader soon realizes Miss Eckhart must be the old woman Loch has seen through his telescope in the downstairs of the house next door. She is not spreading the newspapers for her fire arbitrarily, but effecting a mockery of the way in which she decorated for each year's June recital.

Spontaneous and spirited, Virgie Rainey is the apparent antithesis of Miss Eckhart. A harsh, flat woman with rigid rules and a flyswatter she doesn't hesitate to crack across her students' hands, Miss Eckhart favors Virgie, who plays the piano with the genius and passion we suspect Miss Eckhart once expressed, but now represses. On this afternoon in June, Miss Eckhart's attempts to set a fire in her old studio are as awkward as her long-ago impromptu piano performance during a morning thunderstorm (49). In the last fifteen pages of the story, she manages to set her head on fire but is thwarted from igniting the house by two village men, Mr. Fatty Bowles and Old Man Moody, who afterwards guide her away without much dignity: "The old woman ... held on her head some nameless kitchen rag; she had no purse ... she wore shoes without stockings ... [she] had fallen down and they had to hold her on her feet" (Welty 77–78).

As Miss Eckhart is led away, the disheveled Virgie flees the house with her sailor. The two women—the town's notorious misfits—pass each other on the street. Watching now, with her brother, Cassie expects Virgie to acknowledge Miss Eckhart, but Virgie disappoints her. Later that night, after her hayride, Cassie thinks of the incident: "Both Miss Eckhart and Virgie Rainey were human beings terribly at large, roaming on the face of the earth. And there were others of them, human beings, roaming like beasts" (Welty 85). Here is Cassie's moment of insight, where she appears to realize not every individual succeeds in finding a social niche—that our humanity, in and of itself, doesn't guarantee acceptance, and that many people will spend their lives as misfits. She experiences an epiphany, another signal to classify "June Recital" as a short story.

Yet at nearly eighty pages, her "story" is by no means physically short, and the digression that so elaborately details Miss Eckhart's life in Morgana is itself (33–67) as long or longer than several of the other stories collected here. There is no question that this allowance for Miss Eckhart's development places an unusual demand on the structure of "June Recital." However, by taking this *dip* into Miss Eckhart's life, the author also confuses the reader's expectations. The reader is prompted to change the "activated ... framework for meaning" (Hunter Brown 219); a new schema is introduced, that of the novel.

Frank O'Connor observes that in the novel: "Time is [the author's] greatest asset; the chronological development of character or incident is essential" (21). In this dip into Miss Eckhart's past, we follow just such a paradigm. We are given an overview of the signature events in her life after her arrival in Morgana, sometimes in summary and sometimes in vivid vignette, and through these incidents we discover the complex character of Miss Eckhart.

We learn of her unconsummated affair with Mr. Sissum, Morgana's shoe salesman and cello player (44–49). Through Cassie's point of view, we watch Miss Eckhart allow Virgie to playfully, yet ceremoniously, adorn her with a floral wreath while she sits on a newspaper on the evening grass, listening to Mr. Sissum play the cello at the town political meetings (46). We hear Miss Eckhart's rare laughter from the delight she finds in Mr. Sissum's gift of a Billikin doll, a doll given away with every purchase of Billikin shoes by the department store where he works, a doll her mother spitefully breaks (47). We learn Miss Eckhart has pretty ankles for a large lady (44), and in a poignant moment, we see her public display of grief at Mr. Sissum's funeral after he has accidentally drowned. She "nods" her head at the people gathered at the cemetery, queerly, "increasing in urgency ... the way she nod[s] at pupils to bring up their rhythm, helping out the metronome" (48). These incidents reveal both her passion and her repression. Others demonstrate her entrapment, her deprivation, and her victimization.

One day when Virgie is using Miss Eckhart's piano to rehearse her lesson, Miss Eckhart's mother "screams" at Virgie, "Danke schoen, danke schoen, danke schoen!" (54), mocking the phrase Miss Eckhart often uses to express her pleasure with Virgie after she completes playing a piece of music. In response, Miss Eckhart walks calmly across the room and slaps her invalid, perhaps demented mother on the face, then invites Virgie and Cassie to stay for dinner. They refuse. In this scene, we understand that Miss Eckhart accepts her present situation—the responsibility that she has to care for a disabled parent and the sacrifice of that which she loves. However, she will not allow her mother to suppress Virgie Rainey's gift, as we suspect her mother may have once done to her.

As a German immigrant during World War I, Miss Eckhart is indeed the victim of circumstance, but she is also a victim of a crime. After an attack by a deranged African-American man, and her subsequent lack of "shame" (Welty 51), she is ostracized by the community. In a classic case of "blaming the victim," Cassie suggests that it is this incident, "perhaps more than anything ... that people could not forgive Miss Eckhart" (Welty 51). Eventually the mothers in the community, with the exception of Mrs. Morrison, will not allow their daughters to take lessons from Miss Eckhart. Before this time comes, however, she hosts an annual June recital, an elaborate occasion, where "all of her pupils ... [partake] of the grace of Virgie Rainey" (67).

In this novel-like movement in the story, Miss Eckhart is a protagonist set in conflict with the community—a German in the United States, a yankee in the South, an old maid among families, an artist living in repression. Her conflicts are numerous and allow for a wide range of reader identification, which O'-Connor also posits as novelistic (17). However, in the short-story movement, in which Cassie is the protagonist, Miss Eckhart's contribution is less that of a protagonist and more that of a catalyst. Her imprisonment—within the community and within herself—her alienation, and her relationship with Virgie Rainey are used to facilitate Cassie's epiphany. Surely she could have served in this capacity without appropriating such a disproportionate amount of story time and space.

The "incompatibilit[y]" in these two seeming movements (Hunter Brown 223)—"story" and "novel"—prompts us to take a closer look at the structure of "June Recital." If this elaborate digression into Miss Eckhart's life is not essential for the success of "June Recital" as a short story, why would Welty include this novel-like dip? In a letter quoted in *Katherine Anne Porter: A Life,*

Porter refers to *The Golden Apples* as formally self-indulgent (311). I disagree. I believe the digression in "June Recital" is essential for the collective impact of these seven stories. Although the stories may have been published individually at one time (Harris 131), this fact does not preclude Welty from having had a broader picture in mind, if not from the outset of writing, certainly by some point in their creation. In fact, "June Recital" was originally published under the title "Golden Apples" in the September 1947 issue of *Harper's Bazaar,* where it already had both "movements"—with some difference in details.

The necessity for the reader to "shift frames" created by Welty's novel-like excursus into Miss Eckhart's past encourages the reader to "*reduce*" her life-fable into a familiar schema, enabling its storage in long-term memory (Hunter Brown 220; 217). "[A]ctive ... as well as retrospective interpretation," writes Hunter Brown, "relies on memory" (223). This well-established memory of Miss Eckhart resonates throughout *The Golden Apples* and contributes to its overall cohesion, forming what Robert Luscher refers to in his essay "The Short Story Sequence: An Open Book" (148–167) as the "larger unifying strategies" (149). Ian Reid, in the essay mentioned earlier, discusses the links between stories in a sequence as "intratextual" framing (302). In this sequence, Miss Eckhart acts as what he terms "a part-for-whole-mirror" and provides a "proleptic framing" (302) of the fates of Cassie Morrison and Virgie Rainey as revealed in the final story "The Wanderers."

While Cassie is dyeing her scarf for the hayride and reflecting on Miss Eckhart and Virgie Rainey, we learn that she, rather than Virgie, has been awarded the town's musical scholarship (56). As a result, she resigns herself to a future in which she will take Miss Eckhart's place giving piano lessons in the community. What Cassie doesn't see, but what might be foreseen in the concluding page of the story, is her future as a full-blown version of Miss Eckhart. When Cassie comes home from her excursion to Moon Lake, she thinks about the incident with Miss Eckhart and Virgie Rainey that occurred that afternoon. She considers her behavior at the lake and is proud that she has allowed no one to touch her. Yet, as she sleeps, as her conscious guard is lowered, she dreams a Yeats poem—"all of it passed through her head, through her body" (85).[1] Through this symbolism of Cassie's emotion, we see the authenticity of her ambivalence toward Virgie Rainey (her "secret love ... her secret hate") (Welty 38).

In the next two lines of the story, Cassie sits up in bed and recites the final line of the poem, the last words, "'*Because a fire was in my head.*'" Again, we have a symbolic representation of emotions, of passion. Cassie goes back to sleep, dreaming about a "grave, unappeased, and radiant face ... the face that was in the poem" (Welty 85)—the face of her own repressed feelings and passion. One cannot be surprised then to learn in Welty's closing story, "The Wanderers," that Cassie has become an old maid. She lives in her home among boarders, tending to the memory of her parents and giving piano lessons, an existence more than vaguely reminiscent of that of the tragic Miss Eckhart. Nor is it surprising that the untamable Virgie Rainey continues to defy the community's expectations and intends to leave Morgana now that her own mother has passed away.

In "June Recital," Eudora Welty has written a short story about Cassie Morrison containing the novel-like narrative of Miss Eckhart. In the short story, Miss Eckhart and Virgie Rainey serve as catalysts for Cassie Morrison's epiphany. However, Miss Eckhart could serve the story in this capacity without such an expansive development. Cassie's epiphany is one of several cues encouraging the reader to classify "June Recital" as a short story, but the elaborate digression into Miss Eckhart's life encourages the reader to dip into a "novel" schema. These "incompatibilities" in "selected frame[s]" (Hunter Brown 223) have posed problems for readers and critics from the first publication of the story. Though Welty's dip isn't essential to the short-story movement, it helps the reader to frame *The Golden Apples* in its entirety and enables us to understand Cassie and Virgie's fate as revealed in "The Wanderers."

NOTE

1. This poem is Yeats' "The Song of Wandering Aengus." Its role in "June Recital" and *The Golden Apples* is discussed at length in Patricia S. Yaeger's essay, "'Because a Fire Was in My Head': Eudora Welty and the Dialogic Imagination," originally published in *PMLA*, 99 (October 1984), 955–973.

WORKS CITED

Givner, Joan. *Katherine Anne Porter: A Life.* New York: Simon & Schuster, 1982.

Harris, Wendell V. "The Thematic Unity of Welty's *The Golden Apples.*" *The Critical Response to Eudora Welty's Fiction.* Ed. Laurie Champion. Westport, Conn.: Greenwood Press, 1994. 131–134.

Hunter Brown, Suzanne. "Discourse Analysis and the Short Story." *Short Story Theory at a Crossroads.* Eds. Susan Lohafer and Jo Ellyn Clarey. Baton Rouge: Louisiana State University Press, 1989. 217–248.

Luscher, Robert M. "The Short Story Sequence: An Open Book." *Short Story Theory at a Crossroads.* Eds. Susan Lohafer and Jo Ellyn Clarey. Baton Rouge: Louisiana State University Press, 1989. 148–167.

O'Connor, Frank. *The Lonely Voice: A Study of the Short Story.* Cleveland: World, 1962.

Reid, Ian. "Destabilizing Frames for Story." *Short Story Theory at a Crossroads.* Eds. Susan Lohafer and Jo Ellyn Clarey. Baton Rouge: Louisiana State University Press, 1989. 299–310.

Welty, Eudora. *The Golden Apples.* New York: Harcourt, 1949.

Yaeger, Patricia M. "Because a Fire Was in My Head": Eudora Welty and the Dialogic Imagination." *Mississippi Quarterly: The Journal of Southern Culture.* 39 (1986): 561–586.

2

The End of the World: Closure in the Fantasies of Borges, Calvino, and Millhauser

David Sheridan

In *The Sense of an Ending*, Frank Kermode formulates a theory of closure based on Apocalyptic thinking; how narratives end, for Kermode, can be understood by examining how we mythologize the end of the world; but what about works that are involved in constructing worlds? Such works, it would seem, have a double duty to perform—not only do they need to end a world, but they first need to create one. Fictions by fantasists such as Jorge Luis Borges, Italo Calvino, and Steven Millhauser are frequently concerned with building alternate worlds for the reader—worlds that, like our own, are infinite. Since the infinite is, by definition, without end, closure for these fictions represents a special problem. This paper will explore the narrative strategies employed by these writers to provide an end for the endless.

RETHINKING CLOSURE

> The reader should be carried forward, not merely or chiefly by the mechanical impulse of curiosity, not by a restless desire to arrive at the final solution, but by the pleasurable activity of the journey itself.
>
> —Coleridge

Life is messy; art is neat. Although much recent experimentation challenges this assumption, it cannot be denied that one of the main qualities we look for in art is what we don't find in life: order, form, integrity. A sense of closure is perhaps the single most important ingredient for generating a sense of neatness. Art, as Aristotle says, should be *teleological,* should build toward some goal and should take its shape from that process of building. Though he does not use the term, Frank Kermode argues that this desire for teleology is a manifestation of our larger desire for shape and form in the historical narrative of which our lives are part. It is not satisfying, Kermode says, to live "in the middest"—in the middle of an amorphous historical narrative with no beginning or end, a history that stretches indefinitely before and after a present moment. Therefore we create "concord fictions" such as the biblical stories of Genesis and the Apocalypse, which give history a shape. "The end changes all," Kermode says (47). When we feel the end is near, time ceases to be *chronos*—"one damn thing after the next"—and becomes *kairos,* a "moment of crisis ... a point in time filled with significance, charged with meaning derived from its relation to the end" (47). *Kairos* "is the time of the novelist," Kermode says (46).

John Dewey, thirty years before Kermode, articulates the same argument in less theological terms. In *Art as Experience,* Dewey makes a distinction between "experience," which roughly corresponds with Kermode's "middest," and which "occurs continuously," and "*an* experience" which "is a whole and carries with it its own individualizing quality and self sufficiency." The ending of such an experience "is a consummation not a cessation" (35); this is the matrix, Dewey claims, for the aesthetic experience. Barbara Herrnstein Smith, in her famous study of the subject, echoes Dewey, warning that "there is a distinction ... between concluding and merely stopping or ceasing" (1–2). "Closure" for Smith, is that "sense of stable conclusiveness, finality, or 'clinch'"; it is "distinctly gratifying" (2) and part of what gives a work of art the all-important sense of "integrity" (24–25).[1]

But we need to back up a moment and reread Coleridge's claim that seems to downplay the importance of the end. Perhaps closure is not necessary after all. Thomas Leitch makes such an argument in "The End of the End." Stories, Leitch says, need not be teleological to provide a satisfying aesthetic experience. Their first order of business is to "be tellable," a phrase Leitch borrows from Mary Louise Pratt, thus providing a broader criterion than is attached to the word *telos.* Some stories, like the postmodern experiments of Donald Barthelme, succeed despite the fact that they do not build toward a goal and do not provide a sense of closure as they end. Barthelme's stories are "tellable" because they embrace the value of "elaboration" (Pratt 136; qtd. in Leitch 140); they "flesh out" the world for us, "cataloguing" its objects (140). As Leitch reminds us, the values of *telos* and elaboration are not mutually exclusive; all great works involve both, though often one value is privileged over the other. Leitch cites Barthelme's concept of the "trash phenomenon" which has an "endless" quality. "It is just there," Leitch says, "like a pile of Christmas gifts waiting to be unwrapped, thrown together for the moment in a context that emphasizes their objecthood at the expense of their meaning" (141). Leitch concludes, "In Barthelme's work, a situation need imply no *telos,* neither an intelligible plot, nor a coherent rationale, if it is worth displaying for its own sake" (141). I would argue that much alternate world fiction (AWF) privileges this value of elaboration, often, indeed, falling into a catalogue or listing mode in order to get the alternate world on the page as efficiently as possible. We appreciate AWFs to a large degree not because of how they are shaped or defined by their ultimate goal, but because they present us with one striking elaboration after another. They are worth displaying for their own sake. They amaze, marvel, surprise us as they fill in the canvas with what Leitch labels "bright and eye-catching" details (141). The journey through these amazing worlds is the important thing, not how that journey ends.

LISTS AND THE RHETORIC OF NONNARRATIVE FORMS

Despite the fact that AWFs embrace the formal value of elaboration, they do usually achieve some degree of closure, and the rest of this essay explores some common strategies enlisted in this service. Borges' "The Aleph" will help launch this discussion.

About two-thirds of the way through "The Aleph"—which until this point has been a more or less traditional realistic story—Carlos Argentino Daneri informs the narrator that in his basement there is a tiny world called the Aleph, which contains all things and all time and which allows one to experience all of its contents simultaneously. Overcome by curiosity, the narrator descends into Argentino's basement to experience the amazing Aleph. Because this is one of Borges' *ficciones* and not a realistic story, the narrator does in fact find the promised phenomenon. At this point, the narrative dissolves into a list, a catalogue of what the Aleph reveals. This is the paradigm for world construction.

AWFs are fictions of elaboration, and the most efficient means of elaborating is the list. An inquiry into the way AWFs end needs to begin with an examination of listing as an aesthetic mode. Lists have a tendency (not to say a mandate) to be static, monotonous, and random. In the sequence, "apples, strawberries, pears, peaches, bananas," for instance, there is no movement, no surprise, and no formal or thematic logic beyond the obvious implied heading "common fruits." Lacking this logic, its end is arbitrary, a "cessation" not a "consummation."

If the builder of a world is going to rely on the list as an aesthetic mode, then, the odds are against him from the outset. Yet as soon as one acknowledges the pitfalls of listing, one sees that, if a writer is skillful, they can be avoided. Smith discusses this possibility vis-à-vis Ralegh's famous poem, "The Lie," which is basically a list of things that should be "given the lie." Ralegh's poem avoids what Smith (after the Gestalt psychologists) calls "saturation" by clever variation (42). Ralegh "avoids the poetic problems that are entailed by the repetitiveness of ... [an intensely paratactic] structure" by approaching the items in the list sometimes figuratively, sometimes literally, sometimes through "personified abstractions," sometimes through "synecdoches," and so forth; in short, "although each refrain is never wholly a surprise, the variations prevent us from predicting its exact form" (106). This negotiation between surprise and monotony is exactly what we find in the paratactic forms AWFs often adopt. Consider, for instance, the beginning of the list in "The Aleph": "I saw the teeming sea; I saw daybreak and night fall; I saw the multitudes of America; I saw a silvery cobweb in the center of a black pyramid; I saw a splintered labyrinth (it was London)" (27). On the face of it, this passage should be monotonous. It is, after all, a list of "I saw"s, and we already know, roughly, what will be seen: items from the "real world," for the Aleph is a derivative world, a mere condensation of our own. And yet the list, which spans over a page, avoids monotony, largely by employing the kind of variation Smith discovers in Ralegh's poem. Every item is partly expected, partly a surprise. We open with a teeming sea: an image at once concrete and primordial, recalling cosmogonies such as that found in Genesis. Then we are hit with the concepts of "daybreak and night fall"—not concrete objects, but temporal phenomena, yet equally primordial, again recalling the first day and night of Genesis. Then we get "the multitudes of America" which is not primordial, but relates to the previous two items because it is generic and archetypal. The next item—"a silvery cobweb in the center of a black pyramid"—surprises us by the contrast it provides: it is hyper-specific, concrete, imagistic. Labyrinth relates to pyramid easily enough—they are both icons of ancient Egypt; yet as soon as we make that connection, we are surprised by the reversal in parentheses: this is a figurative labyrinth, not a literal one. And so on. The list Borges offers is a carefully constructed sequence in which the dynamics of expectation/formation and surprise are carefully modulated.

This kind of progression has significant implications for a study of closure. Smith tells us a common device of closure is "terminal modification," the best illustration of which is the Shakespearean sonnet, which achieves closure when the ABAB rhyme becomes in the last couplet GG (81). In a simple list, we could easily employ the device Smith describes. Apples, oranges, peaches, and ... bicycles! The problem for Borges here is that he has made variation the norm. How will terminal modification be experienced as a special modification and not merely another variation that we've come to expect? An examination of the final lines of the list will provide answers:

> I saw the rotted dust and bones that had once deliciously been Beatriz Viterbo; I saw the circulation of my own dark blood; I saw the coupling of love and the modification of death; I saw the Aleph from every point and angle, and in the Aleph I saw the earth and in the earth the Aleph and in the Aleph the earth; I saw my own face and my own bowels; I saw your face; and I felt dizzy and wept. (28)

Before the narrator launches into this list, he observes: "What my eyes beheld was simultaneous, but what I shall now write down will be successive, because language is successive" (26). Borges exploits this successiveness in order to make order out of the chaos of the Aleph. The reference to Beatriz Viterbo (the narrator's recently deceased lover) is important in several ways. First, because it is a reference to death—what Smith calls a "closural allusion" (61). Also, because death is itself a dramatic event, it tends to boost the energy level of this sequence, forming a kind of rising action. Beatriz holds special meaning for the narrator and therefore the mere invocation of her name is felt as a rising. Then we are confronted with the Aleph itself as an item, which is a different kind of surprise than the reader expects: we expect something *in* the Aleph, not the Aleph itself.[2] We are surprised yet again, when the narrator addresses the reader directly, for the first (and last) time in the narrative. Although everything in the list is to an extent surprising, this violation of the "fourth wall" is felt as a different kind of surprise, and therefore functions as a kind of "terminal modification." In this case, there is the added feeling of three worlds being bridged: the world of the Aleph, the world of the story that contains the Aleph, and the world of the reader. This inclusive bridging results in a sense of "ultimate integration," which itself signals closure: all relevant worlds have been reconciled; now we are finished.

As Smith points out, in Ralegh's poem the thematic progression of the list is supported by the formal features of the language. In order to avoid monotony, the syntax of each new item is varied, and this variation allows a general pattern to emerge. For instance, the items tend to get expressed in progressively longer units, supporting the sense of "rising action," noticeably transitioning from a five-word line to the twenty-nine word penultimate line:

> I saw the teeming sea . . .
> I saw the Aleph from every point and angle, and in the Aleph I saw the earth and in the earth the Aleph and in the Aleph the earth

Thus, the final item, "I saw your face," is formally, as well as thematically, a terminal modification, since the expectation is for a longer—not shorter—syntactic expression than the previous one.

The list in "The Aleph" occurs within a larger narrative; but what about the many AWFs that appear to consist entirely as an extended list? One such work is the story "Cathay" by Steven Millhauser, which can be described as a list of the contents and qualities of the alternate world named in the title. The opening line of the story establishes the paradigm for the entire work: "The twelve singing birds in the throne room of the Imperial Palace are made of beaten gold, except for the throats, which are of silver, and the eyes, which are of transparent emerald-green jade" (147). Nothing happens here; we are presented with a static object that exists outside of time. The story is told in a series of subtitled sections—"Singing Birds," "Clouds," "Hourglasses"—all of which treat an object, person, or phenomenon that help to "flesh out" this alternate world. The sections are all relatively short, the longest being about two pages. Although bits of narrative enter the story at times, there is an overwhelming sense of stasis. The sections are not chapters in a narrative; they do not tell what happens next. Instead, they simply introduce a new item in the list.

Like the list in Borges' "The Aleph," this list proceeds by controlled variation, both of formal and thematic features. One formal feature that is varied to stave off saturation is length. Most sections are one-half to one and a half pages long, but we are surprised when we stumble on the section "Blue Horses," which consists only of a short fragment: "The emperor's blue horses in a field of white snow" (160)—a simple haiku amidst a plethora of almost gaudy invention. The kind of phenomena treated also varies: some sections focus on objects, some on people, some on abstractions such as "Summer Nights," "Yearning," "Sorrow." The one thing that never changes from item to item is the striking inventiveness of each new component: we are happy to get a guided tour of Cathay and we do not, as Coleridge warns us, get overly anxious for an end.

Nevertheless, the story does secure closure in a variety of ways. Although most sections are static, the terminal section is a narrative that forms an autonomous story of its own. The mere change from static description to narrative is itself another example of terminal modification, and thus helps secure a sense of closure. This anecdote concerns a contest between two magicians, "a vigorous man of ripe years" and "an old man with a white beard" (162).[3] The switch to narrative opens up all devices native to that mode, and, since the end of this section coincides with the end of the larger work, the closure achieved by this section helps secure a parochial, as well as local, sense of closure. This particular narrative belongs to a subgenre—that of contests—in which closure is normally secured when we discover who wins.

But there are more global and more interesting forces of closure at work. This is a story about a marvelous world called Cathay, but it is also a story about *the nature of the marvelous.* It is a work of art, but it is also a meditation on the nature of art. The story incorporates the implied question, "What are the qualities of a satisfying aesthetic experience?" And this query puts us into a familiar pattern on which many works are founded. A question has been raised; the story can end when it has provided an answer (or when it has proved the question unanswerable).

These questions about "aesthetic experience" and the marvelous are never addressed directly in the catalogue of Cathay's contents; but they are raised and discussed indirectly on every page. In a section called "Concubines," for instance, we find a meditation on the art of love, which

> appears to depend to a large part upon the erotic paradoxes of transparent concealment and opaque revelation. Mirrors, silks, the dark velvet of rugs and coverlets, transparent blue pools in the concealed courtyard, scarves and sashes, veils, scarlet and jade light through colored glass, shadows, implications, illusions, duplicities of disclosures, a profound understanding of monotony and surprise—such are the tools of the concubine's art. (151)[4]

This meditation on the art of love serves as a short treatment of the dynamics of monotony and surprise. As such, the story provides an oblique reflection on its own method and provides a tentative answer to how the larger story of which it is a part can be successful.

The aforementioned section is immediately followed by one called "Boredom," a clever juxtaposition, since boredom is the effect of monotony:

> Our boredom, like our zest, can only be as great as our lives. How much greater and more terrible, then, must be the boredom of our Emperor, which flows into every corridor of the palace, spills into the parks and gardens, stretches to the utmost edges of our unimaginably vast empire, and, still not exhausted, but perhaps even strengthened by such exercise, rises to the height of heaven itself. (151)

This section highlights the problem of saturation—a key aesthetic problem in the story itself. Confronted with one marvelous thing after the next, what keeps us from getting bored? The final section, "The Contest of Magicians," achieves closure in part because it provides the ultimate answer to the question. The contest, of course, is an empire-wide competition to discover the best magician. Eventually the contestants are narrowed down to the old and young magicians mentioned above. The younger one performs first, turning a statue into a living girl—an amazing trick, even by the standards of Cathay. On the older magician's turn there is a moment of keen suspense when, just like the first magician, he asks for a statue. Then the older magician does not merely transform the inanimate statue into a living woman, as his rival does; instead he creates a "living statue" of whom "some said her arms were jade, yet warm, and some said her arms were flesh, yet stony cold" (164). The old magician wins the contest because a living statue, combining both the natural and the artificial, is more satisfying than a living person. What makes a satisfying aesthetic experience? What makes a thing marvelous? Closure is achieved because the work seems to provide an ultimate or definitive answer to these questions, which, loosely paraphrased, is "an intermingling of artifice and nature, of imagination and reality."

By definitive answer I do not mean a conclusion that is "actually true." I mean, instead, what Smith calls "the sense of truth" that is defined as a "certain quality that is experienced by the reader as striking *validity*, a quality that leaves him [sic] with the feeling that what has just been said has the 'conclusiveness,' the settled finality, of apparently self-evident truth" (152). Whether we agree with this "conclusion" after we consider it philosophically is beside the point.

The tension between art and nature is itself one of the primary themes of "Cathay"; indeed, one way the terminal image of the living jade statue achieves closure is that it reminds us of the opening image of the clockwork birds of beaten gold with their eyes of "emerald-green jade." We are told that "it is known that the tones are produced by an inner mechanism containing a minute crystalline pin," but "the shape and motions of the birds are so lifelike that they might easily be mistaken for real birds were it not for their golden forms, and many believe that it was to avoid such a mistake, and to increase our wonder, that the birds were permitted in this manner alone to retain the appearance of artifice" (148). The final image, then, is both cyclical—because it returns to the opening theme of the book—and progressive—because it provides a more striking commingling of artifice and nature. The birds are good fakes; the living statue woman is a new kind of being, part organic creature, part sculpture.

But what should we think about a list that extends not the length of a page or a short story, but an entire book? The premise for Italo Calvino's *Invisible Cities* is that Marco Polo is describing for Kublai Kahn all the cities he has visited. Almost the entire book consists of short sections, each devoted to describing a separate city. Each city is named, and its essence is communicated. The work, proceeding largely through elaboration, succeeds because the cities themselves are "bright" and "eye-catching," like gift-wrapped Christmas presents. And, as in the other lists, controlled variation keeps the reader engaged and makes sure saturation does not set in.

One interesting formal strategy employed by Calvino to solve the problems of formlessness and monotony, and ultimately of closure, is revealed on the title page. I have tried here to reproduce the typography as faithfully as possible:

1	
5	. . . . .
7	Cities and memory. 1.
8	Cities and memory. 2.
9	Cities and desire. 1.
10	Cities and memory. 3.
12	Cities and desire. 2.
13	Cities and signs. 1.
15	Cities and memory. 4.
17	Cities and desire. 3.
19	Cities and signs. 2.
20	Thin Cities. 1.
21	. . . . .
2	
27	. . . . .
30	Cities and memory. 5.
32	Cities and desire. 4.
34	Cities and signs. 3.
35	Thin Cities. 2.
36	Trading Cities. 1.
38	. . . . .

A quick glance at these first two sections as they appear in the table of contents reveals that this list is intricately constructed. The titles shown here—"Cities and memory," and so forth—are not the names of individual cities, but are types of cities. Each type gets introduced into the overall sequence and then dropped according to a strict pattern. All of the middle sections follow the pattern represented in the second section; that is, sections 2–8 all open with a treatment of the frame setting (indicated by the dots) and then proceed to the fifth example of a particular category, and the fourth example of the next category, and so on. Each section ends with the introduction of a new category and the promise of another section. The terminal section is the inverse of the opening sequence: it contains the same number of categories, but opens with the *fifth* example. If we list the category numbers side by side, we can see the correspondence:

1.	5.
2.	4.
1.	3.
3.	2.
2.	5.
1.	4.
4.	3.
3.	5.
2.	4.
1.	5.

Because these sequences are different from the ones in the middle sections, they function as frames just as the opening and closing stanzas in Ralegh's "The Lie." But closure is secured in other ways too. The opening sequence is dominated by the figure "1," emphasizing beginnings. The closing sequence is concerned with filtering out, according to its mathematical pattern, the early examples, and thus is dominated by the figure "5" (which has already been established as the terminal number), until finally it ends with that figure, the final fifth of the final sequence. Calvino's list of cities is much longer than anything we've examined so far, and his formal structure is the most rigid. In fighting the aesthetic dangers of formlessness, which multiply over time, Calvino takes special pains to order and shape our experience; each fifth example in the terminal section of the book functions like a period; after such an extensive list, multiple periods are needed to reinforce adequately our sense of closure.

One final closural strategy native to lists deserves comment here. In the recent Hollywood remake of *Cyrano de Bergerac* (*Roxanne,* 1987), there is a scene in which CD (played by Steve Martin) is the butt of a joke about his oversized nose. Since CD negotiates life by means of his clever wit, his defense is to beat the joker at his own game. He tells the joker to throw a dart at the dartboard and he will tell as many long-nose jokes as the number the dart lands on. The joker gets lucky, however, and hits a high number. Not only does CD need to spontaneously invent a relatively high number of jokes, but his defense will only work if the jokes are actually funny. The tension in this scene is keen: we are acutely curious to see if CD can fulfill his quota; closure is achieved when CD comes through with the final joke. A similar principle operates in all AWF, but especially in *Invisible Cities,* a long work that promises from the outset it will provide X number of marvelous cities—five cities of memory, five of desire, etc. This becomes a tension building device after we read about the first city and recognize the amazing inventiveness involved in its construction. Now we are curious to know if Calvino will be able to make good on his promise: Will he be able to provide us with another city that meets the standards of inventiveness and amazement established in the first one? When we confront the final city and it does indeed fulfill this promise, we experience closure. Calvino has won the bet.

POSSIBILITY AND THE RHETORIC OF INFINITY

One common characteristic of AWFs is that they are concerned with worlds that do not stop—spatially or temporally; AWFs are preoccupied with infinity. The singular thing about the Aleph, for instance, is that, despite the fact that it is only an inch wide, it contains all things and all time. Likewise in Borges' "The Library of Babel," the narrator asserts, "The universe (which others call the Library) is composed of an indefinite and perhaps infinite number of hexagonal galleries" (51). It "exists *ab aeterno*" (52), and the narrator ultimately concludes, "The Library is unlimited and cyclical" (58). Likewise, in Millhauser's "Cathay" we are told that the empire is "so vast that it is said to contain all things" (148). And in *Invisible Cities* we are told on the first page of text that "the empire, which had seemed to us the sum of all wonders, is an endless, formless ruin" (5).

This last example highlights the problem nicely. For infinity tends to make us very uncomfortable. It overwhelms us with its incomprehensible magnitude, makes us dizzy and nauseous with its formless sprawl. Kermode's fear of the "middest" is one manifestation of being overwhelmed by infinity. Popular, self-limiting forms are not available to AWFs. How can there be, for instance, "a day in the life" if the subject is all lives, all days, all things? How can we treat merely the birth, life, and death of an individual when we are concerned with creating an entire universe? In short, how could a list of items from a world that contains an infinite number of items ever stop? And if it did stop, why would it stop with *this particular* item and not some other one? This question is a crucial aesthetic conundrum for AWFs.

One answer to this set of problems is provided by Borges' story, "The Library of Babel," which takes the form of an exploratory essay written by a citizen of the Library who is trying to figure out its essence, unlock the secret of its nature. His task is made simpler by the fact that his world is relatively simple. Every room is, in fact, the same: "This distribution of the galleries is invariable" (51). This is not a world like Cathay, in which everywhere one looks one finds some different object of amazement. The Library can be described with a few descriptive rules; the story can end when the final rule has been stated. This is a world characterized by endless and overwhelming *repetition.*

But in reality the case is not so simple. For the narrator's task is not merely to describe the unusual world in which he finds himself, but to understand it. In short, he needs to understand infinity, needs to come to terms with a world that is *endlessly* repetitious. This is a story, in fact, about infinite monotony, about grappling with Barbara Herrnstein Smith's concept of saturation. Imagine existing in a world of rooms in which every room is exactly the same; all are filled with the same number of books, every book is filled with the same twenty-three symbols arbitrarily combined so that they form page after page of nonsense. This is the artist's nightmare: life is utterly meaningless, repetitious, endless.

To make sense of this, the inhabitants of this world have invented what Kermode would call "concord fictions"—fictions that give a shape to the shapeless. They postulate, for instance, that since the library contains all possible books, it must contain one book that is the compendium of all the rest. Some people spend their entire lives searching for this one book. In this way, they give their lives a teleology: the goal toward which all time and all activity progresses is the discovery of the ultimate book. Since the discovery is always pending, each moment is a moment of crisis or *kairos*.

But the story cannot rely on this ultimate book for closure, since the book is yet to be discovered. Instead, the story ends when the narrator comes to grips with the nature of his world. Some have claimed the library is infinite; others claim it is limited. The narrator reconciles the two:

> I venture to suggest this solution to the ancient problem: The Library is unlimited and cyclical. If an eternal traveler were to cross it in any direction, after centuries he would see that the same volumes were repeated in the same order (which, thus repeated, would be an order: the Order). My solitude is gladdened by this elegant hope. (58)

The narrator's emphasis on "elegance" and "order" is telling; closure is secured here because the narrator has succeeded in giving shape to the shapeless, giving meaning to the meaningless. Infinity has not been exhausted; instead, it has been "solved."

Something similar happens in Calvino's *Invisible Cities*. Again, the story is about a character, in this case Kublai Kahn, who is trying to grapple with the infinite:

> In the lives of emperors there is a moment which follows pride in the boundless extension of the territories we have conquered, and the melancholy and relief of knowing we shall soon give up any thought of knowing and understanding them.... It is the desperate moment when we discover that this empire, which had seemed to us the sum of all wonder, is an endless, formless ruin.(5)

This is the moment Kublai Kahn inhabits at the opening of *Invisible Cities*. But the solution to this problem is also promised from the outset, for in Marco Polo's cataloguing of marvelous cities, Kahn is "able to discern ... the tracery of a pattern so subtle it could escape the termites gnawing" (6). The catalogue of cities takes on significance because we view it through the desperate eyes of

Kahn, who yearns to make order out of his formless empire, to tame infinity. We continue reading, in part, to see how or if this is possible. Can this mystery be solved in the time allotted (whether we see that time as Kublai's lifespan or the length of the book)?

In an attempt to cope with the limitlessness of his empire Kublai turns to things that represent life in neater terms, such as his Atlas and his chessboard, but these fail to provide a lasting sense of clarity and order. In the final section, after marvelous city has been piled upon marvelous city, Kublai Kahn turns to Marco Polo and asks, "You, who go about exploring and who see signs, can tell me toward which of these futures the favoring winds are driving us?" Marco has to tell Kahn that it isn't that simple: "For these parts I could not draw a route on the map or set a date for the landing." Instead, Marco will "put together, piece by piece, the perfect city, made of fragments mixed with the rest, of instants separated by intervals.... If I tell you that the city toward which my journey tends is discontinuous in space and time, now scattered, now more condensed, you must not believe the search for it can stop" (164). Just as the Library of Babel is rendered meaningful by the positing of a book that is the compendium of all other books, Marco Polo tries to help Kublai come to terms with his infinite empire by giving him an image of a single city which transcends the principles of space and time in order to contain all cities in one, the perfect city constructed of fragments from all the others, which will never be found but must always be sought, since looking for it gives us a final destination by which to shape our lives.

AWFs provide answers to the problem of infinity, which is the problem of their own structure. They all provide us with Alephs, which contain all possibilities of time and space in a single time and space. Closure is secured not when all possibilities are exhausted—that would be impossible—but when all possibilities are seen as latent in one final image.

What is striking is the way in which each work comments on its own method. "Cathay" is a story that offers a list of marvels; it is also about the problem of being confronted with one marvel after another. "The Library of Babel" is about giving form to infinity; it is also itself one formal solution to the problem of depicting infinity. *Invisible Cities* is a catalogue of cities, but it is also about how to confront such a catalogue. This meta-cognitive element has important implications for achieving closure in each case. If we are experiencing a list that itemizes phenomena in a given world, and if that world is infinite, how can this list ever end? It can end when this question itself is answered in the abstract and when that answer is performed in the concrete, and these two gestures will take place simultaneously, indeed will be one and the same.

DIALOGUE BETWEEN WORLDS

Closure was secured in "The Aleph" when a bridge was constructed between three worlds: The world of the Aleph, the world of the protagonist, and the world of the reader. In order to complete this inquiry into the nature of closure in AWFs, it is necessary to examine the nature of the relationships that inevitably form between alternate worlds in the fictions that create them. The Aleph will once again serve as an illustrative example.

Simplifying the case for the moment, we can say that in AWFs there are at least two worlds implied: the so-called "real" or "ground" world and the one created by the story. It is immediately apparent that several relationships between these two worlds are possible. First, as with the Aleph, one may encounter a world embedded in a larger fiction. Second, as in "Cathay" and in "The Library," one may encounter a world coterminous with the fiction that creates it, in which there is no explicit reference to the ground world. Third, there is a hybrid possibility, in which the ground world and the alternate world are depicted as two equally strong presences. Fourth, and most complex, there is the case in which the ground world and the alternate world are one and the same world, or are at least hopelessly intertwined. (This last possibility is the case in *Invisible Cities.*)

In the case of "The Aleph," the protagonist is utterly changed by his experience of the alternate world. Since the Aleph introduces him, instantaneously, to literally everything, he feels that his life is used up. That is, all future events are already known; all objects have already been encountered: "I was afraid that not a single thing on earth would ever surprise me; I was afraid I would never again be free of all I had seen" (28–29). The ground world is to an extent "used up" by the Aleph. The alternate world competes with the ground world, takes a hostile stance toward it. If the story were to end at this point, it would be an example of what one critic has called "tragic return," when a return to the ground world from an alternate world does not imply a harmonious or stable close, but instead heightens tension and ambiguity (Gilead 285).[5] But in this case, the protagonist is spared, and is able to repress the experience of the alternate world: "Happily, after a few nights, I was visited once more by oblivion" (28, 29).

Commonly (though not as common in the stories examined here) AWFs adopt a journey and return pattern, and the return to the ground world is a primary means of securing closure;[6] but when the ground and alternate worlds exist side by side, the journey and return pattern is not as simple. Often there are many journeys and returns. One such story is Steven Millhauser's "The Barnum Museum." This story is essentially a list of rooms, a guided tour through the Barnum Museum; a collective (first-person plural) narrator takes us from one room to the next, and gives us a running commentary accordingly. The difference between this story and "Cathay" is that the alternate world is firmly situated in a ground world like our own: "The Barnum Museum is located in the heart of our city, two blocks north of the financial district." (73). But there is no doubt, once we are inside, that this is truly a separate world, and not just a place in our own world. It is suggested that the Museum is infinite. And of course it contains amazing things that could not exist according to the ground rules of our own world.

Unlike Oz, which can be entered only through a dramatic and unusual event, such as a tornado, and can be returned from only through a complex chain of events, involving prerequisite tasks and magic slippers, the Barnum Museum can normally be visited and left at will. Nevertheless, an acute tension exists between the Museum and the outside world. At one point the narrator tells us that "the enemies" of the Museum claim "its exhibits are fraudulent; that its deceptions harm our children, who are turned away from the realm of the natural to a false realm of the monstrous and fantastic" (75). Hannah Goodwin—the only character given a name—serves as an illustration of the danger presented by the alluring Museum. She is drawn out of the ground world and into the Museum. "Her visits grew longer and longer" (82), and even when she is away her mind fixates on the Museum. She becomes "visibly impatient with the dull routines of the day" and "like a woman in love [she] had abandoned herself utterly to ... the always alluring doorways of the Barnum Museum" (82–83). Indeed, just like Aleph, the Barnum Museum threatens to consume or annihilate the ground world:

> It is ... not impossible, that at some moment in the history of the museum our entire citizenry, by a series of overlapping impulses, will find themselves within [the Barnum Museum].... For a moment the city will be deserted. Our collective attention, directed at the displays of the Barnum Museum, will cause the halls to swell with increased detail. Outside, the streets and buildings will grow vague; street corners will begin to dissolve. (80)

Closure, in this situation, will necessarily involve some resolution of this tension between worlds. Near the end of the story, the narrator slips into the first-person singular to offer his personal vision for how the two worlds can be reconciled: "In the branching halls of the Barnum Museum we are never forgetful of the ordinary world, for it is precisely our awareness of that world which permits us to enjoy the wonders of the halls. Indeed I would argue that we are most sharply aware of our town when we leave it to enter the Barnum Museum; without our museum, we would pass through life as in a daze or dream" (90). If we accept this argument, we feel released from the tension between the two worlds, which can now be seen as mutually beneficial—indeed mutually creative of each other—rather than mutually exclusive. The story ends a page later with a reassertion of the Museum's allure, now seen as a positive and healthy force. The final line embraces the Museum freshly: "Welcome to the Museum! For us it's enough, for us it is almost enough" (91). We end where we began, at the entrance of the museum, ready for yet another tour.

Thus it can be seen that a ground world and an alternate world can interact in roughly the same way a protagonist and antagonist can, and that closure in such cases is partly contingent on the resolution of the conflict between those two worlds/characters.

AFTERLIFE

Studies of closure are important. They force us to grapple with the essential nature of any given work. Barbara Herrnstein Smith's classic, *Poetic Closure,* for instance, should always prove interesting to people who love poetry not merely because it is a good catalogue of how poems end, but because it tells us something essential about the nature of poetry itself.

No closural strategy discussed here is the exclusive property of AWF. Nevertheless, it seems clear that certain strategies of closure lend themselves to AWFs more readily than others, and these strategies do comment on the nature of AWFs since they are inextricably bound up with the nature of world construction. To study the way AWFs secure a sense of closure is to study the process of shaping our experience of worlds; which means it is a way of rethinking how we go about shaping our experience of *the* world. How do we deal with the infinite? How do we cope with a world that continually shoves bright and eye-catching details at us (or that fails to)? How do we modulate the dynamics of monotony and surprise in our own existence? How do we keep the marvelous from failing?

AWFs build worlds for us and then allow us to exit those worlds gracefully—something our own world doesn't always allow. If, as John Dewey claims, great works of art create for us well-formed experiences, alternate-world-fictioning is the ultimate aesthetic mode, since the well-formed experiences it creates are versions of the Ultimate Experience—the experience of the entire history of a world. For as Kermode says, it is not satisfying to feel we are merely drifting along in the middest. AWFs give us a chance we would not otherwise have: the chance to experience a complete world history, with a beginning, middle, and an end. What's more, they allow us to contemplate the shape of that history from the outside—from a kind of "afterlife." In short, AWFs, more than any other kind of work, can take us from Genesis to Revelation, and then, by securing closure, allow us to shut the book, set it in front of us, and contemplate it as a whole. For this (among other reasons), AWFs are supremely valuable.

NOTES

1. Herrnstein Smith, in fact, makes exactly the same distinction between experience and *an* experience:

It would seem that in the common land of ordinary events—where experiences are fragmentary, interrupted, fortuitously connected, and determined by causes beyond our agency or comprehension—we create ... "enclosures": structures that are highly organized, separated as if by an implicit frame from a background of relative disorder or randomness, and ... complete.... The sources of our gratification in closure probably lie in the most fundamental aspects of our psychological and physiological organization.... Perhaps all we can say ... is that varying degrees or states of tension seem to be involved in all our experiences, and that the most gratifying ones are those in which whatever tensions are created are also released. (2–3)

2. The image of a mirror held up to itself is one of Borges' favorite images, and, for readers familiar with his work, this intertextual reference secures yet another level of closure: "Yes," we think. "Now he has realized one of his favorite images; now the sequence can end."

3. The pairing of oppositions (which are supported by the assonance of "white beard" and "ripe years") is itself significant, since other oppositional pairs have been introduced previously (e.g., the white and black dwarves). The Doppelgänger is a favorite device of AWFs, and of Millhauser in particular. Just as the double-mirror image in Borges signals a fulfillment of one of his favorite patterns, the Doppelgänger image fulfills one of Millhauser's, and this fulfillment primes the reader to expect closure.

4. Here we have a list within the larger catalogue of the story. Because world construction is so intensely concerned with the efficient transmission of details, there is an almost overpowering tendency for AWFs to break down into lists, even when they try to operate within a different mode.

5. "[T]he tragic mode of return is dominated by a sense of loss unmitigated by the playful or softened tone" (Gilead 285).

6. Sarah Gilead has catalogued the basic form this journey-and-return sequence can take in "Magic Abjured: Closure in Children's Fantasy Fiction."

WORKS CITED

Borges, Jorge Luis. *The Aleph and Other Stories 1933–1969.* Ed. and trans. Norman Thomas di Giovanni. New York: Dutton, 1978.

Calvino, Italo. *Invisible Cities.* San Diego: Harcourt Brace Jovanovich, 1972.

Dewey, John. *Art as Experience.* New York: Wideview/Perigree, 1980.

Gilead, Sarah. "Magic Abjured: Closure in Children's Fantasy Fiction." *PMLA: Publications of the Modern Language Association of America.* 106:2 (1991): 277–93.

Kermode, Frank. *The Sense of an Ending.* New York: Oxford University Press, 1967.

Leitch, Thomas M. "Donald Barthelme and the End of the End." *Modern Fiction Studies.* 28:1 (1982): 129–143.

MacLeish, Archibald. "Ars Poetica." *The Norton Anthology of Poetry.* Alexander W. Allison, Herbert Barrows, Caesar R. Blake, Arthur J. Carr, Arthur M. Eastman, and Hubert M. English, Jr., eds. New York: W. W. Norton & Company, 1983. 1029.

Millhauser, Steven. *The Barnum Museum.* New York: Penguin Books, 1990.

———. *In the Penny Arcade.* New York: Simon & Schuster, Inc., 1987.

Pratt, Mary Louise. *Toward a Speech Act Theory of Literary Discourse.* Bloomington: Indiana University Press, 1977.

Roxanne. Dir. Fred Schepisi. With Steve Martin, Daryl Hannah, Rick Rossovich, Shelly Duvall, John Kapelos, Fred Willard, and Michael J. Pollard. 1987.

Smith, Barbara Herrnstein. *Poetic Closure: A Study of How Poems End.* Chicago: University of Chicago Press, 1968.

3

Genre and the Work of Reading in Mansfield's "Prelude" and "At the Bay"

Suzanne Ferguson

From its beginnings the short story has lent itself to sequencing, by both authors and readers alike: The Hebrew Bible, we now realize, is a cobbled-together short story sequence, as are most epics, romances, and picaresque novels. Put into sequence—chronologically, genealogically, geographically—they "become" a different genre, to be read in parts, perhaps, but understood as a whole. When, in the later nineteenth century, the short story rose to prominence as an artistic genre, sequences (and cycles) grew up side by side with the single story, making possible, for example, the publication and sale of related stories in separate volumes, as in *The Adventures of Sherlock Holmes* or P.G. Wodehouse's many volumes about Bertie and Jeeves. Such volumes we do not think of as "sequences" because, except for the final story in *Tales of Sherlock Holmes*, where Conan Doyle tried to kill off his charismatic hero, they have no governing formal development and denouement. Perhaps Doyle's public so fervently demanded the return of Sherlock Holmes precisely because there was no sequence leading to his "death."

The modernist/impressionist story, however, grew up with "sequences" such as George Moore's *The Untilled Field*, with its themes of Irish emigration and alienation, followed by Joyce's *Dubliners* and Anderson's *Winesburg, Ohio*. The critical enterprise confronting these works must study the meanings of the sequence as a whole as much as of the individual stories. Recently, I have become interested in related stories from this period and after that resist readers' efforts to cast them into sequence: Mansfield's New Zealand stories of the Fairfield/Burnell family from the years 1910–1919; Grace Paley's "Faith Darwin" stories from the 50s through the 80s, Sherman Alexie's "Victor" stories of the early 1990s. These groups have in common that they are autobiographical and were written by authors self-identified as "on the margins" of the mainstream of their society, while they appeal to the mainstream audience and depend for some of their impact on its resistance to their formal challenge: to remain outside the rules of "sequence." Each story tacitly, and sometimes openly (Paley) acknowledges the existence of the others, but doesn't yield to the seduction of plot development, as if denying the authenticity of plot and "sequence."

In their resistance to being read as unified sequences they suggest a curious blurring or overlap of what, just a few years ago, would have seemed fixed: the border between modernist and postmodernist fiction. Rather than a "rage for order" that would respond to New Critical methods of interpretation, these stories confront and accept discontinuity and disorder. They tempt the reader to form sequences, only to leave great gaps and dislocations.

What difference does it make for us as readers whether we read these stories as sequenced or not? One implication of the work of critics Ian Reid, Suzanne Hunter Brown, and others investigating the cognitive side of short-story research is that works whose genre characteristics are mixed or uncertain are more difficult to read (i.e., establish a "reading" of or interpret) and their emotional impact will vary much more from reader to reader than works whose genres are readily identified. Sometimes the mixing of genre characteristics is deliberate: the authors apparently mean to mystify and complicate the reader's task and response, as in Shakespeare's romances or works of postmodern fiction and drama. But sometimes, as when the author is herself trying something new that doesn't seem to fit the conventions of her contemporary mainstream, works emerge that are interesting hybrids, calling on the reader for extra investment of reading effort and perhaps rewarding that readerly work with special pleasures and illuminations.

In writing, the author has available the full arsenal of intentionality, arrangement of episodes, perspectives, diction, imagery, allusion. The reader confronting the printed text has generic expectations internalized and organized from childhood forward. In readers' encounters with generically unusual fictional texts, the work of reading often involves a process of negotiation among conflicting generic expectations. In a short work, full understanding of how to read may develop concurrently with the entire reading experience: only in retrospect, that is, may we be able to "complete" the integration of textual elements into a sense of the work "as a whole." When the reader's sense of the "whole" is a group of "parts" left discrete and separated by the author, the occasion arises for critical interrogation of the formal and social elements that pull the reader toward a sequencing that the author neglected or refused to provide.

On March 25, 1915, Katherine Mansfield wrote to John Middleton Murry that she had begun work on her first *novel.* "I had a great day yesterday. The Muses descended in a ring, like the angels on the Botticelli Nativity roof . . . and I fell into the open arms of my first novel. I have finished a large chunk (*Letters* I, 167–68). She calls the work a "book" in a letter to S. S. Koteliansky of May

4th; to Murry, May 8th and 12th (*Letters* I, 174, 180, 186); and on the 14th of May she declares, "My work is finished my freedom gained.... I have only to polish my work now; its [sic] all really accompli" (188).[1] Nevertheless, in responding to an October 11th, 1917, query from her friend, the painter Dorothy Brett, as to its form, she replied that it was "so difficult to say. As far as I know its [sic] more or less my own invention" (Letters I, 331).[2] This assessment comes after her cuts and revisions to the work gave it the form in which it was to be published, under the title "Prelude," by Leonard and Virginia Woolf at the Hogarth Press in July of 1918 (O'Sullivan, *The Aloe*, 16). Vincent O'Sullivan claims that in this work Mansfield "is discovering a new way to tell a story" which is "not so much a narrative about events shared by several people, as one where several temperaments unfold in the slantings of perspective, in the tilting gradations of time.... The story itself has become how it is being told" (9), and Mansfield herself later referred to "the Prelude method—it just unfolds and opens" (qtd. in Kaplan, 103).

This long story/novella, with its canonical name "Prelude," was also published in 1930 by Murry in its "original" 1915 form, about a third again as long, under its first title "The Aloe." Mansfield's countryman, Vincent O'Sullivan, who has made so many important contributions to Mansfield scholarship in recent decades, made the two versions co-readable in his excellent facing-page edition of 1983, which preserves even passages struck through in the manuscript. The existence of the two versions, in the context of the letters identifying it as a "novel," along with a second work ("At the Bay," 1921) featuring the same characters and a similar form—short sections focusing on different family members unified by an event or a short time period and touching upon a cluster of family themes—and with some additional short stories of more conventionally plotted forms that could nonetheless be seen as related to "Prelude" and "At the Bay," provide a tempting case study for considering generic issues in readers' responses to these works. As Perry Meisel has noted: "In reading 'Prelude,' the issue is not so much creating a subtext or supplement [as it is for other Mansfield stories] as creating a matrix to 'hold' the various strands in a meaningful, coherent whole" (117).

The story, along with its companion piece "At the Bay," has received much critical attention to its form and meaning, notably by such critics as Mary Rohrberger, Saralyn Daly, Sidney Janet Kaplan, Mary Burgan, Vincent O'Sullivan, W. H. New, and Ian Gordon, in his chronological ordering of these stories with other stories of the Fairfield/Burnell and Sheridan families (Mansfield's other autobiographically reminiscent New Zealand family, most notably in "The Garden Party") in *Undiscovered Country* (1974), demonstrates the critical impulse to see them as a sequence. In what follows I will try to focus specifically on elements of the story that point to generic frames by which we determine how to read the story, rather than seeking or espousing a particular interpretation. In the text included in *Bliss and other Stories* (1920), "Prelude" is about 28,000 words long, divided into twelve irregular sections: something already arguably in the "novella" range, already posing problems of generic framing. Are we to abandon ourselves to "experiencing" the fictional world, as in a novel, or are we to grasp all the aesthetic and ideational parts as a whole, as in reading the short story? We begin in medias res (no help from that!) with the scene of a moving day: everything has been loaded up, and all the family have boarded the van except two little girls. We hear their mother, in the free indirect style that immediately puts us on guard as to how to judge what she is saying, announcing that these two will have to be left behind, as the contents already loaded are "absolute necessities." My most recent students, reading this, began to wonder aloud what was wrong with this mother, an appropriate reaction as it turns out, and a question that is unanswered until sections V and XI. No one in the scene, including the children, however, seems to take her seriously, and after the first moment it seems that she has been joking, with the hysterical exhaustion of a moving day. A provisional topos has been set in motion, however, that of the bad mother and of lost or abandoned children—"Hansel and Gretel" in "modern" dress, a tale with moral and psychological resonances for the reader.

This opening scene appears to have set up not just the teasing of one of the girls by a family of children who are, though more worldly wise, of a lower class (the neighboring "Samuel Josephs" who entertain Kezia and Lottie while they wait for the store-man who is to bring them along to the new house), but the girl herself, her farewell to the old house, and her unfamiliar framing of it through colored glass that gives odd (and self-consciously artistic) perspectives on what is soon to be the past.

> Kezia bent down to have one more look at a blue lawn with blue arum lilies growing at the gate, and then at a yellow lawn with yellow lilies and a yellow fence. As she looked a little Chinese Lottie came out onto the lawn.... Was that really Lottie? Kezia was not quite sure until she had looked through the ordinary window. (34)

Thus by following Kezia out of the first scene, the reader frames the "story" to be "about" her reaction to the move. This focus on Kezia continues for more than a quarter of the story, but then, in an elegant "turn" in the scene in which the children are reunited with both their parents and grandmother in the new house, it shifts, playing briefly among several of the adults at the end of section III. The reader's first attempt at a story paradigm is overturned, and s/he must cast about for some other way to establish the unity "story" demands.

Here is the first hint that perhaps we are reading a "novel" after all: we are now following the consciousness of four additional characters—the mother, the father, the grandmother, and the children's Aunt Beryl—and will pick up that of the household maid, Alice, as well, in section X. Certainly one interesting act of reading many have performed with the story and its successor, "At the Bay," is to follow the "stories" of the individual characters: Beryl's "story" of her place in the household as the unmarried aunt and her writing of this to her friend Nan; Linda's story of wishing to sail away from her children and especially her husband, Stanley; Stanley's opposing, dissonant story of his success in marriage and family life; Kezia's story of confronting death and ambiguity in the episode in which the handyman Pat demonstrates beheading a duck, only to have it "pad back to the stream" already headless, distressing Kezia until she is distracted by Pat's little gold earrings. For Alice, the housemaid's "story" is not fleshed out until "At the Bay," in which Beryl has a vivid new strand in her story portraying her relationship with the odious Mr. and Mrs. Harry Kember; there, Linda also has a new episode in which she "falls in love" with her new, male child; and a new character, Linda's brother-in-law Jonathan Trout, appears to juxtapose Stanley's story with a contrasting one of male self-consciousness and regret. In the later story, Kezia is relegated to a minor role as one of a group of children participating in what is, in generic terms, clearly an episode rather than a "story," and extends her own story only in the brief scene in which, teasing with her at naptime, she tries to make her grandmother promise never to die.

Whether we project the "strings" as independent horizontal strands layered as in musical polyphony, or as in the plot and subplot of novels, we are seeing the family as a multileveled system, in which the members interact with and affect one another, even as the whole system evolves. By the time the reader has made it to the middle of "Prelude" the sense of where the story may be leading, in terms of action or change, is almost completely in abeyance. One reads on to see what (if anything) will happen to bring the strands into a pattern. And indeed, nothing does "happen" to any of the protagonists, nor do they do anything to change their status or resolve their problems. Although by the end Kezia has had an experience of confronting death, Linda has admitted to herself her fear of death through sex and childbirth, and Beryl has admitted her false persona, these "discoveries" seem in themselves quite disparate and tenuous as compared to the dramatic conclusions of such Mansfield stories as "Bliss" or "Marriage à la Mode," for example, which deal at least partly with similar themes.

Certainly nothing is concluded in "Prelude" for Kezia. After the episode of the duck, she does not return until the very end of the story, where she appears holding a kitten to call her aunt down to meet "a man Stanley had brought from work," neatly concluding Beryl's "plot" with the notion that she will continue to try to find a husband from among a class of men that in her heart she despises. Kezia's "plot," however, ends with the miraculous *not*-breaking of a face-cream jar lid she has put on the kitten to see it aesthetically arranged and anthropomorphized in Beryl's mirror. Some readers have taken this ending to suggest that Kezia will follow Beryl as a poseur and avoider of responsibility; others that the "mystery" of why things happen embodied in the fantasy of the fearful "them" and "it"—unseen forces in and under our world that both Kezia and Linda Burnell experience—is confirmed in this chance happening of "good" that will spare Kezia from her aunt's wrath.

Although the first scene of "Prelude" could begin either a novel or a story, the last could not conclude a novel of the kind that has been suggested in the various scenes and plot threads. The "to-be-continued" sense is very strong in the suggestion that Linda Burnell will have the male child Stanley foresees in the empty chair of the nursery and she anticipates in section XI: "What am I guarding myself for so preciously? I shall go on having children and Stanley will go on making money and the children and the gardens will grow bigger and bigger, with whole fleets of aloes in them" (142).[3]

In several ways, "At the Bay" does function as a next installment. Beryl's fantasies get her into trouble; Linda has had "the boy" and becomes intrigued with him, suggesting that she will develop into an indulgent and attached mother for the first time with this male child; Stanley continues to be self-centered and self-indulgent; and Jonathan Trout is introduced as a counter to Stanley. The children continue their childhood games and confront the terror that imagination can bring, and Kezia tries to stop the flow toward death by demanding that her grandmother promise not to die, in what could well be a foreshadowing of the grandmother's death in an episode never to be written. The housemaid Alice takes a more prominent role in her visit to her assertive widow-friend Mrs. Stubbs, which results in her revulsion against sex and marriage and longing for the safety of her "kitching." There, the only threat is Beryl, whom, as we saw in "Prelude" (section X), Alice can "vanquish" by imagined repartée, much as troublesome Stanley can be "drowned" vicariously with the teapot in the dishwater.

"At the Bay" uses the same formal method as "Prelude," but instead of the unifying device of "moving house," it has the cycle of dawn to darkness as its spatiotemporal frame. The long set piece with which it opens, establishing the place as special and magical, and the figures of the shepherd and his dog challenged by Florrie the vacationing cat ("silly young female" in the dog's view [4]), seems to most of my student readers very novelistic, and, for a short story, "excessive." Nothing is "done" with the sheep, the shepherd, or the dog later in the story, so they have to carry their full symbolism from connections established within this first scene, and in juxtaposition to the absurdity of the second scene, in which Stanley's morning "constitutional" vacation swim is spoiled by his talkative, ironic, "failed" brother-in-law, who does not have to go back to work for several days, and who doesn't want to, ever. Although one can read "At the Bay" as a separate story, and it has its champions, it seems to depend for resonance on "Prelude" and at the same time to be more contrived in its use of the day cycle to display the differences in the worlds of women and men, the stereotypes and anti-types Mansfield manipulates in the story.

Thus neither work fully conforms to the readerly frame of "novel fragment" or "short story." As "novellae," both are still odd "beasts" requiring much work from the reader to give them aesthetic completeness. Mansfield seems to have recognized that "The Aloe" would not do in the state it was when the Woolfs asked her for something to publish at Hogarth Press. She streamlined it, simplifying its plot lines, characters, and themes as she prepared it for printing.[4] One striking difference that marks an important change of "frame" is that of the title from "The Aloe" to "Prelude," reputedly suggested by Murry (O'Sullivan, 14).

The reader, upon encountering "Prelude," quickly surmises that the moving to a new house is itself "prelude"—something before the *ludus,* the play—to other things that will happen to these characters in their "lives." The "completeness" of the prelude can be evaluated on the basis of how subtly and clearly it does predict what will come "after" the events recounted. A "prelude" is also a free-form musical composition that stands on its own, especially in piano music of the romantic period, successor to the "chorale prelude" of baroque organists—embellishments on a well-known tune or theme, developed freely within established conventions of improvisation. The suggestion of communication through oblique hints rather than direct statement also comes from romantic and impressionist musical "preludes," as does the notion of something small and intimate rather than grand and completely "plotted," like a sonata or a symphony.[5]

The title "The Aloe," on the other hand, was also manifestly wrong for a family novel, but could have worked for a short story, like Lawrence's "Odour of Chrysanthemums" (1911) or Chekhov's "Gooseberries" (1893), both of which use the eponymous plants as focal points for characters' moments of revelation about the meaning of their lives. The aloe plant[6] does work in the story as a many-attributed symbol bringing together Kezia and Linda, and Linda and Mrs. Fairfield, in two memorable scenes. The plant seems to have no direct relation to Stanley or Beryl, though Mansfield's planned cutting-down of the aloe stem while Linda lies ill after giving birth to "the boy" could have brought the other characters into the picture.[7] Nevertheless, like such titles as "Noon Wine," "The Aspern Papers," "The Fox," or "Death in Venice," the titles of "The Aloe," "Prelude," and "At the Bay" suggest central tropes that can easily frame a short fiction—novella or short story—rather than a novel.

With such titles and brevity influencing us on the one hand, and multiple story threads weaving in and out on the other, how do readers decide the appropriate strategies to make sense of and achieve the illusion of wholeness (Poe's "unity of effect") from stories such as "Prelude" and "At the Bay," now widely regarded as trailblazers in modernist short-story form? First, we must accept, and hold in suspension, the sometimes rapid shifts in the objects of our attention. Once the focus has shifted from Kezia, in section IV of "Prelude," it moves first to Beryl, readying herself for bed, imagining "in the garden a young man, dark and slender, with mocking eyes," and thinking "how frightfully unreasonable" her brother-in-law can be; within a few paragraphs, the "eye" of the story, movie-like, shifts to Stanley, talking to Linda, then pauses for a moment on Pat the handyman before shifting back to Kezia and her grandmother (56), and finally out into the night itself, where owls call "more pork; more pork," and a bird—the New Zealand equivalent of a kukuburra, apparently—laughs "far away in the bush" (58) to end the section.

Section V begins with the world's coming back to consciousness in light and sound, with Linda Burnell as the center, for the first time, in the midst of a dream that reveals some of the tensions in her character and marriage. In the dream her father (dead at the time of the story) is walking with her and shows her a tiny chick which, attractive at first, grows large and demanding under her touch (58). The dream is broken by Stanley's pulling up the venetian blind with a clatter. This scene was followed by the largest single cut Mansfield made from "The Aloe," nearly eight full printed pages, about 3500 words, which give more detail on the grandmother, on Linda before her marriage to Stanley, on her father, and on the courtship of Linda by Stanley. These pages filled in background in a conventional novelistic fashion, fleshing out the characters and their interrelationships.

Lacking this background, the "Prelude" reader stays with Linda in her bed, tracing flowers on the wallpaper and feeling haunted by an imaginary "them" reminiscent of the fearful "it" that earlier terrified Kezia in the empty town house. Forced to put these feelings of dis-ease together, both by the fact that Kezia and her mother have similar feelings when left alone and that Linda is now only the second character in the story with whose consciousness we are allowed to have extended contact, we begin to narrow down to a finer sense just who is important and of whose situation we will be asked to judge.

Now at midpoint in the story, with the beginning of section VI, the focalization retreats to a general overview of unpacking activity in the kitchen, where Linda arrives some pages later, and from which she walks out into the garden. Kezia, meanwhile, has also begun to explore the garden, and for two pages (over 700 words) Mansfield describes its flowers, then how Kezia likes to surprise her grandmother with tiny artistic creations put together from flowers and leaves (90, 92). At the end of this section, Kezia and Linda meet in contemplation of the giant aloe, and have their sole conversational exchange in the story (94).

There could be no doubt, whether in a story or a novel, that the aloe is set up as some sort of symbol, because of the extensive description and the convergence of the two most prominent characters in its shadow. Yet it is not until the following evening—in section XI—that its meaning for Linda becomes clear. Like Mrs. Ramsay's lighthouse in Woolf, created nearly ten years later,[8] the aloe "is" Linda's symbol: remote, full of spikes and thorns, able to bloom only once "in a hundred years," and embodying both the aggressiveness of her longing to be free and her fear of Stanley's sexual domination. Thus its projected destruction would symbolize her spiritual "death" as the resisting woman. In section XI of "Prelude" she sees the plant in the moonlight as a great ship powered by sail and oars that can row her "far away over the top of the garden trees, the paddocks and the dark bush beyond" (138).

In the sections of the story between the two "glimpses" of the aloe, Stanley's satisfaction with the move, his plans for his family, the trivial conflict between Beryl and Alice, and Beryl's flirting with Stanley are described, and there is a substantial section (seven-plus pages, over 2500 words) dealing with the children, including the two male cousins and their long-suffering dog Snooker; and the cutting off of the duck's head which so horrifies Kezia but is soon forgotten in the gender puzzle of Pat's earrings. In "The Aloe," another four pages contained a scene with Beryl and Linda's married sister (Jonathan's wife) and additional material on Alice, again appropriate for novelistic development, but unnecessary to the themes of "Prelude," which have begun to emerge more clearly around the motif of how the move brings out tensions and reflections that may have remained hidden in the old environment: Linda's fear of sex and childbirth and her longing to escape (even though she recognizes that she has no real will to do so); Beryl's fear of being an old maid, exacerbated by her new isolation in the country (though she is really only attracted to the men of her dreams, and not the men available in her social group). In "The Aloe" as later in "At the Bay," Beryl is uncomfortably aware of her appeal to women ("The Aloe," 153; "At the Bay," 20–23). A section of the latter also foregrounds Kezia's attraction to and timidity before the spectacle of life and death that unfolds before her.

While the cuts from "The Aloe" seem unexceptionable when one considers the refining and focusing necessary for a short story, all the material would have "fit" perfectly well into a novel, had Mansfield ever chosen to or been able to finish it. She did go on working with the Fairfield/Burnell family after the publication of "Prelude," as she refers in a letter to Murry of December 1917 to a "Bud of the Aloe" which was lost in the mail but later, according to Murry, turned up and formed the opening of "At the Bay" (Letters I, 349). Still later, in 1922, she was working on another "installment," and wrote to her sister Charlotte Perkins: "I am going to write a kind of serial novel for *The Sphere* this summer" that would incorporate both earlier pieces (quoted in Boddy, 186). Although "The Doll's House" (published in February 1922) has a more straightforward short-story plot, with its own exposition of the local social structure, it could also easily have become part of the "novel," extending the characters of the children and Beryl.

That it all might have become a novel, had Mansfield lived and been well enough to pursue it, seems plausible enough, though it would have had to be resolved thematically similarly to Woolf's solution in *To the Lighthouse* (1927). Since the characters were based on her family members, Mansfield might, perhaps, have simply continued to "tell" their lives to some convenient point—Kezia's leaving home, the grandmother's death, some resolution between Linda and Stanley. Beryl's marriage or disgrace or decamping seems only appropriate to a subplot. More interesting than such speculation, however, is how the two long stories became so admired, how they came to seem a new "form" of the short story. The many substantial readings of the stories in recent as well as earlier criticism testify not only to Mansfield's craftiness in interspersing the various episodes dealing with different characters and her success in creating a form similar to the themes and developments of musical preludes, but also in readers' persistence in seeking unities from these pluralities.

Given the basic trope of "moving house" in "Prelude" the reader remains open to each new episode as a revelation of what happens to each part of the family as a result. Kate Fulbrook writes: "Moving house is itself used as a metaphor for the possibility of change as the characters are temporarily dislodged from their habits and set roles," a setting which "prompts a series of moments of self-awareness for the characters" (67–68). Thus Kezia's deliberate defamiliarization of the yard and her sister Lottie (by looking through colored panes of glass) at the old house is extrapolated through the night journey to the new house, the explorations around the new environment, and the discovery of the symbolic aloe. The movement from being "packed up" in the first section to being "at home" in the final three sections, provides a framework within which the reader can examine the dramatic tensions within the family and speculate upon "woman's life" as represented in the different generations and social situations of the women of the story.[9]

In the many ingenious readings of the symbolism and structural echoes of "Prelude" by such insightful critics as Sylvia Berkman, Mary Rohrberger, Sidney Janet Kaplan, Mary Burgan, Saralynn Daly, Robert Robinson, Kate Fulbrook, Patrick Morrow, and W. H. New, we can see the insistent "rage for order" readers bring to bear upon a work they perceive as a short story. The many internal and corroborative clues to the novelistic origin (and planned destination) of the work are set aside or bracketed as each reader seeks to find the unifying elements. Mansfield's arbitrary foregrounding of the aloe as a central symbol and the "natural" unity provided by the instigation and completion of "moving house" actually do seem to satisfy the reader's desire for coherence even if, with Morrow, we concede that "'Prelude' is noticeably incomplete" (51).

Having achieved an improvised formal success in "Prelude," Mansfield was able to use the method as the basis for another installment of her family "novel" in "At the Bay." Having learned to read the former, the reader is prepared for the latter, though this story is even more thematically fragmented than "Prelude," and indeed stands less well on its own. Having used "moving" as the primary structural trope for "Prelude," Mansfield turned more conventionally in "At the Bay" to the time span of the day: a workday (for Stanley) during vacation time, in which the children and the women, along with Jonathan Trout, the unmasculine (because he dislikes work and is thoughtful and sensitive) brother-in-law, engage in their holiday routines of leisure, closer to the elemental rhythms of sea and sun and moon.[10]

The social space of being "on holiday" is a more interesting topos, however, given the tensions between work and leisure, and bondage and freedom that are explored. In this different spatiotemporal setting, a number of the themes raised in "Prelude" are revisited: Linda's distance from Stanley and her children, reframed when she is "seduced" by her boy baby; and Beryl's more dangerous flirting which nearly brings her to grief with Harry Kember. The drawn-out scene of the children's game at the center of the work makes sense only in the context of the characters in "Prelude," however charming it may be. Similarly, Alice's tea with Mrs. Stubbs really draws upon her character as established in the earlier story, and though in itself not lacking for appeal, does not "work" very effectively with the other episodes, even though it opens up a window into a social stratum that mimics the tensions and conventions of the Burnells and their neighbors. The reader does put the pieces of this story together, but it lacks the freshness and intensity of "Prelude," many of whose themes and insights seem repeated with less compelling examples. As further episodes from the "unwritten novel," however, it is enjoyable and meaningful, as well as beautiful.

> In some larger sense, it is impossible not to wish that "the novel" had been written, yet the very fact of its being somehow "behind" the two stories gives them a resonance beyond that of the more conventionally plotted stories. That Mansfield discovered the form of "layering" or "collaging"[11] experiences of several characters to show a range of women's experience within a single "work" essentially by accident—having to give the "woolves" a story to publish at a time when she was desirous of making public her tribute to her dead brother—does not detract from its achievement. As Kaplan writes, "What began as a 'novel' eventually became something new: a mixed genre, a multileveled, spatially ordered narrative." (103)

Though praised as influential, its influence on the short story is difficult, in fact, to follow except in its general principle of presenting episodes that can be read as the traces of a larger theme and plot. The careful neutrality of the omniscient narrator who bridges the episodes and narrates the "dramatic" scenes in which no character's consciousness is observed (and often mediates the characters' consciousness with a dazzling "indirect free style") can also be seen as influential, but as much for novelists (in addition to Woolf, Elizabeth Bowen comes immediately to mind) as later story writers.[12]

Paradoxically, then, it is the fact of "Prelude" and "At the Bay" having histories as drafts toward novels, trimmed for focus but retaining their multiple strands of plot, that creates the reading task of "framing" short stories, or perhaps more properly, novellas, out of them: that is, using their brevity as a rubric to indicate that a thematic and configural unity must be the aim of the reader. That readers have largely been able to find a thematic unity and process the complexity through conflating both "novel" and "short story" reading techniques suggests both how adaptable readers are and how Mansfield managed to make a virtue of necessity with her "Gift of the Muses." By configuration and sequencing of her various plot strands, she calls upon the reader to construct the interrelationship of the family's inner dynamic. Resisting the novel convention of working everything out over time but exploiting its tendency to portray community, she presents a set of examples the reader accepts as a microcosm from which the macrocosm of the family and of the society are projected.

It remains to consider why, then, since the stories did not become parts of a novel, we should also resist "sequencing" them or calling them, even casually, a "sequence" or "cycle." To summarize: like the stories with shared characters by other writers I have listed in the introduction to this paper, Mansfield's fictions about the Sheridans are connected only through the characters and settings. Although they share some themes, the development of the themes is disorganized, and the stories do not form a "whole" with an articulable conclusion. The repeated characters, in Paley's term, are "employed" by the writers to establish a familiarity that can be drawn upon while new themes and emphases are explored by the writer as well as the reader. Although the temptation to forge them into sequences may be irresistible to readers, we should not allow that kind of reading to blind us to the oddities and deliberate strangeness of these stories, nor should we neglect to register the dis-ease that lies behind their refusal to be normalized into sequences. Their very existence resists the pull of plot, the reader's urge to make the crooked straight and the rough places plain: they say to us, "See these lives? See how difficult they are, how marginalized, how fragmented?" As their characters stand outside the mainstream of their social milieux, questioning and challenging their assumptions, so should the reader step aside from the desire to see the tidy fictional package, the reasonable conclusion. Mansfield was right when she wrote to Dorothy Brett that the form of "Prelude" and "At the Bay" was her own invention. So, too, I would argue, is the "form" that resists formulation, the anti-sequence of the Fairfield/Burnell stories.

NOTES

1. Sidney Janet Kaplan notes that in her journal, Mansfield said she was "planning a novel, *Karori*" (216).

2. Mansfield continues with a figure of an island (New Zealand, Atlantis) rising out of the mists of the sea, seen in glimpses and descending again, an image more precisely descriptive of "At the Bay," published three years later.

3. Mansfield also noted her plan to have her brother's birth the conclusion of "The Aloe" in a journal entry.

4. In addition to O'Sullivan, Sidney Janet Kaplan and others have traced and analyzed the excisions.

5. Saralyn Daly likens the appearances and recurrences of symbols as "musical motifs" (91). Compare also T. S. Eliot's "Preludes" as impressionist "glimpses." For a different take on the title, see New, 147–57.

6. The described plant sounds more like the related succulent, the agave, commonly known as "century plant," which blossoms once upon maturing (after thirty years or so), after which the plant itself dies. However new, smaller plants are already growing adjacent to it, in a cluster.

7. Cf. Chekhov's "The Cherry Orchard," or Forster's "Other Kingdom" (ca. 1910) where a Stanley Burnell-like man insists on fencing off a parcel of his forest against his fiancé's will, only to have her disappear, Daphne-like, among the trees.

8. Correspondences between the aloe and the lighthouse, and the possible influence of Mansfield on Woolf here, are explored at length by Angela Smith in her recent *Katherine Mansfield and Virginia Woolf*, 95–105.

9. Thus the third sister can be dispensed with in the short-story version—she merely reiterates aspects of the other women's situation. See also Burgan, 116.

10. Mary Burgan sees in the moon the "female influence.... As a final comment on the anxieties of sex and birth, Mansfield thus provides a vision of eternally recurrent nature which both troubles and consoles" (116). See also Ruth Parkin-Gounelas, 51.

11. Both O'Sullivan and Sara Sandley liken the techniques to those of film (in Robinson, ed., 15, 74–77).

12. Some critics, notably Sidney Janet Kaplan, have argued that what Mansfield created was a peculiarly feminine form of narrative: "What makes 'Prelude' so revolutionary as a narrative is its implicit statement that the construction of gender should be the motivating center of the text.... It is ... a rejection of male modes, and this strategy is apparent in its all-over structure: its multiplicity, its fluidity, its lack of a central climax, and its many moments of encoded sexual pleasure" (114).

WORKS CITED

Berkman, Sylvia. *Katherine Mansfield: A Critical Study.* New Haven, Conn: Yale University Press, 1951.

Boddy, Gillian. "'Finding the Treasure,' Coming Home: Katherine Mansfield in 1921–22." In Robinson, 173–88.

Burgan, Mary. *Illness, Gender, and Writing, The Case of Katherine Mansfield.* Baltimore & London: Johns Hopkins University Press, 1994.

Daly, Saralyn. *Katherine Mansfield.* Revised edition. New York: Twayne, 1994.

Fulbrook, Kate. *Katherine Mansfield.* Bloomington and Indianapolis: Indiana University Press, 1986.

Gordon, Ian, ed. *Undiscovered Country: The New Zealand Stories of Katherine Mansfield.* London: Longman, 1974.

Hunter Brown, Suzanne. "Discourse Analysis and the Short Story." *Short Story Theory at a Crossroads.* Ed. Susan Lohafer and Jo Ellyn Clarey. Baton Rouge: Louisiana State University Press, 1989, 217–48.

Kaplan, Sidney Janet. *Katherine Mansfield and the Origins of Modernist Fiction.* Ithaca: Cornell University Press, 1991.

Mansfield, Katherine. *The Garden Party and other Stories.* New York: Alfred A. Knopf, 1923.

———. *The Collected Letters of Katherine Mansfield.* Edited by Vincent O'Sullivan and Margaret Scott. Vols. 1 and 4. Oxford: Clarendon Press, 1984, 1996.

Meisel, Perry. "What the Reader Knows; or, The French One." In Robinson, 112–18.

Morrow, Patrick D. *Katherine Mansfield's Fiction.* Bowling Green, OH: Bowling Green State University Popular Press, 1993.

New, W. H. *Reading Mansfield and Metaphors of Form.* Montreal & Kingston: McGill-Queen's University Press, 1998.

O'Sullivan, Vincent, ed. *"The Aloe" with "Prelude" by Katherine Mansfield.* Manchester, England: Carcanet New Press Limited, 1983.

———. "'Finding the Pattern, Solving the Problem': Katherine Mansfield, the New Zealand European." In Robinson, 9–24.

Parkin-Gounelas, Ruth. "Katherine Mansfield Reading Other Women: The Personality of the Text." In Robinson, 36–52.

Reid, Ian. "Destabilizing Frames for Story." *Short Story Theory at a Crossroads.* Baton Rouge: Louisiana State University Press, 1989, 299–310.

Robinson, Roger, ed. *Katherine Mansfield, In From the Margin.* Baton Rouge & London: Louisiana University Press 1994.

Rohrberger, Mary. *The Art of Katherine Mansfield.* Ann Arbor, Mich.: University Microfilms, 1977.

Sandley, Sarah. "The Middle of the Note: Katherine Mansfield's 'Glimpses.'" In Robinson, 70–89.

Smith, Angela. *Katherine Mansfield and Virginia Woolf: A Public of Two.* Oxford: Clarendon Press, 1999.

4

Death and the Reader: James's "The Beast in the Jungle"

Arthur A. Brown

In his 1936 essay, "The Storyteller," Walter Benjamin writes:

> The reader of a novel actually does look for human beings from whom he derives the "meaning of life." Therefore he must, no matter what, know in advance that he will share their experience of death: if need be their figurative death—the end of the novel—but preferably their actual one. How do the characters make him understand that death is already waiting for them—a very definite *death* and at a very definite place? That is the question which feeds the reader's consuming interest in the events of the novel.... The novel is significant, therefore, not because it presents someone else's fate to us, perhaps didactically, but because this stranger's fate by virtue of the flame which consumes it yields us the warmth which we never draw from our own fate. What draws the reader to the novel is the hope of warming his shivering life with a death he reads about. (101)

For Benjamin, the "actual death" of a character is preferable to the figurative death of the end of the novel because in our modern world death has been hidden from us, and in our search for the meaning of life we cannot do without it. "[Not] only a man's knowledge or wisdom," he writes, "but above all his real life—and this is the stuff that stories are made of—first assumes transmissible form at the moment of his death.... This authority is at the very source of the story" (94). When we consider, however, that the "actual death" of a character is a representational death, that it takes place in a world where death is an impossibility, we might begin to wonder in what way precisely the authority of the dying enters the narrative act. The death of a character is most effective in literature that is aware of its own nature as literature, as "*the life that endures death and maintains itself in it,*"[1] so that the contradiction between literature and real being becomes part of the drama—and the reader one of the participants.

The meaning of life depends on death—not to wrap things up or provide closure, so that we might walk away from life with meaning in hand—but to distinguish life itself from represented or figured or constructed life—in a word, from literature, or from any "consciousness" that survives death. The end of a novel or story is not only a figurative death; it is the moment that restores the reader to his own mortality. Of course this "moment" exists throughout the story—the story could not begin without its having already become, as Benjamin says, "transmissible."[2] The authority at the source of a story comes not so much from the death of a character as from the death that takes place in the act of its being told—an act in which the reader may be the only living player. Thus it is in fact his own death with which the reader warms himself—the actual and ever-present possibility of it—without which the narration could not take place. It is the act of storytelling itself, at moments dramatized by what takes place within the story, that warms our shivering life.

According to Maurice Blanchot, death "humanizes nature"—"it raises existence to being, and it is within each one of us as our most human quality" (55). Literature, on the other hand, "manifests existence without being, existence which remains below existence, like an inexorable affirmation, without beginning or end—death as the impossibility of dying" (47). Yet literature claims the right to death in its contact with a mortal reader—that is, in the act of narration, which is as dependent on life and death as the act of speech. "[W]hen I say 'This woman,'" Blanchot writes,

> real death has been announced and is already present in my language; my language means that this person, who is here right now, can be detached from herself, removed from her existence and her presence and suddenly plunged into a nothingness in which there is no existence or presence; my language essentially signifies the possibility of this destruction; it is a constant, bold allusion to such an event. . . . Therefore it is accurate to say that when I speak: death speaks in me. My speech is a warning that at this very moment death is loose in the world, that it has suddenly appeared between me, as I speak, and the being I address: it is there between us as the distance that separates us, but this distance is also what prevents us from being separated, because it contains the condition for all understanding. (42–43)

Like the meaning of life, the acts of speech and of narration depend on death. The meaning of literature lies in its ability to turn us away from its immortal world and remind us of our mortal being.

In an article that appeared in *Harper's Bazaar* in 1910, Henry James asked, "Is There a Life After Death?" and concluded that there was, or that he liked and had every reason to think so. His artistic consciousness had opened the door to a life of far greater possibilities than those any mortal life could hold, and his own death would usher him into it. But James's fiction constitutes a different response to the question "Is There a Life After Death?" The task of literature is to affirm mortality not to deny it—or even as it denies it.

"The Beast in the Jungle" can be placed roughly in the middle of what appears to be a change in James's thinking from seeing death as the final and determining fact of life to seeing it as the end of one term of being and the beginning of another. In his headnote to "The Beast in the Jungle" that appears in *The Ghostly Tales of Henry James,* Leon Edel traces the story's origins. He cites James's notebook entries of January 9, 1894, and February 5, 1895, written eight and nine years before the story. In the first of these two notebook entries, James writes, "The idea of *death* both checked and caught me; for if on the one side it means the termination of consciousness, it means on the other the beginning of the drama in any case in which the consciousness survives." Here he goes on to explore the ways the consciousness can be "said to" survive so that the story of death can be told. It survives a death that is a death in life—a metaphorical death, such as artistic or moral failure, or, as he sees a year later, "a love that is formed too late" (143–44, 183). In the notebook entries, James perceives actual death as "the termination of consciousness." Metaphorical death, on the other hand, generates stories—more than one story, as Edel and Matthiessen and Murdock have pointed out.[3] Thus the idea of death-in-life is turned to plot. The death of James's characters is the life of his stories and of his own artistic consciousness.

In turn, the life of his artistic consciousness comes round to convincing James of a life after death—not merely metaphorical but actual death. In the 1910 article, James writes that, as "more or less of" an artist,

> I deal with being, I invoke and evoke, I figure and represent, I seize and fix, as many phases and aspects and conceptions of it as my infirm hand allows me strength for; and in so doing I find myself—I can't express it otherwise—in communication with *sources;* sources to which I owe the apprehension of far more and far other combinations than observation and experience, in their ordinary sense, have given me the pattern of. (224)

James seems to be saying that in the act of figuring and representing being—in the act of writing realistic fiction (in which "the air of reality" is "the supreme virtue"[4])—his resources for writing, for apprehending being or reality, become unlimited. In the context of the essay, however, the distinction blurs between James's sense of his own unlimited ability to perceive realistic "combinations" and his conviction that these perceptions give him an insight into an unlimited reality. According to the thesis of "Is There a Life After Death?," if John Marcher had been able to write about his tragedy, he would have been not "too late" but just in time. The tragedy would disappear, and so would the story. In other words, James, who *had* been able to write about Marcher's tragedy, had taken from it—or from the ability to write it—the conviction that no such tragedy could exist. To perceive the tragedy, to "figure and represent" being, leads to a way out of it.

James writes in the article that he is interested only in a "personal" immortality, and he realizes that to have one the signs by which he recognizes himself must remain with him after death:

I practically know what I am talking about when I say, "I," hypothetically, for my full experience of another term of being, just as I know it when I say "I" for my experience of this one; but I shouldn't in the least do so were I not *able* to say "I"—had I to reckon, that is, with a failure of the signs by which I know myself. (212)

To perceive at all, to be conscious, is to perceive and be conscious of the self. Yet this self can be known only, apparently, by signs—that is, by things external to it. The ability to say "I" and to know oneself by the perception of signs is heightened in the artist's ability to imagine and construct worlds of his own. In other words, James's sense of himself is inseparable from his sense of himself as an artist, and it is his sense of himself as an artist that affirms his sense of personal immortality:

Living, or feeling one's exquisite curiosity about the universe fed and fed, rewarded and rewarded—though I of course don't say definitely answered—becomes thus the highest good I can conceive of, a million times better than not living (however *that* comfort may at bad moments have solicited us); all of which illustrates what I mean by the consecrated "interest" of consciousness. It so peoples and animates and extends and transforms itself; it so gives me the chance to take, on behalf of my personality, these inordinate intellectual and irresponsible liberties with the idea of things. And, once more—speaking for myself only and keeping to the facts of my experience—it is above all as an artist that I appreciate this beautiful and enjoyable independence of thought and more especially this assault of the boundlessly multiplied personal relation (my own), which carries me beyond even any "profoundest" observation of this world whatever, and any mortal adventure, and refers me to realizations I am condemned as yet but to dream of. (222–23)

For James, living is an opportunity to develop his artistic relationship with the world. What he dreams of today as an artist is proof of the extended relationship with the world that he will have in reality after death.

James's insistence on a "personal immortality"—on the ability to say "I" in a world where death would no longer be a possibility—seems in keeping with his lifelong attempt to reconcile his personal life with his life of letters. To have a life of letters is, in a sense, to have a life after death, and to have a life after death is, in a sense, to justify a life of letters. But only in a sense. In actuality, a life in letters, like a life after death, would be a horror; it would be, as Maurice Blanchot says of literature, "*my* consciousness *without me*" (47). To have a life in letters and a life after death would be to lose that which makes us human.

John Marcher is not an artist, but his own ability to say "I" and to know himself by the perception of signs is heightened by the sense he has had "from [his] earliest time, as the deepest thing within [him], . . . of being kept for something rare and strange, possibly prodigious and terrible, that was sooner or later to happen to [him]" (71). He lives in relation to this thing that will happen, which he or the narrator or both name the "beast in the jungle" (79), as if his life were a story and he himself the main character. The parallel between Marcher's life and our act of reading is conspicuous: like Marcher, we watch for the thing that will happen—we figure his life by the image of the beast; like us, Marcher reads "the open page of his story" (125). At the same time, the difference between Marcher's life and our act of reading, since it is an act that takes place in the world where death is a possibility, is so apparent as to remain *in*conspicuous. Yet we ought to ask—and the story makes us ask—what it means to believe what we are told by an omniscient narrator, or writer, and to take our place as a privileged yet disembodied listener, or reader. Our own ability to find *and lose* ourselves in language duplicates the artist's "immortality"—his ability to say "I" after death—and actualizes Marcher's death in life—his inability to live except by figuring and marking his life.

John Marcher knows himself by his sense that something prodigious will happen to him and by the knowledge, finally, of what this something is—the present that has passed him by and continues to pass him by in his unending figuration of it. He sees that his own self-consciousness is the thing that he had been waiting for and seeing all along, the thing that had made him blind to everything else. He had been unable to love May Bartram "for herself" (125); he had used her the way a writer uses a reader, or vice versa—to corroborate his way of seeing the world. What John Marcher wants is mortality; what has done him no good at all is the artistic consciousness that has made him read his life as we read his story, which is to say, endlessly.

In the preface to *A Portrait of a Lady,* James suggests that the novelist's task is to *place* "the breath of life," the true subject of the work, in novelistic form without limiting or interfering with his own awareness of its truth (43). He writes that "the worth of a given subject" is determined by its being the genuine and sincere "result of some direct impression or perception of life." The "moral" sense of a work of art depends "on the amount of felt life concerned in producing it." He adds: "The last touch to the worth of the work" is given by "the enveloping air of the artist's humanity" (45). One would think that the artist's humanity is defined less by his "communication with *sources*" than by his "observation and experience, in their ordinary sense"—and that the artist's "direct impression or perception of life" and the life that is "felt" in the production of his work are similarly dependent on his connection, for better or worse, to life in *this* world.

To "deal with being," or to "seize and fix" being, is to put being on one's own terms, to put its fundamental value in question in a way that James seems well aware of as a writer of fiction. The value of being is *the* moral question in James's fiction. Characters in his novels and stories must decide whether other characters are worth believing in, even as they construct fictions around them or become part of others' fictions. Their belief is continuously measured against a worth that runs parallel or counter to that which they perceive or construct; otherwise, there would be no story to tell.

May Bartram's belief in "*the* thing" that will happen to John Marcher (73), in "the real truth" about him (80), constitutes her love for him. "I understand you. I believe you," May tells Marcher at Weatherend. "You mean you feel how my obsession—poor old thing—may correspond to some possible reality?" he asks. "To some possible reality," she confirms (74). Reality is exactly what she does confirm—for Marcher and for the reader. What "reality" means is the possibility of death. May's role in the story is precisely to die. Marcher must feel the loss not merely of the sense of himself that she had given him but of her very being: "*she* was what he had missed" (125). The extent to which he had "thought of her" in "the light of her use" is the extent to which we do (126), and to this extent we will be mistaken as to what she is worth.

Writing in *Harper's Bazaar* of his "infirm hand" (in the year following the publication of the twenty-four volume New York Edition of his work), James seems a little too pleased with its powers and a little too content to have seized and fixed things with it. He seems to belittle what he might see as the one thing *not* subject to perception or belief—"the termination of consciousness," or death itself. What James is able to express in "The Beast in the Jungle" is not only Marcher's or the reader's mistake but the mistake of literature. Literature, a formation of the artistic consciousness, looks not for immortality but for death, without which there would be nothing to write about and no way to write—no being to displace and no way of displacing it. But the more elaborate its construction of signs the more it disguises its own effort, until it sees nothing more than itself, or at best, its own mistake.

As Edel writes of "The Beast in the Jungle," "the surface of the story suggests the long passage of wasteful futile frustrating years" (670). It does so, however, not merely in its way of presenting events—summarizing and explicating more than dramatizing—but in the very act of presenting them. To write or to read is to have something prodigious happen to you—it is to become immortal, which is to say, it is to live in a death that does not die. For a time, actual death loses its meaning; it becomes nothing more than the principle of substitution and displacement that makes language possible, and life turn into signification. The person who can die, like everything else—like being itself—is no longer there.

In his essay "The Dramatics of the Unspoken and Unspeakable in James's 'The Beast in the Jungle'" Herbert Perluck positions himself against "the numerous commentaries" on the story that, in Perluck's view, "are in general agreement over its essential meaning" (252). According to this "essential meaning," Marcher is, as he says himself, "an ass" (68), though at the time he calls himself one he is not half such an ass as he turns out to be. Speaking for Marcher, who experiences the horror of self-knowledge, the narrator spells out the moral of the story at the end of it. Having kept himself "for something rare and strange, possibly prodigious and terrible, that was sooner or later to happen" (71), Marcher becomes "the man of his time, *the* man, to whom nothing on earth was to have happened" (125). It is to the fifty or so pages in between that Perluck wants to call our attention.

According to Perluck, to read the story as an indictment of Marcher is to distance ourselves from the act of reading the story; Marcher's detachment from life parallels the detachment we all feel in "the thick, bewildering opacity of language and experience" (252). Perluck continues: "nothing ever really 'happens' to anyone" (251). The dramatic meaning of the story lies in the "misreading" of it; any "essential," or allegorical meaning that we find in the text points to our taking too easy a way out of it.

Perluck sympathizes with Marcher, who "has confounded his sense of separateness, of difference, with egotism, reproving the inescapable 'detachment' in all selfhood as lovelessness" (251). According to Perluck, the real egoist is he who believes he *can* selflessly love. May Bartram, who truly loves Marcher, knows that detachment is part of love, that claims made by marriage of inseparability are inevitably "unredeemable." For Perluck, the story's tragic irony lies not in Marcher's having felt nothing but in his *thinking* that he had. "[T]o whom," Perluck asks, "under similar circumstances" (by which presumably he means having survived a loved one), "has it not occurred that he alone truly sinned, that only he felt nothing, lived nothing, hadn't really loved?" (250). He points out that the pity Marcher himself feels for a grieving stranger in the cemetery works against the judgment that the stranger's appearance seems to make: that Marcher could not feel for anyone—"He had seen *outside* of his life, not learned it within, the way a woman was mourned when she had been loved for herself" (124–25).

Perluck is right to call our attention to the act of reading the story; though we may wish to see *outside* of it, the story forces us to *learn it within.* He is brave in identifying himself and the rest of us with Marcher. But he is wrong—and his own reading becomes too easy a way out of things—when he says that "nothing ever really 'happens' to anyone." However much our consciousness may distance us from what happens, however "thick" and "bewildering" our language and experience may be, things happen—different things to different people. The play between what happens and what we perceive, between the reality of mortal life and the fictional constructions we make of it, is what brings stories to life and life to stories. In "The Beast in the Jungle," the Beast springs "in Time" (97); "what was to happen *had* so absolutely and finally happened" (117)—in the events that make up Marcher's life, not all of which are determined by his attendance on the Beast.

When their acquaintance is renewed at Weatherend to begin the story, Marcher is attracted to May by his sense of her having suffered. While he believes their former meeting could have had "no importance," his "actual impression of her" seems to have had a great deal of importance, yet he finds the explanation for this discrepancy in his having "penetrated to a kind of truth" about her: "She *was* there on harder terms than any one; she was there as a consequence of things suffered, one way and another, in the interval of years." (63). Against this *truth,* the Weatherend house, with all its "fine things," in which May serves as a kind of guide, flattens into a transparent figure for the house of fiction—for Marcher's fiction in particular. *She* is the real thing, and fiction cannot do without it.

Thanks to the death of May's great-aunt, May is able to set up a home in London; in turn, she and Marcher can meet frequently. James dramatizes three of their meetings. While the discussions invariably center on the thing that is to happen, the occasions mark May's birthday—and Marcher's own definite aging—May's illness, and May's dying. Take away these mortal events and we have no story. Against Marcher's sense, finally, that "he had been the man of his time, *the* man, to whom nothing on earth was to have happened" (125), we have May's dying word for it that "Whatever the reality, it *is* a reality" (105), and that what "*was* to" happen *had* (107). And it is May we believe, for she speaks with the authority of death. Until her death, May dedicates herself to watching Marcher, to proving the truth about him—to proving that there *is* a truth. The truth, finally, is that, in endlessly figuring his life under the image of the beast, Marcher affirms mortal being even as he denies it. He marks its very presence. And he does so most effectively by marking our own presence, our own mortal being, as we figure his life with him. We are May and Marcher both.

In "Is There a Life After Death?" James acknowledges that real things happen, though he does so reluctantly:

> Those to whom such dreadful things have happened that they haven't even the refuge of the negative state of mind, but have been driven into the exasperated positive, so that they but long to lay down the burden of being and never again take it up—these unfortunates have an equal chance of expressing their attitude and of making it as eloquent and as representative as they will. (226–27)

How "equal" the chance of those to whom "dreadful things have happened" actually is, we might assess, minimally, by James's tone. James suspects that "these unfortunates" will not belong "to the class of those the really main condition of whose life is to work and work their inner spirit to a productive or illustrative end" (227)—in other words, to the artist's class, the class to which he belongs and to which he must presume his audience wishes to belong.

In his headnote to the story, Edel writes that in all the "fantasies" that led to "The Beast in the Jungle," "there is the recurrent, the deeply felt, note of the *unlived life.* James the celibate, who had renounced the world on the steps of 'queer little old Dane Hall' for letters, had never completely resolved his conflict" (668). In "Is There a Life After Death?" the conflict is resolved, to the extent that the article helps us see the fiction more clearly. "I don't mean to say," James continues,

> that no sincere artist has ever been overwhelmed by life and found his connections with the infinite cut, so that his history may *seem* to represent for him so much evidence that this so easily awful world is the last word to us, and a horrible one at that: cases confounding me could quite too promptly be adduced. The point is, none the less, that in proportion as we (of the class I speak of) enjoy the greater number of our most characteristic inward reactions, in proportion as we do curiously and lovingly, yearningly and irrepressibly, interrogate and liberate, try and test and explore, our general productive

and, as we like conveniently to say, creative awareness of things ... in that proportion does our function strike us as establishing sublime relations ... . [I]t is in a word the artistic consciousness and privilege in itself that thus shines as from immersion in the fountain of being. Into that fountain, to depths immeasurable, our spirit dips—to the effect of feeling itself, *qua* imagination and aspiration, all scented with universal sources. (227–28)

James's spirit seems to be so proportionately free of his body at this "well-nigh final pass" that it is in danger of evaporating.[5] To separate the artistic consciousness or privilege so completely from the artist himself and his mortal circumstances is to remove that consciousness from all things dramatic and give it nothing to live by. Whether James's characters take part in a life with others or are excluded from it in a private life, they are not so finished with being that they can celebrate "immersion in the fountain of [it]" without a sense of loss.

"Is There a Life After Death?" might well be taken as a eulogy for James's brother William, who was ill and died the year it was written. In *Human Immortality*, written in 1898, William James acknowledges that the "'transmission-theory' of cerebral action"—which interested him more than the idea of life after death—leaves open "the doorway to immortality" (v, 3). According to this theory, the brain's function is not to *produce* consciousness but to *transmit* it, to define and limit a larger and preexisting consciousness. The extent to which this larger consciousness is felt or is operational in an individual varies according to a "threshold" level: "When [this level] falls, as in states of great lucidity, we grow conscious of things of which we should be unconscious at other times; when it rises, as in drowsiness, consciousness sinks in amount" (24). Henry James's "artistic consciousness" corresponds to his brother's "[state] of great lucidity."

In the article, Henry James writes that the "exclusively present world" offers the personality a chance to experiment in preparation for its greater freedom. James compares this "chance" to "the sustaining frame on little wheels that often encases growing infants, so that, dangling and shaking about in it, they may feel their assurance of walking increase" (229–30). Matter may aid the spirit, or obstruct it, but "has no more concern in producing [it] than the baby-frame has in producing the intelligence of the baby" (231). The danger to fiction—and to life—posed by this entertaining metaphor is that "the baby" steals the show; the artistic consciousness or spirit that might enlarge our experience walks out from under it, into a world where experience—actual experience, mortal experience—no longer matters. And if we take actuality and mortality out of experience, what have we left?

In the real world, babies remind us of our humanness, our mortality. Our love for them is inseparable from our awareness of the possibility of death. And so James's metaphor is not so dangerous to life and fiction as it seems, because it is inside out. The frame ought to represent not actual experience but the artistic consciousness; and the baby not the artistic consciousness but actual experience. James had the metaphor right in "The Beast in the Jungle," when Marcher, believing in May's assurance that the thing *had* happened, sees himself, now that she is dead, living only to guess what it was: "The lost stuff of consciousness became thus for him as a strayed or stolen child to an unappeasable father; he hunted it up and down very much as if he were knocking at doors and enquiring of the police" (117–18). Actual experience is what Marcher has lost—it is what walks away from the artistic consciousness. Not that experience is not subject to consciousness; but it is subject above all to death.

In the years after 1910, James became more concerned with real suffering in the real world than with anything else. In Edel's "Chronological Table" that appears at the end of *The Ghostly Tales,* we read for the year 1914: "Deeply shaken by outbreak of war, nevertheless begins war work, visiting hospitals, writing for war charities, aids Belgian refugees" (765). Without real death in the real world there would be no literature and no difference between literature and real life. There is plenty of difference. Without it, literature would lose its meaning, in a way that real life—the actual experience of life and death—never does.

As Perluck shows, James's fiction is effective in part because we feel the passage of real life in the *detachment* that we feel from it, and which the act of reading represents and reproduces. But James's fiction is effective in greater part because it does not leave us without obliterating this detachment. In spite of Marcher, in spite of James, and in spite of our act of reading, "The Beast in the Jungle" transgresses its own nature as literature to achieve the right to death. It does so in its contact with a living being—which is to say, in the act of narration. Its strength lies in its ability to restore us, even as we enter the world where death is an impossibility, to our mortal lives. James's fiction is the dramatic antithesis to the thesis he supports in "Is There a Life After Death?" What we feel at the end of "The Beast in the Jungle," before we can remark the feeling, is a loss of self-consciousness—of the artist's and reader's power to know themselves by certain signs.

In the graveyard, with death all around him, figuration and reality merge for Marcher: "He saw the Jungle of his life and saw the lurking Beast; then, while he looked, perceived it, as by a stir of the air, rise, huge and hideous, for the leap that was to settle him. His eyes darkened—it was close; and, instinctively turning, in his hallucination, to avoid it, he flung himself, face down, on the tomb" (126–27). Turning, ourselves, away from the text and into being, we feel the presence of death. If only for a moment—a moment that has passed once we have felt it—the rush of the beast and Marcher's reaction to it have taken us out of the text. In the next moment, we find ourselves back in it—that is, back in the text—with the image of John Marcher, who, having "flung himself, face down" on May Bartram's tomb, cannot die and is interminably in it.

NOTES

1. Blanchot, 54.

2. See Lacan and Felman. Lacan writes that "the signifier . . . materializes the agency of death" (38). Of *The Turn of the Screw,* Felman writes: "It is thus *death* itself which moves the narrative chain forward, which *inaugurates* the manuscript's *displacements* and the process of the *substitution* of the narrators. By so doing, death paradoxically appears not as an end but rather as a starting point: the starting point of the *transferral* of the story, that is, of its *survival,* of its capacity to go on, to subsist, by means of the repeated *passages* it effects *from death to life,* and which effect the narrative" (173–74). What the frame of *The Turn of the Screw* dramatizes takes place in effect each time a story is told—in its passage from narrator to listener, or writer to reader.

3. See Edel's headnote to "The Beast in the Jungle" and Matthiessen and Murdock's notes in *The Notebooks,* 143, 145, 149, 184. Stories in addition to "The Beast in the Jungle" that dramatize the theme of life-in-death and death-in-life include, "The Death of the Lion," "The Private Life," "The Friends of the Friends," "Maud Evelyn," and "The Altar of the Dead."

4. See James, "The Art of Fiction," 172–73.

5. In the *Critique of Judgement* (1790), Immanuel Kant writes that "in all free arts, there is yet requisite something compulsory, . . . without which the spirit, which must be free in art and which alone inspires the work, would have no body and would evaporate altogether" (147).

WORKS CITED

Benjamin, Walter. "The Storyteller." *Illuminations.* Ed. Hannah Arendt. Trans. Harry Zohn. New York: Schocken Books, 1969. 83–109.

Blanchot, Maurice. "Literature and the Right to Death." *The Gaze of Orpheus.* Trans. Lydia Davis, Ed. P. Adams Sitney. Barrytown, NY: Station Hill Press, 1981.Trans. of "Littérature et le droit à la mort." *La Part du feu.* Paris: Editions Gallimard, 1949. 21–62.

Edel, Leon. Headnote to "The Beast in the Jungle." *The Ghostly Tales of Henry James.* Ed. Leon Edel. New Brunswick, NJ: Rutgers University Press, 1948. 667–70.

Felman, Shoshana. "Henry James: Madness and the Risks of Practice (Turning the Screw of Interpretation)." *Writing and Madness.* New York: Cornell University Press, 1985. 141–247.

James, Henry. "The Art of Fiction." *The Art of Criticism.* Ed. William Veeder and Susan M. Griffin. Chicago: University of Chicago Press, 1986. 165–83.

———. "The Beast in the Jungle." *The Novels and Tales of Henry James.* Vol. 17. New York: Scribner's, 1909. 61–127.

———. "Is There a Life After Death?" *In After Days: Thoughts on the Future Life.* By W. D. Howells, Henry James, et al. 1910. New York: Arno Press, 1977. 199–233.

———. *The Notebooks of Henry James.* Ed. F. O. Matthiessen and Kenneth B. Murdock. 1947. Chicago: University of Chicago Press, 1981.

———. "Preface to *The Portrait of a Lady.*" *The Art of the Novel.* Ed. Richard P. Blackmur. New York: Scribner's, 1934. 40–58.

James, William. *Human Immortality: Two Supposed Objections to the Doctrine.* Boston: Houghton Mifflin, 1898.

Kant, Immanuel. *Critique of Judgement.* Trans. J. H. Bernard. New York: Hafner Press, 1951.

Lacan, Jacques. "Seminar on 'The Purloined Letter.'" *The Purloined Poe: Lacan, Derrida & Psychoanalytic Reading.* Ed. John P. Muller and William J. Richardson. Trans. Jeffrey Mehlman. Baltimore: Johns Hopkins University Press, 1988. 28–54.

Perluck, Herbert. "The Dramatics of the Unspoken and Unspeakable in James's 'The Beast in the Jungle.'" *Henry James Review* 12 (1991): 231–54.

5

Sandra Benítez[1] and the Nomadic Text

Andrea O'Reilly Herrera

Over the past twenty years the academy has witnessed an increasingly lively debate among writers and scholars regarding the formal properties or characteristics of the short story and its structural affinities with other genres.[2] In the wake of the postmodern age, however, theorists of the short story are, to borrow Susan Lohafer and Jo Ellyn Clarey's terminology, *at the crossroads* once again, for scores of contemporary authors are penning nomadic texts that resist categorization and definition in that they freely cross generic borders and openly defy the formal characteristics employed to distinguish among literary forms.[3] In *A Place Where the Sea Remembers* (1993), for example, Sandra Benítez explores with direct simplicity and spare prose the fragmentary and subjective nature of human experience in a kind of intricate tapestry that weaves together the lives of eight central characters. Not unlike a photo album, *A Place Where the Sea Remembers* is laid out in short, lyrical chapters which feature seemingly isolated or random incidents or "slices" of the title characters' lives. (The only character who has more than one chapter devoted to her is the mystic *curandera* Remedios, whom I will discuss at a later juncture.) Although many of the chapters are elliptical and highly metaphoric, each has its own integrity and meaning and, therefore, can be treated as an independent entity—a separate episode or short story as it were (hereafter referred to as epi-story). It isn't until the fifth chapter—nearly a quarter of the way through the text—that the reader becomes conscious that the characters' epi-stories are indeed interconnected, and each contains within it a thick web of symbols and themes that are taken up and developed throughout Benítez's work. In other words, despite the fact that *A Place Where the Sea Remembers* is classified as a novel, in truth it reads more like a collection of short, interlinked epi-stories bound together by an overarching narrative, and a complex network of unstable symbols and recurring themes whose larger meanings stand in relation to the entire text.

In chapter two, for example, we are introduced to the title character Candelario Marroquin (*el ensaladero*/the salad-maker); his childless wife, Chayo (*la ramilletera*/the flower girl); and his pregnant sister-in-law, Marta (*la recamarera*/the chambermaid), who was raped, abandoned and, as a result, is considering aborting her illegitimate child. Candelario, who had recently been promoted to the position of salad-maker in his *patrón* Don Gustavo del Norte's restaurant, proudly offers to raise Marta's child in light of his new position and his wife's apparent inability to have children. On the following evening, however, Candelario loses his job simply because he serves a wealthy doctor, Federico (who, incidentally, would have performed the abortion on Marta) and his wife the unwholesome Caesar salad he had been instructed to prepare according to Don Gustavo's special recipe.

When read in isolation, Candelario's epi-story can be treated as a meditation on fate or destiny; a commentary on the class system in Mexico; and a painful lesson in *machismo* and/or *hubris.* Although it lacks closure, it bears all of the marks of a short story, for it can be defined according to its length, internal unity, and its revelation of theme and character. In this single epi-story, however, Benítez (unbeknown to the reader at this point in the text) introduces a series of interrelated themes and issues that reappear like leitmotifs throughout the entire work and whose meanings transform and, in their cumulative effect, deepen.

More specifically, Candelario's epi-story reveals the author's neo-Marxist leanings, for it puts into relief the chasm that exists among the classes in Mexico, epitomized first by Don Gustavo's obsequious attitude toward Federico and his wife and second by Candelario's unquestioning obedience to his *patrón.* Through the characters of Federico—who has earned at least a portion of his fortune by capitalizing on the misfortunes and victimization of women—and Don Gustavo, Benítez exposes the detached, elitist attitude of the rich toward the poor, an attitude typified by Don Gustavo's suggestion that education is the panacea for solving the problems of the Mexican people and the doctor's ironic response that the "filth" of Mexico's indigent is a "symptom" of the "corruption" of society (14). In effect, Federico and Don Gustavo blame the victims themselves for their victimization. "How easily the rich spoke of solutions," Candelario thinks to himself, as he ponders his own inability to read or write: "How untroubled and simple their lives seemed to be" (14).[4]

In several parallel sequences Benítez takes up the same theme as exemplified in the epi-story (chapter five) in which Rafael (*el maestro*/the teacher) travels to his truant student Beto's home to scold him for his excessive absence from school and realizes that his own relative wealth and comfort (though he is by no means rich when compared to Federico and Don Gustavo) has blinded him to the fact that the boy must stay home and contribute to earning the family's livelihood in order for them to survive. In effect, this epi-story takes Candelario a step forward for it illustrates in very specific terms the complexity of the issue and, inadvertently, serves to reemphasize the shallowness and utter simplicity of Don Gustavo's "solution" and Federico's comment.

Benítez further complicates the matter at a later juncture (chapter eight) when we meet Beto's father César, who has suffered the loss of his wife and two younger sons in a bus accident. Functioning as a kind of corrective to Rafael's mistaken impression that the family's extreme indigence must translate into misery, a view which he shares with Don Gustavo, César ponders with great sorrow the loss of his wife and children who, despite their poverty and the rustic simplicity of their lives, were happy together. In a word, he sees himself as "a man who lacked little" before the loss of his family; and Rafael in turn realizes that his own life "contained a different kind of bleakness" in spite of his material comfort (88, 77). Rafael is then prompted to readjust his vision once again when he eventually learns that Inés, an illiterate Nahuatl girl who works for his mother, Doña Lina, suffers from an abusive marriage to a man whom Rafael mistakes for her father. Though the girl benefits from the education *el maestro* offers her, it is painfully clear to the reader that illiteracy is the least of her problems—she must first break the cycle of abuse in which she is caught by escaping her husband. At the conclusion it becomes apparent that Rafael is the one who undergoes an education, and the lesson he learns is that book-knowledge alone will not save women like Inés and, in the case of Beto and César, money and education do not ensure personal happiness.

Candelario's epi-story also introduces the author's feminist concerns regarding women's positions and roles in Mexican society. In her preliminary characterization of Chayo and Marta, Benítez lays bare the traditional Mexican patriarchal ideology that defines women according to their bodily functions and suggests that their labor is only meaningful and their desires legitimate or valid in relation to their domestic duties, which include among other things producing a male offspring to insure the continuity of the patrimony and, as Candelario reminds us, make men of their husbands. Treating the controversial subjects of rape and abortion, this epi-story also suggests that the notion of *machismo,* which is supported by the Catholic ideology inextricably interwoven into Mexican thought and culture, accounts for and perpetuates the sexual victimization, vulnerability, and oppression of women such as Marta.

Although this theme echoes throughout *A Place Where the Sea Remembers* in regard to women such as Inés, Luz (who is abandoned by her husband and left to care for two young children), and Esperanza (the midwife who was raped as a young girl by her employer and, therefore, sees herself as stained, ruined, and unworthy of love), Benítez eventually complicates or counters this negative and, perhaps, stereotypical view of Latin men by introducing male characters who demonstrate their abilities as caretakers and nurturers, such as Rafael (who looks after his aging mother) and César (who assumes Concha's domestic duties following her death). In addition, she exposes the ironic and controversial notion that oftentimes women themselves comply with these cultural gender roles and modes of behavior and thereby perpetuate the very system which oppresses them, as exemplified by Luz's characterization of her husband as blameless and innocent and her conviction that he had "no choice but to fall for [his mistress's] charms" (47); the nameless grandmother who remains silent, though she knows Esperanza is being raped; Doña Lina, who immediately assumes Inés had seduced Rafael; and Marta, who no one except for Remedios believes was impregnated against her will.

The salad-maker's epi-story also puts into relief the subject of Mexico's economic relationship to the United States. Like Don Gustavo and, ultimately, Candelario, most of the characters in Benítez's work are economically dependent upon American tourism for their livelihoods. Many, such as Marta (who longs to flee to El Paso and names her son after Richard Burton), harbor a kind of romanticized, glamorized vision of *el norte* based on magazines and Hollywood films. In short, characters such as Marta nurture a false ideal, which is based upon stereotypes portrayed in the media and popular culture at large. This notion is corroborated in parallel sequences that invert and overturn Marta's vision, such as the revelation that Luz Gamboa's husband ran off with his mistress Tula to El Paso, and through the experiences of characters such as Esperanza, who traveled to the States, accepted a position similar to the one Marta envisions for herself and eventually obtains in El Paso, and was consequently raped by her employer.

Fulgencio Llanos' epi-story extends Benítez's exploration of false ideals and stereotypes when the photographer completely misjudges the motives of a *gringo* from "just north of the border," whom he first takes for a cowboy and then for a "heepee," a stereotype he has formed on the basis of a "popular" movie "about a band of them traveling across the country in a dilapidated van" (29). Benítez consequently examines this theme through characters such as Doña Lina, who clings to a racist stereotype of Indians and, therefore, discriminates against Inés because of her heritage; and the text is filled with moments in which the characters base their assumptions on appearance, rather than reality, an idea expressed in Luz's ironic observation that "Esperanza doesn't make mistakes" (51).[5]

The recurring image of the photograph can also be regarded as yet another false image or ideal, for, as Roland Barthes reminds us, it is "pure contingency," despite the fact that it "gives itself out as [being] complete—integral" and, one might add, objective (1982, 210).[6] In essence photographs, like stereotypes, are merely fixed constructions which bespeak a longing for order or control and, moreover, the desire for historical significance and immortality. This notion is perhaps best illustrated by the photographs of César's wife and sons, which he and Beto place in the roadside shrine and the "instant" photo of Richard that Fulgencio takes at Rafael and Esperanza's wedding. For passersby the pictures of Concha and her sons are essentially without meaning, whereas for Beto and César they function as a kind of testimony to their loved one's lives and deaths.

In the same vein, the snapshot of Richard preserves an image that is at once uncharacteristic and false, for the photographer "catches" him smiling, "something [he] did not often do" (155).[7] Despite Fulgencio's statement that "the camera does not lie," the reader is constantly reminded throughout the text that appearance is not always reality, as seen, for example, in Marta's impressions of the United States, which are based on photographs in a magazine.

Finally, Candelario's epi-story takes up the subject of fate and determinism, as witnessed by the salad-maker's mistaken assumption that luck had brought his promotion and, conversely, "fate" or the "whims of tourists" had revoked his good fortune by placing him at the doctor's table (16). Although certain events in the text seem to suggest that human destiny is unpredictable, as demonstrated by Concha's death or Richard's fatal fall after the lime tree was swept away in the flood, more often than not the characters' "vision" is "turned ... so entirely upon themselves" (as in the case of Doña Lina, Marta, and Chayo) that they lose all sense of perspective and objectivity (126). Frequently, their assumptions about freedom and determinism are informed once again by their particular situations or positions in the social hierarchy. And thus characters such as Marta cannot envision themselves rising beyond the lowly social status they maintain in Santiago.[8]

Despite the fact that all of the characters are identified in their respective chapter titles by name and profession—tags which clearly establish socioeconomic status and constructed categories such as gender and ethnicity—Benítez repeatedly inverts traditional paradigms in order to demonstrate that the gender roles they have assumed and their positions in relation to society are not necessarily fixed. Rafael and César are obvious examples. In effect, their assumption of domestic responsibilities traditionally assigned to women refutes a gender-based notion of social determinism and suggests that gender roles in particular, and the social order or hierarchy in general, are human constructs that can be altered. More often than not, however, human beings blame fate or credit chance or luck for the paths that their lives take, as seen when Esperanza nearly misses her opportunity for happiness by convincing herself that "fate" would determine her future destiny, and Rafael blames his meekness and fear on a "biological deficiency" (131, 75). The malleability of the social system is also subtly suggested at alternate intervals in the text by the fact that various characters manipulate and break the law, such as Federico (who performs illegal abortions), Fulgencio (who robs flowers from shrines for his backdrops), and Luz (who takes money from tourists' rooms).

Rather than relying on their own internal strength, and thereby taking control of their lives and responsibility for their actions, many, such as Luz and Marta, seek external assistance from Remedios and Don Picho Lara, *el brujo*. Although most of the characters place their trust in "unseen powers" and remain largely unconscious of the long-term ramifications of their actions and choices, we as readers eventually see that every action or choice sparks some reaction (54). For example, Rafael's decision to seek out Beto ultimately becomes the reason why the boy is not killed in the bus crash. Despite the fact that *A Place Where the Sea Remembers* seems to affirm the existence of a transcendent order in its presentation of what Ernest Cassirer calls a "bimodal approach to reality," it simultaneously suggests that human beings can exercise control over their lives insofar as they possess the ability to make decisions that alter not only their lives but the lives of others.[9] As Inés' decision to leave her husband and Rafael's to take a stand against his mother and forgive and marry Esperanza demonstrates, the characters' ability to effect change in their lives often resides within themselves, a lesson which Chayo—who has consciously refused to forgive her sister—and Don Justo—who waits for his daughter to bridge the chasm he has forged between them—learn only after it is too late.[10]

Despite its chronological and geographical specificity and its culture-specific elements (such as language), *A Place Where the Sea Remembers* ultimately points toward more universal themes, for the epi-stories depicting the lives of the inhabitants of Santiago collectively illustrate—in microcosm and macrocosm—the painful realities of the human condition, the subjectivity of human perception in regard to reality, and the sometimes imperceptible motivations that prompt human behavior. Benítez emphasizes the characters' "shared humanity" in that oftentimes their lives run parallel courses. Subtly reminiscent of authors such as Virginia Woolf, she creates a kind of "tunneling" effect in *A Place Where the Sea Remembers* which reveals the characters' similarities and relationships to one another, despite the fact that their experiences are delineated and distinguished by their individual perspectives and desires. It is an idea encapsulated in the loosely parallel sequences in which Beto mistakenly blames himself for his mother's and brothers' deaths and Esperanza feels responsible for her rape; Doña Lina and Beto go mute in response to loss (the former when her sons leave her and the latter at his mother's death), just as Esperanza and the grandmother remain silent about the rape; and Rafael's breaking of the soup bowl is paralleled by Inés shattering Doña Lina's meat platter.[11] Benítez also links characters according to their "professions," such as Federico, Remedios, Esperanza, Don Picho Lara, and the priest, all of whom are "types" of spiritual/physical healers. In the same vein, Don Picho and Federico both claim the ability to "cause the child to no longer be a burden" (60); Fulgencio and Roberto are both described as flatterers; and Luz, Marta, and César are all single parents. *A Place Where the Sea Remembers* is also filled with parallel yet inverted occurrences. For example, Doña Lina's arthritis, which swells her limbs, threatens to keep Esperanza and Rafael apart, whereas Tonito's severe allergic reaction, which swells his throat, becomes the catalyst-event which brings the couple back together again; Fulgencio bargains with God and Esperanza with Fate; both Luz and César lose their spouses; and Fulgencio breaks his promise to God, just as Chayo breaks her promise to Marta.[12]

In spite of her characters' similarities, Benítez also reveals the complex and variegated nature of human response and offers profound insights into human nature and desire by demonstrating not only the complexity of specific issues such as poverty or oppression, but by illustrating the subjective and often erratic nature of human behavior, which more often than not is based on incompatible and contradictory assumptions and positions which are relational, subjective, and subject to change. As the work progresses it becomes increasingly apparent that the author does not advocate any particular position regarding the host of issues she raises. Rather, her text functions as a kind of prism, which refracts and reflects a wide range of unstable subject positions or points of view. This idea is best exemplified by the manner in which she handles the central trope in *A Place Where the Sea Remembers*—the parent/child relationship. On the one hand, César agonizes over the loss of his two sons, "on whom he'd rested much of his hope for the future," whereas Marta fears that Richard will destroy her future. In the same vein, Chayo's longing for a child and Candelario's for a son is countered by Marta's desire to rid herself of her child; Doña Lina's rejection of Rafael, "the son whose mother never considered him"; Roberto's abandonment of Marta and, consequently, their child; and Don Justo's renunciation of his daughter, Justina (82). Functioning as a variation on the same theme, César's sister-in-law offers to take in her dead sister's child, and Marta and Chayo are raised by their aunt, Tía Fina, after their mother's death; conversely, Chayo refuses to raise Marta's son when she learns of her own pregnancy and, ironically, Richard dies when he is in her care.[13] Assuming a kind of "devil's advocate" posture, Benítez inverts this trope at a later juncture and allows us to view it from a different perspective by juxtaposing Rafael's desire to rid himself of the burden of caring for his overbearing and implacable mother with characters who mourn over the premature loss of their mothers, such as Marta and Chayo, Don Justo, Esperanza, and Beto.

As previously mentioned, Benítez's postmodern exploration into human epistemology and human existence directly implicates her readers, for the gradual manner in which the characters are introduced into the plot and their stories unfold give us only fleeting and sometimes fragmentary glimpses into their lives—glimpses which only begin to make sense when we consider the text as a whole. In effect we—like many of the characters—must continually readjust our vision as we move from what Charles May calls "one province of meaning to another"; and, in the process of seeking out the "truth," we must also confront our own limitations. Integration thus demands that the different facets of the characters' complex situations and "realities" be viewed through an increasingly wider lens, which converts each individual epi-story into a new whole that is larger than its constituent parts. Ultimately, we as readers must make a final leap and synthesize all of the alternately conflicting and asymmetrical constituent parts represented by each epi-story in order to apprehend the text's more universal, overarching themes. In so doing it becomes apparent in retrospect that there exists some discernible pattern to human life, for we, as privileged reader-spectators, not only have access to information which is either withheld from the characters or which they withhold from one another, but we can trace the chain of cause and effect.

Through the character of Remedios, Benítez also seems to suggest the existence of a larger cosmic order that transcends the human social order. Although she appears at regular intervals throughout the text, the old woman is featured in four chapters, which punctuate the other characters' narratives at key points in the text. From the very outset of *A Place Where the Sea Remembers* it is established that Remedios, unlike the reader, literally and figuratively possesses a "bird's eye" perspective of the lives of the people of Santiago. Moreover, she seems to partake in a cosmic order that is simultaneously atemporal, ahistorical and mythic, as suggested by her mystical association with the elements and the four directions. In effect, these sequences not only frame the entire work and serve as a connective tissue, but they stand in a kind of Cassirerian "opposition" to the constructed and subjective world of "experience and perception," the world of everyday reality depicted in the characters' individual epi-stories.

Even the circular form in its relation to the content of *A Place Where the Sea Remembers* seems to affirm this larger mythic perspective, in that it points toward a fundamental aspect of Mexican ideology and cosmology that lays claim to the concept that life and death are part of a seamless continuum which the characters (with their limited vision and knowledge) and we as readers (who are attempting to make sense of the individual epi-stories) tend to see as separate and distinct. Drawing upon a tradition that hearkens back to writers such as James Joyce, the beginning of Sandra Benítez's work is quite literally the end, and the end is the beginning. *A Place Where the Sea Remembers* is also scored by details and scenes that contain in a paradoxically harmonious balance what seem to be contradictory elements which reinforce this ideology. For example, the clinic where babies are "saved" is also the place where fetuses are aborted; Inés's miscarriage is an event that culminates in the end of her marriage and the beginning of her new life, and she is transported on the same vehicle in which Concha and her sons meet their untimely deaths; Richard's drowning is a coda to the same episode in which Esperanza and Rafael marry, and Luz and César go on what may possibly be their first date; the attempt to save the pig—a necessary source of sustenance and life—caught in the branches of the lime tree results in Richard's death; Esperanza is a midwife who delivers infants into the world and tends to the aged (Doña Lina) and the dying (Tonito); Santos's taxi delivers Concha's shrine, carries Tonito to the hospital where he is saved, and transports Richard's corpse; and the beach is the site of Esperanza's confession and Richard's conception, and it is the place where the boy's corpse returns, Chayo and Don Justo earn their livelihoods, and Fulgencio has his "lucky break."

Again and again we are subtly reminded of the overarching themes of birth, death, and rebirth throughout Benítez's work. Concha's death and Doña Lina's departure to Veracruz (the event which allows Esperanza and Rafael to cultivate their relationship), for example, occur during the Christmas season—the birth of Christ; Marta dreams of her future while leafing through the pages of *Life* magazine; Doña Lina religiously watches the *novela The Right to be Born;* and Luz's name recalls the Spanish expression *dar a luz* (give birth or, literally, give to light). In addition, the author employs protean symbols that alternately connote life and death. The paper flowers that represent the source of Chayo's livelihood, for example, are also used to ornament the shrines of the dead and "liven up" the backdrops in Fulgencio's photographs (35). In Chayo's dream, moreover, the sapphire-tinted flower is symbolically linked to Richard's death. Though *A Place Where the Sea Remembers* is a retrospective that primarily dwells on the past, toward the latter half of the text Benítez points the reader toward the future, for simple gestures such as Don Justo replacing his dead bird, Rita *bonita,* with Carolina, or the prospect of Luz's and César's budding relationship affirm the notion that "life goes on" despite sorrow and loss.

Perhaps more than any other image or symbol the sea, with its eternal cyclic patterns and tides, simultaneously functions as a metaphor for life and death. Not only does it provide sustenance for the people of Santiago, who are nearly all economically dependent upon it, but it is linked both directly and indirectly to death through the characters of Concha (the Spanish word for shell) and Richard. The sea, moreover, functions as the repository of the townspeople's past and present histories, an ever-present source which becomes the site, as scholars such as Edouard Glissant and Derek Walcott suggest, of infinite renewal, diversity and protean change.[14] The sea preserves and "remembers" the truths of the past—located somewhere within the collective memory—regardless of how painful it may be. It is the place where nothing is forgotten and nothing is lost, where "Nothing dies away because it is remembered," Remedios reminds us, as she "retells" the characters' stories (142, 105). In its depths, in its salty brine, the sea contains and preserves the stories "that save us," she continues, for it unites the past, the present and the future in what Glissant would call "a prophetic vision of the past." [15] In other words, the survival of the individual and ultimately the community—both in the present and the future—is dependent upon knowing where one has already been.

In the act of oral repetition, Remedios is performing a kind of ritual that mirrors the cyclic rhythms of the sea and, in the process, she allows for the possibility of transforming the errors of the past and thereby altering the future, rather than being "condemned," to borrow Santayana's notion, "to repeat it." At the conclusion of *A Place Where the Sea Remembers,* therefore, it is made clear that Richard's death and Marta and Chayo's reconciliation signal the completion of a cycle in the characters' lives. At the same time, however, Benítez reminds us that life, like fiction, oftentimes lacks closure, and thus the story of the people of Santiago concludes at the point at which Esperanza and Rafael begin their new life together and Marta decides to move to El Paso. In effect, their stories are just beginning to unfold.

NOTES

1. A special thanks goes to Sandra Benítez for her feedback and her warm and enthusiastic support.

2. See, for example, Susan Lohafer and Jo Ellyn Clarey's edited collection *Short Story: Theory at a Crossroads* (Baton Rouge: Louisiana State University Press, 1989) and Charles E. May's *The New Short Story Theories* (Athens, Ohio: Ohio University Press, 1994).

3. Although my argument focuses upon the work of Sandra Benítez, it could easily apply to texts such as Sandra Cisneros' *The House on Mango Street* or Maxine Hong Kingston's *The Woman Warrior.*

4. Although this epi-story typifies the attitude of the rich toward the poor, Candelario's comment suggests that his assumptions are also based on stereotypes, for we learn later in the text that material wealth does not necessarily ensure peace, happiness, and "an untroubled existence"—an idea best exemplified by Rafael.

5. The text itself seems to emphasize this notion, for it is extremely complex and sophisticated, despite its apparent simplicity.

6. *A Barthes Reader.* (New York: Hill & Wang, 1982).

7. Fulgencio's insistence that Doña Lina "seize the moment" rings hauntingly true, for the photograph, like the characters' individual epi-stories, is nothing more than an isolated moment in time which has little to do with the "reality" it purports to capture and preserve (84).

8. Marta's desire for her own room functions as a darkly comic play on Virginia Woolf's concept of "a room of one's own."

9. See Charles May's discussion of Cassirer in "The Nature of Knowledge in Short Fiction," which appears in his edited collection *The New Short Story Theories,* 135–36.

10. Ironically, Don Justo—the birdman—sells fortunes to tourists on the beach and lacks the "bird's eye" vision that Remedios possesses.

11. Benítez also subtly links characters together through names. Santos, for example, is the name of the cabdriver and the wrestler whom Fulgencio photographs; César shares the name of the salad which ends Candelario's career, and his employer's surname is del Norte, a name that links him to Marta and Luz's husband, Tito. In the same vein, she employs recurring symbols such as the color blue, which is not only linked to the sea but is associated with male babies and with the Virgin Mother. She also binds together the action through the lime tree, which "bears witness to life," and links her characters through the image of the bus (the vehicle that literally transports much of the action, as well as the characters), and the photographer (who appears at several key points in the characters' lives) (51).

12. In addition, words such as freedom and happiness become completely relative terms. For example, Marta wishes to free herself of her "obligation" to Richard, Chayo of her promise to Marta, and Rafael to his sense of duty toward his mother. Benítez also plays with various themes such as trust, betrayal, and forgiveness.

13. This theme is taken up in the folktale about the witch who hatches a baby from an egg and raises it as her own son (67).

14. Indeed, the sea is not only present in each and every chapter, but it is characterized as corresponding to the characters' moods and feelings (bathos).

15. "The Quarrel with History," *Caribbean Discourse, Selected Essays* (Charlottesville: University of Virginia Press, 1989), 64.

WORKS CITED

Barthes, Roland. *A Barthes Reader.* New York: Hill & Wang, 1982.

Benítez, Sandra. *A Place Where the Sea Remembers.* New York: Scribner's, 1993.

Glissant, Edouard. "The Quarrel with History," *Caribbean Discourse, Selected Essays.* Charlottesville: University of Virginia Press, 1989.

Lohafer, Susan and Jo Ellyn Clarey, eds. *Short Story: Theory at a Crossroads.* Baton Rouge: Louisiana State University Press, 1989.

May, Charles. "The Nature of Knowledge in Short Fiction." *The New Short Story Theories.* Athens: Ohio University Press, 1994.

Part II

Exploring the World of the Short Story

The cultures discussed in the upcoming section share similar concerns over preserving and defining identity within their respective environments, frequently in opposition to outside influences. The short stories discussed here seek to impose their own sense of identity on the lives and surroundings of their subjects.

Donald Petesch's chapter examines how incongruity, a staple technique of postmodern literature, informs Jean Toomer's presentation of the conflicting worlds of the American North and South in *Cane.*

In "The Virtuous Complaint," Rivanne Sandler discusses a generation of Iranian short-story writers bent on stripping down prose "overdressed in multiple adjectives and long, convoluted sentences" into something more like "everyday speech." Sandler further appraises how these writers, working in prerevolutionary Iran of the 1960s and 1970s and "devoted to social change," utilize "suggestion, symbolism, [and] irony" in order to effect an "affable" exploration of the "gap between the ideal and the possible."

For Donna Davis, in her chapter on Janette Turner Hospital, it is the nature of the land itself that exerts a far more dominant influence than humankind on the development of her characters, Australian Aborigines and European colonizers alike. This focus on nature, according to Davis, allows Hospital to address a stew of "overlapping postmodern issues, including diversity, ecofeminism, and postcolonial concerns."

The themes of postcolonialism return in Catherine Ramsdell's chapter dealing with the theories of Homi K. Bhabha, and a strong case is made for the inextricable link between postmodernism and postcolonialism. One notable area is in the ambiguity of the definitions themselves, weighted as they are with the influence of their predecessors, the "shifty" use of "post," a prefix which should indicate an end but in literary study "meaning only to have moved past, not beyond."

6

Postmodern Issues in Janette Turner Hospital's Nature-Dominated Short Stories "The End-of-the-line End-of-the-world Disco" and "Our Own Little Kakadu"

Donna J. Davis

In exploring Janette Turner Hospital's use of nature imagery in her two short stories, "The End-of-the-line End-of-the-world Disco" and "Our Own Little Kakadu," readers can identify numerous often overlapping postmodern issues, including diversity, ecofeminism,[1] and postcolonial concerns. In this chapter I shall attempt to show how in her use of nature imagery Hospital touches on these postmodern issues while addressing and subverting a variety of imperialist agendas, including European techno-capitalist dominance, white-male monoculture and dominance, European linguistic dominance, and European versions of history and ways of knowing (Ashcroft, Griffiths, and Tiffin 33).

The landscape of Australia contains much more than the European mapmakers saw, according to Hospital, because those mapmakers were blinded by their own cultural biases (qtd. in Connolly 88–89). To Aborigines, as with peoples of many other cultures, the land, not humankind, is central. T. C. McLuhan writes in *The Way of the Earth: Encounters with Nature in Ancient and Contemporary Thought:* "In Aboriginal Australia there is no geography without meaning or sacredness. Life is lived out in a constellation of relatedness anchored in the land. The whole of Aboriginal countryside is one living ageless family tree" (40). Indeed, W.E.H. Stanner "had seen an Aboriginal lie down and embrace the earth he walked on" (qtd. in McLuhan 42).[2] Further, in reporting on her studies of the similarities and differences in the views of the nature of six cultures, McLuhan explains that for the Aborigines of Australia "perhaps more than in any other society, land is a fountain of energy that invigorates their world" (42). Indeed, the land is perceived in that culture as a living, sentient being; says one Aborigine, "That country knows who is walking about in it. It can feel who is there. It knows if a stranger comes. And it can get angry—start a bush fire, or something. Not people, doing that—just the country itself" (qtd. in Berndt and Berndt 16).

Hospital recognizes and includes nature as this sentient essence in her short stories. In a panel interview with Selina Samuels during the Fourth International Conference on the Short Story in English, "Many Cultures, Many Voices," Hospital told the audience that the Aborigines of Australia say, "We don't own the land, it owns us" (Hospital, Samuels interview). However, in a private interview during the same conference, Hospital commented that she as well as other Australian writers sees that human beings' relationship with the land is of equal importance to their relationship to other humans, a far less nature-centered stance than that of the Aborigines (Hospital, Personal interview). The question we want to consider now is which of these views her writing actually reflects.

In the course of examining her short stories, "The End-of-the-line End-of-the-world Disco" and "Our Own Little Kakadu," I shall attempt to show that Hospital's use of nature and landscape in setting and imagery shows nature as a far more dominant influence than humankind on the development of her characters. Further, I submit that this stance is part of Hospital's postmodern approach to addressing, resisting, and successfully subverting colonial linguistic, economic, technical, race-based, gender-based, and epistemological agendas.

In these two stories Hospital's main characters are affected by nature and the landscape of, respectively, the outback or bush country of Queensland's southwestern section and the "Garden of Eden rainforest" of the coastal area of the Northern Territory, near Darwin and the Kakadu National Park (Hospital, Samuels interview) In "End-of-the-line," nature in the outback is clearly in control. Its capacity for near total devastation is clear in imagery, Biblical comparison, and direct report. Hospital uses nature imagery in descriptions of characters and their thoughts: mundane, sexual, and spiritual. Gladys, the primary human character in this story, becomes like nature as we shall show, to the point that she merges, indeed mates, with it in a rapturous sense of freedom. Again, in "Kakadu" Hospital reveals nature's power over human characters in both its unstoppable vitality and the conscious and subconscious revelation of the interconnectedness of all life. The main human character, Jug, who once believed in the European colonials' value system of human beings' superiority over nature, is seen as evolving into a devoted servant of the all-powerful living earth. As in "End-of-the-line" Hospital shows in "Kakadu" that the psychological and spiritual victory belongs to the characters who identify with nature and willingly surrender to her vital power.

By the end of each story, neither Gladys nor Jug sees themselves as equals with nature. Both become her devotees, readily admitting their subordinate role. We shall attempt to show in this exploration of Hospital's use of nature imagery that this Australian-born writer clearly gives precedence to the human-nature relationship over the human-human one, joining her fellow Australians, the Aborigines, in full.

First, Hospital addresses the postcolonial issue of European forms of linguistic dominance. In "End-of-the-line," this issue is mildly and humorously reflected in the writer's use of updated, outback, settler-class appropriation of the King James version of the Noah's ark story of nature in flood time: "every living thing upon the ground was destroyed, ... (except the bloody mosquitoes and flies, it goes without saying)" (Hospital 1995, 425). The outback setting, the Millennium Hotel, becomes the ark, ironically likened to the multilevel slang term for the man-made inversion of nature, a "zoo" (425). Although this passage may be designed simply to "foreground the act of transplantation" of the white settlers from Great Britain (Thieme 2), it is likely that it was meant, as postcolonial literatures often do, to co-opt the colonial language with imitation and parody that can amuse even while it appropriates the language and raises consciousness of difference on several levels (Villanueva 659). The authors of *The Empire Writes Back* have examined in depth the frequency and breadth of such uses of the ironic mode in postcolonial works to reflect "language-place disjunction" and the widespread employment of "appropriation" of the language of the imperial culture for the postcolonial's own purposes (Ashcroft, Griffiths, and Tiffin 28, 38).

Far more deeply, the postcolonial issue of European linguistic dominance is seen in the position of silence taken by the one(s) colonized. Because "imperialism results in a profound linguistic alienation," silence, not only when imposed on, but also as a reply from, the postcolonial Other is the first position of the subjugated (Ashcroft, Griffiths, and Tiffin 10, 83–84). As a woman who has been victimized by her ex-husband and by her male-dominated culture, Gladys, in "End-of-the-line," has a profound wish for silence and wordlessness, for escape into the wordless natural world, and for freedom from having to explain her plight, shedding words as a "snake discarding the skins of past lives" (430). The "dead explanations" Gladys hopes to escape may refer to what Gayatri Chakravorty Spivak calls the "epistemic violence" of the European legal system (25). The white-male and upper-class-dominated legal language of marriage and divorce have betrayed Gladys, leaving her so impoverished after twenty-seven years of unpaid labor and child-rearing services that she must tend bar (Salleh 14, 60); or the "dead explanations" may refer to the social requirements of repeatedly explaining why she is, in the male- and class-dominated world which she knows, an Other of an even lower caste than a married woman, a divorcee, a previously-owned woman now without a man, and therefore assumed to be prey for men in general. Whether that Other is female, lower-class, rural, from a non-temperate climate (as with Maggie, in "Kakadu," facing the Melbourne sophisticates' ridicule of her "troppo" family, an Australian term meaning "from the tropics" and, therefore, "wild and crazy"), or a person whose color relegates her to a lower caste, silence is the first position chosen in defense.

However, it is important to note that in "Kakadu" the silence of the First Ones comes not from a position of weakness or defense; its origin is the strength, vitality, and ineffable power of rootedness in the natural world and, consequently, in its simultaneous existence with all time. More vivid than Gladys's silence of refusal and escape, the Dreamtime First Ones' presence and silence overturns the relationship between white settler-colonizer, Jug, and all Aborigines past-present and present-present. As a result of that encounter, Jug abandons what Albert Memmi calls the "profit, privilege, and usurpation" of the colonizer altogether (9).

Second, Hospital subverts techno-capitalist dominance with her deft employment of nature imagery. The "vultures" reference on the first page of "End-of-the-line" adroitly exposes the urban news media's exploitation of the devastation of the outback region; to the media the flood and its destruction are merely spectacle, a capitalist way of making money off suffering.[3] In "Kakadu" Hospital specifically compares Western European and white Australian settler notions of order and progress to nature and its wholeness as interpreted by the Aborigines. She visually, tactilely, and metaphysically contrasts the natural-*cum*-metaphysical world of the Aborigines and the divide-and-conquer, exploitative consciousness of the European colonizers. The strike against the road building through the Kakadu National Park becomes the defining event in which techno-capitalism meets Aboriginal deep ecology and Dreamtime spirituality. Here the transitory nature of techno-capitalist dominance loses the struggle for power when it attempts to subordinate nature as Other. We shall explore this issue in more depth below.

In the third subversion, Hospital addresses white-male dominance. The crisis-driven, near-death opportunism of the men in the Millennium Hotel seeking to have sex with any available woman appears to be a shared frenzy, as the couples go into the rooms of the hotel off the upper floor veranda, where, to Flutie, they generate "the fizz and spit of concentrated life" (428). Flutie is surprised to realize that Gladys is indifferent to him. She has had enough with the routine and oppression of being with a man and chooses nature, not Flutie, for her partner. It is nature for whom she shakes her hips, the one who will make her euphoric and "free as a bird" (431). In "Kakadu" Jug epitomizes male dominance in the extreme. He physically and verbally abuses his children, even when they are adults; he verbally abuses his Aborigine daughter-in-law, Liz, and seeks to abuse the land of the Dreamtime, even after Liz announces her pregnancy in telling him it is his unborn grandchild's inheritance. In Hospital's story Jug's abusive behavior does not succeed; rather, she draws the reader into the point of view of the abused Other. The Aborigines, through their First Ones, win, and in the process transform Jug into a person who, despite his resistance, acknowledges the ubiquity of their existence. Indeed, Jug becomes a nurturer of the Aborigine's land by completely abandoning his support both of human exploitation of nature and of any human control over nature whatsoever. As we have seen in "End-of-the-line" neither the woman nor nature is bested by a man or men. Similarly, in "Kakadu" the Aborigines and the land are not dominated, but make a new, boundary-crossing connection to, and conversion of, the former road builder.

Fourth, Hospital utterly subverts the epistemological stance of the European world in these two stories. As do many other postcolonial writers, Hospital "deliberately sets out to disrupt European notions of 'history' and the ordering of time" (Ashcroft, Griffiths, and Tiffin 34). In both of these stories the perspective shifts from that of a dominator (albeit an intermediate one, as white-settler culture in Australia is itself dominated by European culture) to privileging the point of view of the dominated, where history and time take on different dimensions and meanings. To disrupt the hegemonic dominator perspective, in "End-of-the-line" Hospital uses parodic references to the King James version of the Noah's ark story and the survival of the chosen few. She inverts and revises Flutie's belief that the crisis-time sexual encounters between men and women are "sensible ... telling death to f—off," in Gladys's own version of real sexual and mythic encounters with nature (428). She upends his male power value with Gladys's "sheer indifference" toward him (430) and concludes with Gladys's euphoric ride, surfing belly-down in the dinghy in the floodwaters. She rides away, alone, from "intolerable ordinary life" controlled by European and male hegemonic values, for her physical escape and her spirit's freedom (430). In "Kakadu" the European Great Chain of Being hierarchy is dismantled. What will survive as ways of being and knowing are not hegemonic values of hierarchy and linearity but complexity and diversity, what Wilson Harris describes as a pluralistic "cross-culturality" (Harris 17), and Jug, in awe, describes as simultaneous existence. "They are *with* us," he said, explaining to Maggie how, in his epiphanic vision, the Aboriginal First Ones appeared to him in the thousands, watching him in silence (*sic* 408). Both visible nature and the unseen universe are not subservient, but, indeed, as Australian Aborigines and Harris see it, the Ground of Being (McLuhan 41), "linked with the cosmos" (Harris qtd. in Possi 260). In turn, nature seems to honor Jug for his recognition; he is canonized by the cosmos: haloed in the "moon, bright orange, [which] sits behind his head like a plate" (408). In Hospital's story the linear way of knowing of European culture has met and bowed to the more inclusive, simultaneous consciousness of the Australian Aborigine culture.

With the most prominent postmodern issues Hospital addresses in mind, a deeper exploration of her use of nature imagery to influence her characters' development and relation to nature will be fruitful. In "End-of-the-line" nature is introduced as the main opponent in the very first paragraph. Flutie, a sheepherder, shearer, and pub regular speculates on whether the emergency workers will arrive on time before the floodwaters overwhelm the pub of the Millennium Hotel where they are partying. It is a flood party, a defiant gesture to the elements by people who refuse to evacuate a threatened area.

The power and enormity of nature are directly reported in several passages. Early on we learn the river is "coming down like a seven-foot wall" (423).

Nature's capacity for near-total devastation is again alluded to, this time with humor and a merging of local history with the Biblical story of the Great Flood: "And the flood was forty days and forty nights upon the earth ... and they can prove it from the *Courier-Mail,* though the figures were disputed in the Sydney papers" (425). To the people who do scurry away from the coming flood, nature is not mindless but sentient and intentional, as reflected in the narrator's report of apparently conscious inter-waterway collaboration: "all the rivers running in packs" and "the watercourses rising up in convocation" (426).

Earth, water, and animal imagery appear in descriptions of the characters or their thoughts, forcing the reader to reflect on each character's relationship with nature. Shortly after her first appearance in the story, Gladys, the barmaid, is described from Flutie's point of view as having "watery blue eyes" (423). Later, she imagines the river as a "black snake ... nosing south" (426). To its "wet blunt snout" Gladys offers an invitation, "Here, baby, she murmurs, moving her hips" (426). Even though just prior to this natural image of the river as snake, Hospital's narration likens a man-made machine to the sweetness of a lover; her placement of the hip-moving sentence makes the powerful coital imagery connect Gladys and the "wet blunt snout" of the river (426). It is nature's force and vitality, not something man-made that charms Gladys. Thus Hospital foreshadows Gladys's readiness to merge with nature and to choose it over all other suitors, in perhaps one of the most radical responses to male dominance a female can make. Later, the snake image appears again in association with Gladys after a passage in which letting go of the limits of words is compared to the freedom of a snake to shed its skin: "You felt like singing your new self without any words at all. You felt like a snake discarding the skins of past lives" (430). The magic-making power of being free of words is evoked here with reference to "singing," an English translation of an Aboriginal term used to name the act of making something happen or come into being by ritual magic; that is, the power of calling upon the metaphysical, spiritual worlds, by means of an elaborate ritual song, as the Aborigines do. To "sing a person" also can mean to request his or her death by magic (as occurs in "Kakadu"). Being wordless, a way of being more like nature, gives freedom, in Gladys's metaphysics.

Like nature, Gladys is beyond Flutie's reach not only physically, but also psychologically and spiritually. In the final scene, nature dominates again, in the freedom of flying with no mechanical means. Gladys, surfing on the dinghy in the rapids of the flooded river, sees as if from the rope swing of her childhood in Brisbane. She is riding on "that wild delicious arc of the swing, soaring up, up, and out from the broken rope" (431). Flying "beyond the farthest branch of the mango trees," Gladys feels "euphoria bear[ing] her upward, she is free as a bird" (431). As in her childhood experience, Gladys is again merging with nature, this time escaping beyond the reach of, and retrieval by, human hands. It is likely that the end is not merely the fractured leg of the child whose rope swing breaks, but the "euphoria" of the disconnection of the silver cord, the freedom of union with the All in death; though, in keeping with much in postmodern discourse, Hospital leaves the ending of the story ambiguous.

If for Gladys the rope of the metaphorical swing breaks disconnecting her entirely from what holds her to social conformity and physical safety, this is not the case for Flutie. Although also affected by the landscape and by nature, Flutie's experience is profoundly different from Gladys's. His response to the threat of annihilation by flood is in the classic "macho mate" style: half recognition of the danger, and half denial and bravado. In the opening line of the story, both halves of Flutie's reaction are clear; he believes in a fifty-fifty probability that "the world will end" very soon and concludes that they should live it up (423). Flutie's hedonism is characteristic of the "deep North" of Australia, according to Hospital (Samuels interview). It is also characteristic of the "nowhere to go but up," dispossessed point of view of Australia's first European settlers, emigrees from prisons and poorhouses. As Albert Memmi has described so clearly, in the chain of colonization there are "small colonizers," middlemen, who are not at the top and who experience both being colonized and colonizing others (11); the Australian white settler often falls into this category. The white settler-colonizer voice will appear again in "Kakadu."

In "End-of-the-line" nature is not only a setting but also a major player, reflecting power and, when met and joined, freedom. Landscape, both in the end-of-the-line, marginal Australian outback and also in the mounting, uncontrollable flood, has a profound but idiosyncratic effect on each of the characters. While Gladys greets the growing danger as the excitement she's been waiting for, embracing the danger and probable annihilation with a sense of euphoria and liberation, Flutie's response combines both the macho bravado-*cum*-denial and also the hedonist pragmatism that has helped make him one of the survivors of past floods. The pub dwellers have hope not in God nor in nature but in the large, proven, physical shelter of the biggest man-made structure around, the Millennium Hotel, their own ark (425). Of those two responses, the one showing the nature-human relationship as more powerful and important than the human-human relationship is the one with which Hospital closes her story and supports, by quantity, quality, and positioning.

This same stance, that the nature-human relationship trumps the human-human one, albeit differently evoked and presented, appears in "Kakadu." Here, though, the power implied in nature is less that of nature's physical strength and emotional attractiveness, and more of the unstoppable vitality and interconnectedness of all life. Hospital specifically compares the European, white-settler concept of order and progress to the Aboriginal idea of nature and its wholeness. The contrast is made visually, tactilely, and metaphysically between the natural-*cum*-metaphysical world of the Aborigines and the divide-and-conquer exploitative consciousness of the European, white-settler colonizers.

From the very opening of the "Kakadu" story, the European colonizers' imposition of monoculture cash crops and gardening by rows is contrasted to the wildness of diverse nature taking its course on the family acreage: "When [Maggie, the returning daughter] steps carefully between pineapple rows ... she puts her foot on at least a dozen eggs" (395). Maggie's mother reports the cause: Jug, Maggie's father, is inexplicably "against anything being penned in now. Against pruning" (395). The main characters differ in their views of the returning dominance of nature. Maggie's mother is upset, as the change foils her attempt to have an orderly life. Maggie's own initial reaction is the sensory unpleasantness of stepping on the undetected chicken eggs. Jug's idea of his relationship to nature before his epiphany is completely reversed afterward. Confronted by Liz, his rejected (because Aboriginal) daughter-in-law, at the planned site of a new road from Jabiru through Kakadu National Park and Aboriginal sacred land, Jug had responded that he was obliged to do this road building because it was his livelihood, claiming his working-class status for argument. In that pre-epiphanic time his ethic extended no farther than his own family's survival; that is, until he found out just how large that family was.

Maggie, the character whose point of view governs the story, begins to take the reader over the line between the dualistic European way of seeing nature versus alleged "civilization" and the Aborigine's holistic view of human beings' relation to nature and to each other. This transition passage explains "what was impossible about Melbourne.... She couldn't bear to expose her perfectly ordinary strangeness, her loony family's ordinary Darwin madness, to people who knew so very little" (397). The passage ends with Maggie's rueful but welcomed realization and acceptance of her belonging to, indeed, being owned by, this place: "I'm just a part of this blissed-out vegetable world" (398).

Liz reflects and represents the Aboriginal view of nature and human beings' relation to it: nature is their home, the source of their spiritual, physical, and mental wholeness. The land and its wholeness and health are the Aborigines' birthright and nurturance; damaging them in any way is sacrilege. So Liz, with other protestors, confronts Jug to prevent the building of a road on sacred ground. To illustrate the emotional, mythical, and practical levels of the Aboriginal valuing of the natural world, here is an actual report on the sacredness of the land, from the former chairman of the Aborigines' Northern Land Council, Galarrwuy Yunupingu who begins by noting his age: "When I was sixteen ...

> One day, I went fishing with Dad. As I was walking along behind him I was dragging my spear on the beach, which was leaving a long line behind me. He told me to stop doing that. He continued telling me that if I made a mark or dig, with no reason at all, I've been hurting the bones of the traditional people of that land. We must only dig and make marks on the ground when we perform or gather food. (*sic* qtd. in McLuhan 56)

After his vision of the First Ones, the ancient ancestors of today's Aborigines, Jug radically changes his perception of, and relation to, nature. In verification of nature's approval of his new worldview, Hospital describes him as he tells the story of how he came to leave his job as a road construction worker. Through

Maggie's eyes we see him canonized by nature, with the moon haloing his head (408). First Jug tells his daughter that right after Liz had confronted him, he had gotten on his steamroller, preparing to flatten the gravel for the road. "I suddenly had the giddy feeling I was on the spine of a razorback. Each side of me there was nothing. *Nothing*" (*sic* 408). Then Maggie sees his transformation into prophet-saint. Jug continues, "I turned around . . . and there were hundreds and hundreds of them, thousands maybe, just standing there with their spears in their hands, watching me. They didn't make a sound" (408). Jug concludes by telling Maggie, "'They are *with* us'" (*sic* 408). He adds that although they were silent he knew what they were waiting for and he got down, left the site, and never returned to roadwork (408). Finally, Jug pulls this all together for himself and Maggie, quoting the Biblical reference to *"a cloud of witnesses,"* conflating the Biblical passages of Jesus's preaching that in the life to come "the last shall be first," with the First Ones of the Dreamtime, and referring to their simultaneous presence with his culture and time (*sic* 408–09).

Thus, the reader and Maggie understand why Jug has let nature take over everything on the acreage to such an extent that the family's land and the rusted vehicle frames are so covered with indigenous vegetation that Maggie had to ask herself whether anyone could identify the boundary (405). Until Maggie listened, Jug had believed that no one but the Aboriginal daughter-in-law he had once rejected would understand why and how he had changed so radically in his relationship to nature. In Jug's new world there is no boundary; the dominant/subordinate dichotomy is completely annulled by new knowledge and a new epistemology.

In both "The End-of-the-line End-of-the-world Disco" and "Our Own Little Kakadu" Hospital brings us characters whose relationship with nature becomes greater than their relationship with other human beings. Here the colonized Other transcends and is empowered by powerful and wordless nature, and by relationships with human beings who recognize and welcome that intimate connection. With Gladys, the longing for freedom from ordinary life draws her to the simultaneously life-enhancing (because independent and thrilling) and life-threatening ride alone on the floodwaters in the fragile dinghy. Jug realizes that all of the human family, from the First Ones to those living now, are together, simultaneously present, and irrevocably interconnected; that what one does to the land one does to all human beings, past and present, because all coexist. This insight transfigures Jug, changing him from a pawn of Euro-white Australian settler exploitation of the Aboriginal land to a radical environmentalist and profound mystic. Hospital has created, especially in Jug, a "hybridity" which, as Ashcroft, Griffiths, and Tiffin interpret Wilson Harris's use of the term, would replace "a temporal linearity with a spatial plurality" (35–36).

It is informing to read Wilson Harris here on what he calls the "visibles and the invisibles," the man-made and the natural:

Whereas the road is man-made and the earth under the road is much more primordial. It belongs to some sphere of being or non-being, and non-being and being ... could be a link, because there is an arterial reality running through all landscapes, and the landscape seems inactive or passive, but it's alive, and therefore there are arteries running through.... The landscape is alive. If we misjudge the landscape, if we abuse it, it could turn upon us, in all sorts of peculiar ways. Because the landscape ... is linked with the cosmos. All these things are linked. (*sic* qtd. in Possi 260)

Compare that commentary with the Aboriginal view of land and nature, as described by T. C. McLuhan, "the world-forming marvels of The Dreamtime—the heroic acts of the ancestors that sustain and validate Aboriginal traditions—continue to provide a philosophy for contemporary Aboriginal life. It is a system of knowledge that regards man and nature as one corporate whole, sacred and eternal" (52).

Facing substantial postmodern issues of diversity, ecofeminism, and postcolonialism, with all the latter's concerns of anti-imperialism, antiracism, feminism, and rejection of language and epistemological dominance, Janette Turner Hospital has produced what Bharati Mukherjee would call wonderfully "subversive" writing (Address). Hospital makes her readers hear some voices not commonly heard, see in ways that make heads turn, accomplishing what Mukherjee has said is the function of "an imaginative work ... [to] enlarge the heart and soul; [to] expose ... selves to thoughts and feelings to which we have no armor" (Address).

NOTES

1. Ariel Salleh's description of one purpose of ecofeminism is "to highlight the relational [as opposed to exploitative] character of a particular human sensibility that has been marginalized, censored, repressed" (83). Hospital, like Salleh, sees the falseness of the European imperialist distinction between nature and history which leaves nature, females, and people of color as passive and only white males as active (14, 95).

2. See W.E.H. Stanner, *White Man Got No Dreaming* (Canberra: Australian National University Press, 1979), 230.

3. Coverage of disaster and suffering makes for increased media ratings and advertising revenues, an observation commonly noted in the United States since the attacks of September 11, 2001.

WORKS CITED

Ashcroft, Bill, Gareth Griffiths, and Helen Tiffin. *The Empire Writes Back: Theory and Practice in Post-Colonial Literatures.* London and New York: Routledge, 1989.

Berndt, Catherine H. and Ronald M. Berndt. *The Aboriginal Australians: The First Pioneers.* Carlton, Victoria: Pitman, 1983.

Connolly, Kevin. "Threads of Order." *The Power to Bend Spoons: Interviews with Canadian Novelists.* Ed. Beverly Daurio. Toronto: Mercury Press, 1998. 78–89.

Harris, Wilson. "The Age of the Imagination." *Journal of Caribbean Literatures.* 2.1–3 (2000): 17–25.

Hospital, Janette Turner. *Collected Stories: 1970–1995.* St. Lucia: University of Queensland Press,1995. 395–409; 423–431.

———. Interview with Selina Samuels. Fourth International Conference on the Short Story in English: Many Cultures, Many Voices. University of Northern Iowa. 8 June 1996.

———. Personal interview. June 10 & 11, 1996.

McLuhan, T. C. *The Way of the Earth: Encounters with Nature in Ancient and Contemporary Thought.* New York: Simon & Schuster, 1994.

Memmi, Albert. *The Colonizer and the Colonized.* New York: Orion Press, 1965.

Mukherjee, Bharati. Address. Fourth International Conference on the Short Story in English: Many Cultures, Many Voices. University of Northern Iowa. June 8, 1996.

Possi, Monica. "A Conversation with Wilson Harris." *Journal of Caribbean Literatures.* 2.1–3 (2000): 260–70.

Salleh, Ariel. *Ecofeminism as Politics: Nature, Marx, and the Postmodern.* London & New York: Zed Books, 1997.

Spivak, Gayatri Chakravorty. "Can the Subaltern Speak?" *The Post-colonial Studies Reader.* Eds. Bill Ashcroft, Gareth Griffiths, and Helen Tiffin. London and New York: Routledge, 1995. 24–28.

Thieme, John, ed. *The Arnold Anthology of Post-Colonial Literatures in English.* London: Arnold, 1996.

Villanueva, Victor. "On the Rhetoric and Precedents of Racism." *College Composition and Communication.* 50.4 (1999): 645–61.

7

The Virtuous Complaint: Iranian Short Fiction of the 1960s–1970s

Rivanne Sandler

The nature of Persian prose was altered forever with the appearance of the short story in Iran in the 1920s. In the same decade the world of poetry too was on its way to lasting change with a poem that broke the traditional rules and led to what in Persian letters is termed *she'r-e no* (new verse).[1] The "new poets" minimized the all-important basics of classical poetry: the conventions of form, language, meter, and rhyme, regarding them simply as "tools" for the primary purpose of expressing the poet's feelings.

The first generation of short-story writers delighted in the freedom afforded to them by the new genre. They concentrated on the telling of amusing tales, satirizing states of mind, highlighting human foibles, particularly of members of social groups who, for better or for worse, played a significant role in a changing society. However, the look of the new short story was recast in its infancy by a poet, Nima Yushij (1895–1959), who is accorded preeminence among the progressive elements of second-generation Iranian storytellers and poets. Nima Yushij introduced the startling notion of "my pain" as "the basic, underlying, source of my poetry … . I write poetry for my pain and the pain of others."[2] The innovative ideas and techniques of Nima Yushij and his dynamic inheritor, the poet Ahmad Shamlu (1925–2000), dominated the literary achievements of fellow poets, and the second generation of short-story writers as well. Many, if not the majority of the stories of the 1960s–1970s exhibit a haunting poetic sensibility. Furthermore, a tone of grievance dominates the expression and unfolding of the tale.

The "new poets" (and the "new" short-story writers) were the inheritors of a classical literary tradition that assumed an intimate knowledge of every item in the classical "literary cupboard." The poetic innovators insisted that the well-established conventions of poetry regarding subject matter, rhythm, rhyme, and imagery should be recast so as to be readily available to an audience of ordinary citizens. Similarly, the short-story writers of the 1950s and 1960s insisted that the story should not be overdressed in multiple adjectives and long convoluted sentences like the prose of the past. Ahmad Shamlu declared (in a "poetic manifesto" entitled "She'ri Keh Zendagi Ast" (Poetry Is Life)[3] that a poet working in the modern milieu "searches among those passing by on a busy street for his subject matter, his meter and rhyme." Short-story writers too drew upon the lives and everyday speech of ordinary people. No longer valued by the primary taste of the writing community was the conventional and specialized literary language of the past. Language should not be a barrier to an ordinary person's understanding of a prose piece. The short story of the 1960s–1970s followed the example outlined in Ahmad Shamlu's "Poetry Is Life": "Today's poet is no stranger to the pain of being human; he laughs like ordinary men/ He infuses his very being with people's pain and hope."

The tone of this poem is affable, even cajoling. The poet addresses his audience directly, attempting to win them over through convincing argument, rather than lecturing from a position of authority, as in the past. "Come with me, dear fellow citizen!" The next several lines of the poem read as if the poet has indeed made friends with his audience, and feels comfortable enough to share his experience of writing poetry. The poet assumes the listener's understanding, sympathy, and interest because all the features of his poem—subject matter, rhyme, meter—are drawn from life itself. "No longer is he separated from his audience by a different life experience. No longer does the poet of today work in the "hothouse" atmosphere of the court and write for the pleasure of royal patrons only. "New poets" tell the story "of pleasant mornings and dark nights."[4]

The "new" short story often adopted the same cozy conversational tone exhibited in Shamlu's poem "Poetry Is Life," assuming a close relationship with the audience. A notable example of the amiable conversational mode of narration (but with a sardonic twist) is Bahram Sadeqi's (1936–1986) short story "Tadris Dar Bahar-e Del-Angiz" (Teaching in a Pleasant Spring).[5] The story begins by addressing a generic "you" politely, with an invitation: "Let's suppose, if you will that both of us are sitting in a classroom." The narrator, whose exact identity remains a mystery throughout the story, is distinguished only by his (not likely her) voice; an unfailingly polite, solicitous, and measured tone dominates the progression of the tale. "But if you think this is a bit absurd or you're afraid to be alone, or you want this to be more official and nearer to reality, it doesn't matter, we can all be sitting in a classroom" (Persian 206; English 53). The narrator then goes on to describe the kind of classroom evidently found only in dreams: spacious, clean, with plenty of fresh air and light. Every element of the imagined classroom is ironically on the order of the most basic of classroom amenities. The reality of the opposite intrudes into the dream in the narrator's ironic comment: "It's fortunate that these thoughts have entered our minds in a favorable season, during this pleasant spring, so we won't need a heater or a fan" (Persian 206; English 53).

It is clear to the reader that there is a gap between the ideal and the possible. In spite of this discrepancy, the narrator never becomes angry or frustrated. He is unwavering in his consideration for his audience; every now and then, just when interest or patience might be flagging, he interjects a polite directive: "let's assume ... " or "we are still imagining ... " Although the narrator is obviously making a concerted effort to interest his listeners, he seems to know that people are busy; they have other pressing concerns, and a tendency to look the other way, to ignore what they see in front of them, to pretend that everything is just fine. But, as the narrator points out, there is the promise of "a propitious future" (Persian 206; English 53) for all of them, if the splendid scenario, they as a group are busy imagining, is realized.

Narrators, students, audience; all are waiting for the class to begin. But the teacher has yet to make an appearance. When he does appear, he is a formless hazy figure. He asks the students what they wish to read but his question remains unanswered because teacher and students are unable to see each other clearly. In a telling reference to reality, the teacher can only make out a mass of similar shapes and sizes. However, in a surreal twist, a sudden ring of the school bell startles the teacher into seeing clearly. But the classroom is empty save for an old man at the back of the classroom, sleeping. The others have already left, following the lead of an angelic blond-haired girl who was sitting at the front of the classroom. The blond angel had, early on in the drama, excused herself from the classroom's shortcomings.

The old man, too, is able to see clearly. He sees a young man with a strong build whose eyes and nose are cut off, with unruly hair, protruding crooked teeth, cold eyes. The old man stares at the teacher and asks him: "You ... why are you ... like that?" In an obvious miscommunication, the teacher asks whether the old man enjoyed his lecture. The old man tells the teacher that his lecture was of no use and that all his high hopes for learning have been disappointed: "I didn't understand one word" (Persian 212; English 59). The teacher slaps him and berates him for his rudeness, and threatens to fail him. The old man responds by apologizing, pleading for mercy and forgiveness, for himself, and each and every one of his family members.

The conversation between the only two verbal participants in the classroom experience meanders on for a time; the teacher is righteously indignant and the old man dutifully penitent. Finally, the teacher gives the old man a failing grade for all the old man's attempts to placate him. As the teacher walks out of the classroom, leaving the old man in tears, the old man comes into focus clearly, and he cries out, "Where are you going? Looking like that ... you unfortunate .... Okay, do what you want to" (Persian 214; English 61). His strong voice, an angry voice is unheard in the emptiness.

The complaint of this tale is wrapped in sarcasm. The narration is eerily reasonable and measured, except for odd bursts of anger from the teacher and the old man. Told throughout in a conversational style, mixing the absurdity of reality and the reality of the absurd, the author draws the audience into the theater of his own despair that he shares with the other participants in the educational drama.

"I write poetry for my pain and the pain of others." The students in this story forsake the useless classroom, the teacher leaves in frustration. The old man, representative of the many like him who have been abandoned for skilled and more valued segments of the modernizing economy, is left behind, shouting into the wind. The text clearly points out that "the basic problem is money" (Persian 211; English 58). But truth is buried in the confusing mix of reality and obliviousness, in the story, as well as in the reality of the situation depicted in the story. None of the characters except the old man demonstrates any capacity for straight thinking and action. The story is a sustained cry of pain—the pain of awareness, of unlocked opportunities. It is an expression of the author's underlying frustration and anger which he shares with disgruntled elements of society who have no way of expressing their complaints. And if they did, they would not be heard.

Socially concerned writers were a thorn in the side of a government that had a glorified vision of Iran that bypassed the likes of the simple old man and the frustrated, "handicapped" teacher in the story "Teaching in a Pleasant Spring." More angry old men make their appearance in writer and dramatist Gholamhosayn Sa'edi's (1935–1985) short story "Maskhareh-ye Navankhaneh" (The Orphanage Clown).[6]

Sa'edi's ability to dramatize the absurdity of reality is amply demonstrated in this story. An antiques dealer shows a gullible patron, a retired employee of the archive branch of the Justice Department, a coin he claims is from a historic period. "It was only at that time that the gazelle's foot on a coin bore a resemblance to the tail of a dog. If you look closely, this foot bears a very strong resemblance to a dog's tail." Dealer and patron collude in the sham: "You're perfectly right. I didn't even realize ... it's a dog's tail," says the retiree. But the antiques dealer comes back with "It's not a dog's tail, it's the foot of a gazelle" (Persian 128), proving that he can manipulate the civil servant to his heart's content. There follow several obviously ridiculous tales about history, mirroring the official manipulation of the past at the expense of the needs of the present.

It seems that the antiques dealer can claim anything about his objects. His gullible customer will believe him. He will even make a purchase although, as a record of a quarrel with his wife further on in the story lets us know, he has little enough money to spend. His wife "wanted food supplies, convinced that however valuable old things are, they can't replace a meal and a full stomach" (Persian, 132–33).

The retired civil servant stops on his way home from the antiques shop at a café he frequents. Failing to find an empty table, he asks an old man if he can join him. The retiree refuses a newspaper because, as he tells the newsboy in a self-congratulatory manner, "I am informed about everything." The old man says, "Are you serious? Do you know everything? ... Then can you tell me how is it that things have gone so wrong for us?" The evasive answer is: "There's nothing wrong with us, it's the world" (Persian 130).

The retiree boasts to the old man that he has just purchased two valuable and distinctive coins: "It's likely that none of the retirees who gather here have had this privilege." The old man's forthcoming exclamation interjects a note of reality into the ridiculous sketch: "What use are old things.... Nothing is more antiquated than I am ... how much am I worth?" (Persian 131).

The retiree is unfailingly optimistic and hopeful in meetings with the unhappy neglected old men who cross his path, advising one to "keep busy." "Take me, for example. I'm busy collecting old things and pursuing this hobby has brought a wonderful warmth to my life" (Persian 131). Obviously the civil servant is living a dream and the reader waits for reality to catch up with him. The next morning at his wife's insistence, the retired civil servant sets out to return his antique objects. He stops for a rest in the National Garden and meets another old man with a beatific look on his face. They engage in conversation and the retired civil servant complains that "something strange has happened to me and I don't know what to do. What should I do?" (Persian 134). Now it's the turn of the old man to offer platitudes: "Nothing is unsolvable. Since the beginning of time, millions of problems have been solved" (Persian 134). The civil servant responds with a denial of any solution for "the strange puzzle I'm involved in" (Persian 134). "Turn to 'one of the *Aghas*' (literally: 'Sirs') to help you with any problem, spiritual, financial, it doesn't matter," says the old man, and offers to set things right for him.

The story ends with both men walking hand in hand, in blissful ignorance. Still gullible, joining another naive person who believes that help is just around the corner, the retiree shouts to some passing birds in flight, meaningless empty words of hope: "Good-bye my friends. The road to salvation has been found at last. The angel of mercy saved me from misfortune. May you be happy and never forget the sound of happiness" (Persian 135).

Gholamhosayn Sa'edi (a practicing psychiatrist in the slums of south Tehran as well as a dramatist and short-story writer) has explained the creation of his characters as mirrors of his own constrained life as a writer and the life of his fellow Iranians.[7] In the story discussed above, he manages, despite the veil of absurdity and confusion that dominates the conversations, to reveal to his reader the well-kept secret of government neglect of pressing social problems and, at the same time, to point a finger at the complacent middle class. The characters say nothing really, but the reader discerns the truth.

That Nima Yushij's dedication of his poetry to the expression of "pain" determined the generally serious tone of short fiction and poetry of the 1960s and 1970s is well illustrated by Beh Azin's (1915–c. 1989) autobiographical short story, "Az Dehaneh-ye Chah" (Through the Opening in the Well).[8] The story consists of the dream-like musing of the narrator as he considers the world around him.

The author was a poor student who went to France to study engineering at government expense after completing high school in Iran. In this sense, he bears a close resemblance to the students in Bahram Sadeqi's story who abandoned their underfunded classroom for the golden opportunities that awaited them with the acquisition of a foreign degree. (Beh Azin returned to Iran in the 1930s and was employed in the Iranian Navy and the Ministry of Education.) In Iran, the narrator continually searches for a way out of his sense of confinement and oppression. "I cannot be myself except when I escape, through my vision and fantasies, from the tight space and the darkness of my well" (Persian 40).

Scenes in which the affirmative power of "light" overcomes the burden of "darkness" follow. Looking at "a little garden without any flowers or plants and surrounded by dusty brick walls on every side ... borders of small box trees formed a dark, thick screen, contributing to the sad and hopeless quality of our everyday life" (Persian 40), the narrator turns his gaze on "a weeping willow tree, like a huge, black fountain, leaping out of the earth's heart, a thousand delicate trembling branches newly covered with a delicate green coating pouring down" (Persian, 40–41). He turns westwards, where

> the sky was still bright, green and yellow and translucent like satin. The crescent moon, beside shining Venus, sprinkled light from above, down on this simple scene ... all at once I found myself changed ... I was being drawn out of myself. I was like flowing air. It was delightful, disturbing, maybe death. (Persian 41)

Returning from France, Iran seems unbearably ugly and decrepit and backward.

In the "smoke-filled" kitchen of his home in the slums of south Tehran, "the thin face of my mother, weary, wrinkled, pained me more than anything else." However, once again, the magic of the blue sky and a thousand stars turns gloom into brilliance. "Oh Lord. How many stars there were in the heart of this dark night. And how pleasant, how peaceful, how mystical the darkness can be" (Persian 42).

The experience in France is a reversal of his Iranian experience. Watching an airplane make a terrifying dive toward earth, and finally hit water, the narrator finds that he "wanted the earth, the dark and strong calming earth." He reaches the conclusion after this electrifying experience that, for better or worse, "I am a child of the earth after all" (Persian 44).

The story concludes with a visit the narrator makes with his father to a family friend, a noble, hardworking gentleman who had suffered a bad fall and is not expected to survive. The room where the man lies is dark; any scrap of light causes the gravely ill man distress. The narrator confesses to a feeling of dread in the room's gloom. A marked contrast exists between the man who happily showed them around his sun-filled garden and the man overtaken by a desire for the "darkness" of death (Persian 45).

This story seems extremely close to poetry in its reflective and haunting consideration of life's contradictions. It also echoes Beh Azin's view of the writer as the most enlightened member of society and advocate for the disadvantaged. Literature, for Beh Azin, was to be a guiding light, showing the way to a better world. Speaking to the newly formed Writers' Union in the late 1960s, Beh Azin expressed his view that writing should be devoted to social change; if not, it was unworthy of being called literature. "Art is a report of the artist's observations, experiences and thoughts, arranged to convince the audience. Literature acts as a fermenting agent in society."[9]

Some writers chose to portray characters who have no way out of their predicament. Bahram Sadeqi in his story "Vesvas" (Obsession)[10] enters the mind of a young educated man who lives an isolated, lonely existence. The story opens with "He's on his way to the movies. He told the landlord's wife who lives on the second floor. He should get in line now. After the film, he'll go for a little walk" (Persian 20). The language is spare, the story reads like a documentary. We see the young man walking, then lining up for his ticket. At this point the author permits a glimpse into the young man's state of mind. He worries endlessly. Will he have enough money left over by the end of next week to see the coming attraction. He makes a mental note of his expenses: bus fares, bread, cigarettes (the cheapest brand). The name of the movie "The Blue Lamp" sets off another round of nagging worries: "I didn't turn off the light in the room.... They tell me I use too much electricity. They'll add it on to the rent" (Persian 21).

The young man is obsessed with worries about money. But this is only the beginning. One day a stranger arrives on the doorstep and rings the landlord's bell. When the landlord's wife asks the tall stranger what he is looking for, he replies: "A man, single, civil servant, about twenty-three or twenty-four, fair hair. He just moved here" (Persian 21). The landlord's wife informs the stranger that the young man is at the movies. The stranger says politely: "That's really too bad, madam. I have some very urgent business with him" (Persian 21). After pacing up and down the street for a while, he leaves, telling himself he'll return.

Not much time elapses before the stranger returns again. This time the veil of civility is abandoned. When the landlord's wife tells the stranger that the young man is still not at home, he says that he'll return tomorrow and almost as an afterthought adds aggressively, "Tell him I'll be back for sure" (Persian 23). Hearing the landlady's report of the incident with the stranger adds another obsessive worry to the already extensive list of the young man's compulsive anxieties. Who is the stranger? He has no idea. How does the stranger know him, know his name? He has no idea. The problem overwhelms him and he adds it to his concern about the lights, the stove, the keys for the door. The reader suspects the young man will never stop worrying.

The predicament of this harmless young man and the unidentified, but menacing stranger who suddenly enters his life is reminiscent of "a persistent stranger who represents the administrative power of the day" who meddles in the artistic and everyday life of the writer Beh Azin, causing him heightened agitation and apprehension.[11]

The next two stories unconventionally enter the homes and the thoughts of two female characters, one told by a little girl and the other by a woman of thirty-four years. Both characters tell stories of injustice, the little girl to her doll and the woman to a conjectured listener. The plight of the young girl and the older woman are not of their own making, but rather stem from their environment. Furthermore, in neither of these stories is the female character (or any of the other characters, for that matter) allowed to voice her complaints directly and frankly to those around her.

The plot of Hushang Golshiri's "Arusak-e Chini-ye Man" (My China Doll)[12] unfolds through the conversation of the young girl with her doll. We quickly ascertain that the crisis the young girl and her family are facing is the arrest of the child's father. The story begins hopefully: "Mama says he'll come back." The action is spare, moving between home and prison. There is little in the way of characterization. It is the use of language that provides the reader with the guide to the fact that there is an important story within the story. The conversations are colloquial and familiar. The reader senses a rare opportunity to penetrate the normal walls around family life and partake of intimate family affairs. Not only does the reader cross over into the private space of the family but also he or she is permitted to enter the inner space of an individual. Seeing what transpires through the seemingly naive but insightful conversations of the child with her doll, the reader gathers that the hub of this tale is the unwillingness of any of the characters to face up to, confront, or challenge the injustice of their situation.

Not one of the characters pierces the veil of silence that covers "the truth" and also constrains family relationships. Unfailingly, the author succeeds in showing that a patina of politeness blunts the effect of every word, except those spoken by the child to her doll. In prison, "Daddy" tells his wife: "Don't let me see you lose face in front of them [i.e., the prison guards]" and "Esmat, dry your tears. I don't want them to see you crying" (Persian 67; English 335). If a character departs from the code of silence and courtesy that dominates relationships, even within the intimate circle of the family, the offending character is quickly notified not to speak, not to cry. "Mama said, 'didn't Daddy tell you not to cry?'" (Persian 68; English 336). Grandmother, who is a little more outspoken, is continually told not to speak or cry "in front of the child." "Mama's bad. Not always; just when she doesn't let Grandmother talk, talk about Daddy. She's bad when she says loudly: Grandmother!" (Persian 68; English 336).

Reality is coated with evasion. Sharp, dangerous edges are blurred. The female guard in the guileless words of the child is "pretty, like my own china doll .... She was like those ladies that talk on television, no, those who read from the newspaper and smile" (Persian 70; English 338). The child wants to say "But Daddy isn't coming back" (Persian 70; English 338). Instead, she speaks to her doll, acting out what has happened to her for the doll, instructing the doll to say this or that in imitation of what has happened. "Daddy, he looked like the china doll, like when that brat Mehri broke her. His face looked funny" (Persian 74; English 342). "Daddy got like my china doll. He was broken" (Persian 75; English 343).

The story ends with the child venting her anger and frustration on her doll, threatening to tear off its legs and arms and head and throw it in the garbage can. "I won't cry for you either. But I can't not cry" (Persian 75; English 343).

The woman who narrates her tale of woe in Jalal Al-Ahmad's "Zan-e Ziyadi" (The Unwanted Woman)[13] takes her listener into her confidence because: "To whom can one speak? If a person doesn't tell someone, her heart will burst" (Persian 187; English 71); the story is told by a first-person narrator but shifts to the impersonal from time to time.

The "unwanted woman" of the title is thirty-four, betrothed, and then married to a man who works in her brother's office. They meet briefly for the first time in the home of the woman's parents. She goes to live in her new husband's home with his mother and sister. He spends less and less time with his wife in their room and more and more time with his mother and sister. Finally, he returns her to her father. The story is primarily a record of the woman's "complaints," her inner thoughts following her return to her father's home. "It's as if the walls of my father's house were clasping my heart.... Nothing has changed but I am suffocating. Everything has changed for me" (Persian 185; English 71). "How can a person not know that her existence is the cause of all this torment.... How can someone possibly not feel that they are unwanted?" (Persian 186; English 71).

Although the narrator tells all to her listener, she is extremely reticent about saying what is on her mind to members of her own family, as well as to her in-laws. The story is dotted with lines such as: "God is my witness. When I was in the room, I wanted with all my heart for him to find out that I wear a wig. But I couldn't say anything" (Persian 190; English 74). "Do you think there were words? Or that we quarreled? Or that I spoke out of turn, to bring about this disaster?" (Persian 192; English 75). She chides her mother-in-law cautiously for not attending the wedding, with no effect at all (Persian 194; English 76).

Ultimately, the woman regrets never having learned to read and write, never having enjoyed any kind of social life, never having spoken up for herself, never having complained, accepting whatever came her way. Where did it get her? She could not believe that her husband would return her to her father's house. "It was like I knew what he wanted to do to me. But once again I put it out of my head" (Persian 198; English 78).

Only at the end of her story does she allow herself to cry without stopping. The tears are followed by anger for lost opportunities: "I wanted my own home, to be the mistress of my home" (Persian 191; English 74). "Damn it, who's to blame? Why did I just sit there and let them destroy my life?" (Persian 198; English 79).

The woman's question is left unanswered. Who or what is to blame for her predicament? The woman is illiterate. Who is to blame? She cannot support herself. With whom does the fault lie? The woman has no one to listen to her complaint, care about her situation. The story begs for answers, solutions to the problem of women as society's outcasts.

Among the literary agendas of the 1960s–1970s was the emphasis on forthright language. The writer Simin Daneshvar (1921–) comments that in the period following the Second World War, writers, including herself, began

> to pay attention to the common people and to use a language that the people could understand. I very quickly came to the conclusion that the duty of every writer in this country is to write very simply because of the low rate of literacy.... I use simple prose and defend the workers.[14]

A prime example of plain, straightforward language is Ahmad Mahmud's (1930–) short story "Masibat-e Kabk-ha" (The Partridge Tragedy).[15] The story has an arid, monotonous tone which itself tells another story. Under a seemingly calm surface there lies a seething anger that finally erupts into the story itself.

The palm tree in the dry, empty courtyard of the man, his wife, and son who inhabit the story is "only a blurred outline" of "spear-tipped, dark dusty leaves ... mingled with the dark blue expanse of the sky" (Persian 6). The very opposite of the weeping willow tree whose branches, covered with a new growth of "delicate green coating" outlined against a bright sky, hold out such hope for the narrator of Beh Azin's "Through the Opening in the Well."

Rather than speak directly of the miserable lives of the characters in the woebegone, neglected area of southern Iran, which is the setting of the story, the language suggests the aridity and hopelessness of life: "There was the humidity of the air and the salty smell of the sea" (Persian 5). "The dusty lantern threw a faint light on the wall. The air in the courtyard was suffocating" (Persian 7). "All the stars hanging from the sky like lanterns radiated a dull glow" (Persian 10).

Once again, as in the other stories discussed in this chapter, the truth of the situation is buried in suggestion, symbolism, irony, and in the apathetic, lethargic conversations of the characters. The father wants the radio turned off. The son wants it on: "Maybe we'll learn something from the news" (Persian 7). The lackadaisical woman is the surprising harbinger of reality, as is the wife of the retired civil servant in Sa'edi's "The Clown of the Orphanage." "That's a long time off," (Persian 7) says the woman in this story who is described as "sitting ... like a brooding hen ... her eyes, yellow and predatory like a hawk" (Persian 5). It is unlikely that any "real" news, especially of internal issues, will be discussed in public. Following a broadcast about "waste" and "the budget must be utilized for the improvement of the economic situation" and promises to rectify matters, the three characters "looked at one another in silence for a few moments, uncomprehending, silence" (Persian 8).

In this story, as in other stories discussed in this chapter, customary sources of communication such as newspapers and the radio are unreliable. After the radio is turned off, reality reasserts itself. "The son sighed, turned off the radio and said: 'Unemployment is coming again.' The father frowned and added: 'And hungry times too'" (Persian 9).

There is no one to take responsibility for miserable lives, for promises made but not kept, for the blanket of evasion and repression enveloping society. Thus the blameless family partridges are martyred, in an illogical and ultimately useless transfer of accountability (Persian 10).

The writers of the 1960s–1970s cloak their ideas in symbols, insinuations, and absurdity. Characters, even those with grievous complaints, tend to pretend in front of others that nothing is wrong. Uncomfortable facts and controversies are cloaked in politeness. But the stories cast a wide net over society; they share what citizens experience. The underlying reality is discernible, at least between the lines.

In the first days of the 1978–1979 revolution that changed the government and the culture of Iran, the writer Sa'edi spoke with optimism of a "fresh, vital feeling; people were free to discuss and exchange opinions and air 'hopes and anxieties.'" Both women and men, and people from all walks of life participated in the excitement of openly airing views and complaints in public squares, on university campuses "and even remote cross-streets." Sa'edi found the lack of fear and the newfound freedom exhilarating.[16]

The stories discussed in this chapter put unexpressed opinions, hopes, and fears into words for public display. In the 1960s–1970s, writers joined their fellow citizens to articulate a "virtuous complaint."

NOTES

1. Translations from the Persian are by the author of this paper. References to English translations are noted when available.

2. *Az Nima Ta Ba'd* (Nima and After). Tehran: Fourth Edition, 1363/1984, p.11.

3. Shamlu, Ahmad. *Hava-ye Tazeh* (Fresh Air: Poems from 1945–1956). Tehran: Entesharat-e Nil, 1353/1974–5.

4. If "the night" is taken to be the symbol of evil and oppression, the poet assures the people of an inevitable dawning, or "awakening." Leonardo P. Alishan, "Ahmad Shamlu: The Rebel Poet in Search of an Audience," *Iranian Studies,* Vol. XVIII, nos. 2–4, Spring-Autumn 1985, p. 379.

5. First appeared in 1963 in an Iranian journal and then in a collection of Sadeqi's short stories, *Sangar Va Qomqomeh-ha-ye Khali* (Fortification and Empty Flasks). Tehran: Ketab-e Zaman, 1349/1970. Translated into English in *Modern Persian Short Stories.* Edited and translated by Minoo Southgate. Washington, D.C.: Three Continents Press, 1980.

6. *Shab Neshini-ye Ba-Shokuh.* Tehran: Second Edition, 1349/1970.

7. Although pressed mainly for details for a record of the times in which he was living (for an oral history project), the writer managed to say a few words about his writ-

ing. The interview is published in the journal (in Persian) *Alefba* (new series), no. 7, Autumn 1986, pp. 70–139.

8. *Shahr-e Khoda* (God's City). Tehran: Agah, 1357/1978. Although Beh Azin's stories date from the 1950s, they saw the light of day only for a short while in the year or so preceding and following the 1978–1979 revolution, due to the writer's political affiliation.

9. *Goftar Dar Azadi* (A Talk on Freedom). Tehran: Agah, 1979. First published in 1977.

10. *Sangar va Qomqomeh-ha-ye Khali* (Fortification and Empty Flasks). Tehran: Ketab-e Zaman. First published in 1349/1970. Fourth printing 2536 (c. 1975).

11. *Goftar Dar Azadi,* pp. 54–55.

12. *Namazkhaneh-ye Kuchek-e Man* (My Little Place of Prayer). Tehran: Ketab-e Tehran, 1364/1985. First published 1354/1975. Translated in *New Writing from the Middle East.* Edited with an Introduction and Commentary by Leo Hamalian and John D. Yohannan. New York: New American Library. First Mentor Printing, 1978. Translations from the Persian tend to follow the English translation.

13. *Zan-e Ziyadi* (The Unwanted Woman). Tehran: Entesharat-e Ravaq. First printing 1331/1952. Fourth printing 1356/1977. Translated in *Iranian Society: An Anthology of Writings by Jalal Al-e Ahmad.* Compiled and edited by Michael C. Hillmann. Lexington, KY: Mazda Publishers, 1982.

14. *Alefba* (new series), no. 4, 1983, p. 148. The irony of the insistence on language that was accessible to a wide audience is the low rate of literacy in Iran. In the late 1940s, 12.5 percent of Iran's population was literate. By 1956, the literacy rate had risen just .3 percent. By 1980, less than 45 percent of all Iranians could read and write. *Iranian Studies,* Vol. XVIII, nos. 2–4, Spring-Autumn 1985, p. 408.

15. *Za'eri Zir-e Baran* (A Visitor in the Rain). Tehran: Entesharat-e Farhang, 1347/1968. First published in 1345/1966.

16. "Deculturization in the Islamic Republic," translated by Michael Beard and Hosein Qadimi. *Fiction International,* 15:1, 1984, pp. 180–89. The period of relative freedom of expression was, however, short-lived.

WORKS CITED

Al-e Ahmad, Jalal. *Zan-e Ziyadi* (The Unwanted Woman). Tehran: Entesharat-e Ravaq. First printing 1331/1952; fourth printing 1356/1977.

Alishan, Leonardo P. "Ahmad Shamlu: The Rebel Poet in Search of an Audience," *Iranian Studies,* Volume XVII, Nos. 2–4 (Spring-Autumn 1985), 375–422.

Az Nima Ta Ba'd (Nima and After). Tehran: n.p., fourth edition, 1363/1984.

Beh Azin, M. E., *Shahr-e Khoda* (God's City). Tehran: Agah, 1357/1978.

———. *Goftar Dar Azadi* (A Talk on Freedom). Tehran: Agah, 1979. First published, 1977.

Golshiri, Hoshang. *Namazkhaneh-ye Kuchek-e Man* (My Little Place of Prayer). Tehran: Ketab-e Tehran, 1364/1985.

Hamalian, Leo and John D. Yohannan, introduction and commentary. *New Writing from the Middle East.* New York: New American Library. First Mentor Printing, 1978.

Hillmann, Michael C., compiler and editor. *Iranian Society: An Anthology of Writings by Jalal Al-e Ahmad.* Lexington, KY: Mazda Publishers, 1982.

Mahmud, Ahmad. *Za'eri Zir-e Baran* (A Visitor in the Rain). Tehran: Entesharat-e Farhang, 1347/1968. First published 1345/1966.

Sa'edi, Gholamhosayn (Sa'edi, Gholam-Hossein). *Shab Neshini-ye Ba-Shokuh* (A Splendid Soirée). Tehran: n.p., second edition, 1349/1970.

———. "Tarikh-e Shafahi-ye Iran. Mosahebeh-ye Daneshgah-e Harvard ba Gholam-Hossein Sa'edi" (Harvard University Interview with Gholam-Hossein Sa'edi), *Alefba* (new series., Paris) (in Persian), no. 7 (Autumn 1986), 70–139.

———. "Deculturization in the Islamic Republic," translated by Michael Beard and Hosein Qadimi. *Fiction International,* 15:1 (1984), 180–89.

Sadeqi, Bahram. *Sangar va Qomqomeh-ha-ye Khali* (Fortification and Empty Flasks). Tehran: Ketab-e Zaman, first published 1349/1970. Fourth printing 2536 (c. 1975).

Shamlu, Ahmad. *Hava-ye Tazeh* (Fresh Air: Poems from 1945–1956). Tehran: Entesharat-e Nil, 1353/1974/5.

Southgate, Minoo, editor and translator. *Modern Persian Short Stories.* Washington, D.C.: Three Continents Press, 1980.

8

Jean Toomer's *Cane*

Donald Petesch

In my book *A Spy in the Enemy's Country* I suggested that *Cane* is many books. To begin with, it is a young man's book, whose women tend to be dream-visions, mythic rather than naturalistic; it is a philippic against the city, that place of locks, bolts, houses, grime, straight lines, the look of the other; it is an evocation of roots, of place, of home; it is an experimental work; and it is a study in ambivalence.[1]

While I believe that *Cane* is all of these, for the purposes of this chapter I will focus on the tensions created by Toomer's placing various elements in opposition. The first and third Georgia sections clearly contrast with the middle Washington, D.C./Chicago section, but the tendency can also be found at both the level of the sentence and the paragraph. To illustrate: Fern (from the first Georgia section) is imagined in an incongruous setting: "picture if you can, this cream-colored solitary girl sitting at a tenement window looking down on the indifferent throngs of Harlem. Better that she listen to folk songs at dusk in Georgia, you would say, and so would I."[2] From "Calling Jesus" (in the second Washington, D.C./Chicago section): "Her breath comes sweet as honeysuckle whose pistils bear the life of coming song. And her eyes carry to where builders find no need for vestibules, for swinging on iron hinges, storm doors" (58). And, finally, from the third—"Kabnis"—section, set in rural Georgia. Kabnis is speaking: "Dear Jesus do not chain me to myself and set these hills and valleys, heaving with folk-songs; so close to me that I cannot reach them. There is a radiant beauty in the night that touches and ... tortures me. Ugh. Hell. Get up, you damn fool. Look around. Whats (*sic*) beautiful there? Hog pens and chicken yard. Dirty red mud. Stinking outhouse. Whats [*sic*] beauty anyway but ugliness if it hurts you?" (85)

Toomer, in a letter to Waldo Frank upon completing *Cane,* wrote that "*Cane*'s design is a circle." He elaborated: "Aesthetically, from simple forms to complex ones, and back to simple forms. Regionally, from the South up into the North, and back into the South again."[3] Toomer's "circle," looked at closely, could as usefully be described as a line, the endpoints representing polar elements: South versus North, natural versus mechanical, spiritual versus material, feminine versus masculine. These opposing, polar elements infuse *Cane* and help to create the recurring dramatic tensions. Similar contrasts at the level of characterization express the ambivalence in such divided characters as Dan and Muriel in "Box Seat," John in "Theater," Paul in "Bona and Paul," and Kabnis in "Kabnis."

We know—from Toomer's autobiographical statements and from biographical criticism—how closely *Cane* mirrors Toomer's own experience of Georgia and Washington, D.C., and to what extent the text bodes forth Toomer's own ambivalent racial choices. We can appreciate, for example, the impact of Toomer's Louisiana governor grandfather, but an important *literary* forebear has been generally ignored. W.E.B. Du Bois—another black northerner gone South—viewed the southern rural folk in his 1903 *The Souls of Black Folk* with both the depth of empathy and sensitivity we will see two decades later in Toomer's *Cane,* but he also, as Toomer, does his viewing within a set of contrasts, which creates dramatic tensions and oppositions throughout *The Souls of Black Folk.* These contrasts are established in the first chapter, appropriately titled "Of Our Spiritual Strivings." There Du Bois describes the freed Black in terms of spiritual qualities: "[F]ew men ever worshipped Freedom with half such unquestioning faith.... [H]ow faithfully, how piteously, this people strove to learn.... [S]aw in himself some faint revelation of his power, of his mission.... [N]o truer exponents of the pure human spirit of the Declaration of Independence."[4] Du Bois contrasts the spiritualized quality of Blacks with the materialism of American society: "we black men seem the sole oasis of simple faith and reverence in a dusty desert of dollars and smartness" (11–12). The contrasts are sustained throughout *The Souls of Black Folk,* as Du Bois contrapuntally opposes hopes, yearnings, beliefs, strivings to the materialistic logic of finance capitalism in the southern Black Belt, a logic that once had held black souls as personal chattel and now squeezed black souls in systems of debt peonage.

Du Bois is a profound cultural critic, in the tradition of Thoreau. His is not simply the objective, and often detached, "car-window sociologist's" view of the South. Rather, it is more like Toomer's own self-appraisal. Toomer wrote of his experience teaching school in rural Georgia: "As I worked with my children in school and met with their parents in the homes, on the farms, and in church, I found myself studying them with a sympathetic objectivity, as I could realize they were something apart; but in an instant's reflection I could realize they were me, and I was they; that a force stronger than blood made us one."[5] Du Bois similarly wrote of the family of one of his students: "I saw much of this family ... and grew to love them" (53).

The similarities between the two books in terms of empathy, passion, sensitivity, and thematic structuring are so extensive that I can only suggest their effect in this chapter. But let me note two rather concrete elements shared. A key word in both works is "soul," a term occurring in Du Bois's first chapter: "the very soul of the toiling, sweating black man is darkened by the shadow of a vast despair" (9), and in the last chapter: "sometime, somewhere, men will judge men by their souls and not by their skins" (214). In Toomer "soul" also recurs, and, when it does, it is generally linked with a congeries of terms evocative of the South, as in the movingly personal poem "Song of the Son," where "soul" alliteratively mixes with "sun," "son," "soil," "slaves," "slavery," and "song." *Song* is central to both Du Bois and Toomer, and their understanding of its importance places them in a line that stretches back to Frederick Douglass's 1845 *Narrative,* where, speaking of the spirituals Douglass wrote, "To those songs I trace my first glimmering conception of the dehumanizing character of slavery."[6] In the closing chapter of *The Souls of Black Folk* titled "The Sorrow Songs," Du Bois describes the spirituals as "the most beautiful expression of human experience born this side the seas" (205); and ten of his fourteen chapters are prefaced by bars from the spirituals. Earlier I cited three passages from Toomer to illustrate his use of opposing elements—each contained a reference to song or folk song. Fragments of spirituals and references to song recur throughout *Cane.* The book concludes: "The sun rises. Gold-glowing child, it steps into the sky and sends a birth-song slanting down gray dust streets and sleepy windows of the southern town" (117).

The basic opposition Toomer poses in *Cane* is that between the South (specifically Georgia)—which is viewed as the homeland and the potential source of ripeness, growth, possibility, drama, passion, art, sensuality/sexuality, qualities which inhere potentially in the southern woman—and the city (generally Washington, D.C. but also Chicago) which is viewed as mechanical, unnatural, and repressive. Characters, too, are divided, as I noted earlier. Their division, their ambivalence, perhaps reflecting Toomer's reading of Freud is generally expressed by a conflict between those impulses which ideally might have had their source in the id of the South, the homeland, and those conventions/rules/mores/superegos imposed by middle-class urban respectability.

In the South there is the *potential* for wholeness, unity, fertility, perfection. Karintha, even as a child, carries "beauty, perfect as dusk when the sun goes down" (3). The "whole countryside seemed to flow" into Fern's eyes (16). In "Carma" the world is seen as a natural extension of Africa: "The Dixie Pike has grown from a goat path in Africa" (12). Traces of the South blow through the Washington, D.C./Chicago stories, just as Proust's remembered Madelaine, and when they do they momentarily emphasize the city's infertility and the character's felt sense of displacement, contrasted to the South's naturalness, its fertility and fruitfulness, as in "Avey": "And when the wind is from the South, soil of my homeland falls like a fertile shower upon the lean streets of the city" (48).

The sketch "Rhobert" furnishes a good example of the transformation of southern traces in an urbanized setting. Rhobert owns a house, but the house owns him (as in Emerson's "things are in the saddle/And ride mankind" and Thoreau's farmers who daily push a barn fifty feet long down the road). He has become the house—Rhobert the robot. He wears it like a diver's helmet. In this surreal sketch the weight of the house forces Rhobert underwater, and Toomer salutes his passing: "Let's open our throats, brother, and sing 'Deep River' when he goes down" (43). Toomer's allusion ironically recalls the opening line of the spiritual: "Deep river, Lord/My home is over Jordan." "Home," which figures so profoundly in the Afro American experience (as in the spiritual "I got a home ina dat rock, don't you see?" and in Leadbelly's secular boll weevil who's "jus lookin fuh uh home/just lookin fuh uh home") becomes a house, which is an early instance of its use by Toomer as a symbol for constraint, for spiritual death.

The "house" is centrally symbolic in "Box Seat," the longest story in the second section. The opening paragraph introduces an opposition between houses and the street: "Houses are shy girls whose eyes shine reticently upon the dusk body of the street. Upon the gleaming limbs and asphalt torso of a dreaming nigger. Open you liver lips to the clean white spring. Stir the root-life of a withered people. Call them from their houses and teach them to dream" (59). Just as Whitman, who in "Song of the Open Road" and *Song of Myself* called upon the reader to come out from the cultural context of houses, Toomer will depict the ideological molding of the house as a cultural construct, but his principal guide through the urban middle-class Inferno will be T. S. Eliot. As in Eliot's "The Love Song of J. Afred Prufrock," Dan too makes his visit, but he is, as Muriel tells herself, a "timid lover, brave talker" (61) (recalling Prufrock and the earlier Hamlet). Muriel tells him he "ought to work more and think less" (62). Prufrock's "a hundred visions and revisions" becomes Toomer's "a hundred platitudes" (62). Echoing *The Wasteland*'s "Ta ta. Goodnight. Goodnight," Dan tries to dismiss Mrs. Pribby: "Ta-ta, Mrs. Pribby" (60), but, just as Prufrock, Dan is unable to force the moment to its crisis:

> A sharp rap on the newspaper in the rear room cuts between them. The rap is like cool thick glass between them. Dan is hot on one side. Muriel, hot on the other. They straighten. Gaze fearfully at one another. Neither moves "It's time." [In both Eliot's world and Toomer's.] A clock in the rear room, in the rear room, the rear room, strikes eight. Eight slow, cool sounds. Bernice. [The encounter concluded, Muriel's actions recall the post-assignation actions of *The Waste Land*.] Muriel fastens on her image. She smoothes her dress. She adjusts her skirt.

In the opening lines of Eliot's "Geraontion" an old man waits for rain; in the opening lines of *The Waste Land* spring rain stirs dull roots; and in the opening lines of Toomer's "Box Seat," it is the spring that might "stir the root-life of a withered people." But spring does not come to "Box Seat." Nor does Christ come, and the gaseous waters He might walk upon seem as bereft of possibility as Eliot's "sweet Thames." Nor will a Moses lead his people out of bondage: "Suppose the Lord should ask, where was Moses when the light went out? ... Oh, come along Moses, you'll get lost" (64, 67). Roots, the South, and salvation are *suggested* in the theater section of "Box Seat":

> He shrivels close beside a portly Negress whose huge rolls of flesh meet about the bones of seat-arms. A soil-soaked fragrance comes from her. Through the cement floor her strong roots sink down. They spread under the asphalt streets. Dreaming, the streets roll over their bellies, and suck their glossy health from them. Her strong roots sink down and spread under the river and disappear in blood-lines that waver south. Her roots shoot down. Dan's hands follow them. Roots throb. Dan's heart beats violently.

But there is no rain, no salvation in Toomer's wasteland, and Christ will not ascend the subway stairs. Nor will the mermaids sing to him; rather, Muriel is sung to by the bloodied dwarf, who has himself engaged, with another dwarf, in a perverse parody of the battle royal.

Salvation/redemption occurs only in the closing lines of *Cane,* and only in the South, where Kabnis's ambivalence, like a fever, is drawn from him by Carrie, a black southern woman, close to and rooted in the soil. The *potential* of the black southern woman, suggested in both the Georgia and urban stories, is finally realized in a scene that is poetic, mythic, and religious. Important Christian imagery coalesce in the closing lines:

> Carrie's gaze follows ... [Kabnis] till he is gone. Then she goes to the old man and slips to her knees before him. Her lips murmur, "Jesus, come."
>
> Light streaks through the iron-barred cellar window. Within its soft circle, the figures of Carrie and Father John.
>
> Outside, the sun arises from its cradle in the tree-tops of the forest. Shadows of pines are dreams the sun shakes from its eyes. The sun arises. Gold-glowing child, it steps into the sky and sends a birth-song slanting down gray dust streets and sleepy windows of the southern town.

The scene is one of nativity, where Carrie and Father John merge with Mary and Joseph, and the love of Carrie and Kabnis becomes the child Jesus, becomes the sun that sets in "Bona and Paul" and rises in the closing lines to suggest a new world, a new dispensation. In the opening paragraphs of the "Kabnis" section, Ralph Kabnis had seen himself as a dream, and "dreams are faces with large eyes and weak chins and broad brows that get smashed by the fists of square faces" (83). The violence of this beginning becomes the natural mixing of dreams and pines and sun in the closing paragraphs. The "Kabnis" section, which begins in darkness, ends in light.

NOTES

1. Donald A. Petesch, *A Spy in the Enemy's Country: The Emergence of Modern Black Literature* (Iowa City: University of Iowa Press, 1989), pp. 197–201.

2. Jean Toomer, *Cane* (1923, New York: W.W. Norton & Company, Inc., 1988), p. 17. Subsequent citations are from this edition.

3. Cited in Cynthia Earl Kerman and Richard Eldridge, *The Lives of Jean Toomer: A Hunger for Wholeness* (Baton Rouge: Louisiana State University Press, 1987), p. 99.

4. W.E.B. Du Bois, *The Souls of Black Folk* (1903, New York: Viking Penguin, 1989), pp. 7, 8, 9, 11. Subsequent citations are from this edition.

5. Cited in Kerman and Eldridge, *op.cit.*, p. 83.

6. Frederick Douglass, *Narrative of the Life of Frederick Douglass* (1845, New York: Penguin, 1982), p. 58.

WORKS CITED

Douglass, Frederick. *Narrative of the Life of Frederick Douglass.* New York: Viking Penguin, 1982.

Du Bois, W.E.B. *The Souls of Black Folk.* New York: Viking Penguin, 1989.

Kerman, Cynthia Earl and Richard Eldridge. *The Lives of Jean Toomer: A Hunger for Wholeness.* Baton Rouge: Louisiana State University Press, 1987.

Petesch, Donald A. *A Spy in the Enemy's Country: The Emergence of Modern Black Literature.* Iowa City: University of Iowa Press, 1989.

Toomer, Jean. *Cane.* New York: W.W. Norton & Company, Inc., 1988.

9

Homi K. Bhabha and the Postcolonial Short Story

Catherine Ramsdell

The term "postcolonial" may be somewhat of an oversimplification. It seems to imply merely that which happened after colonialism, which in turn would imply that all literature written by once colonized people is postcolonial literature. While this definition may sound acceptable, numerous critics including Albert Wendt, Frantz Fanon, and Homi K. Bhabha would be quick to disagree because in the beginning of the twenty-first century, postcolonial literature is supposed to be something more than simply the literature written after colonization. Postcolonial literature must be more than literature written during a certain time period; it must also be something very different from colonial literature. And this dilemma presents postcolonial writers with a difficult task because postcolonial literature uses the same genres and often the same language as the literature that formerly helped to oppress postcolonial authors. Albert Wendt summarizes some of the problems with postcolonial fiction in his introduction to *Nuanua: Pacific Writing in English Since 1980,* stating that not all postcolonial literature succeeds in its desire to be "different from and opposed to colonial literature" (Wendt 3). He contends that "[c]olonial literature created a whole mythology about us. This is still being perpetuated in some of the supposedly post-colonial anthologies" (Wendt 2). Neither can postcolonial literature merely portray the once colonized as "[h]apless victims and losers in the process of cultural contact and interaction; [whose] cultures have been 'diluted' and 'corrupted'" (Wendt 3). Changing definitions of what is truly postcolonial versus poststructural or postmodern further complicate the issue. In actuality, postmodernist themes appear regularly in postcolonial works. Perhaps because "[l]ike the postcolonial, postmodern literature is still defining itself, clearing a space for itself, declaring itself against some of the tenets of modernism," an overlap between the two schools should not only be expected but might also be necessary (Wendt 4). This overlap should not be regarded as a negative entity; it simply complicates further the issue of what is truly postcolonial. Of course, for every question or puzzle there is a critic or theorist who believes he or she has the answer or solution. One such theorist is Homi K. Bhabha, who believes he has answers to some of these questions; he contends that all we need to do is "move beyond."

In his book *The Location of Culture,* Bhabha introduces many theoretical perspectives including cultural difference, cultural knowledge, mimicry, hybridity, all of which, according to Bhabha, are part of the moving beyond process, a theory that is much more complicated than it might originally sound. This idea encompasses much more than simply moving from the past to the present; it involves seeing, writing, recording from an entirely new perspective, a new perspective that is neither one nor the other. As soon as Bhabha begins to define moving beyond in the introduction to *The Location of Culture,* he introduces the idea of neither one nor the other as he states "[t]he beyond is neither a new horizon, nor a leaving behind of the past" (1). The implication here is that moving beyond is an in-between, that it is neither the past nor the present but something in the middle. However the idea of neither the one nor the other goes much further than time; it expands to touch on almost every categorizing entity, including literary theory. Bhabha chastises modern literary criticism, stating

> [t]he language of critique is effective not because it keeps forever separate the terms of the master and the slave, the mercantilist and the Marxist, but to the extent to which it overcomes the given grounds of opposition and opens up a space of translation: a place of hybridity, figuratively speaking, where the construction of a political object that is new, neither the one nor the other, properly alienates our political expectations, and changes, as it must, the very forms of our recognition of the moment of politics. (25)

Bhabha also maintains that literary criticism has not yet moved beyond; that literary criticism is too caught up in categorizing and in doing so allows only for two sides. Literary criticism is also too involved with class and gender instead of focusing "on those moments or processes that are produced in the articulation of cultural differences. These 'in-between' spaces provide the terrain for elaborating strategies of selfhood that initiate new signs of identity" (Bhabha 1). Then there is the problem with the term "post," as in postcolonial, postmodern, poststructural, and so forth. Bhabha refers to the word "post" as "shifty" as it is used in criticism, arguing that it means only to have moved past, not moved beyond. "Post" suggests an ending, a finalized state. Postcolonial suggests the end of colonization and the beginning of another state. And while, "[b]eginnings and endings may be the sustaining myths of the middle year ... in the fin de siecle, we find ourselves in the moment of transit where space and time cross to produce complex figures of difference and identity, past and present, inside and outside, inclusion and exclusion" (Bhabha 1). "Post" connotes only *after* when Bhabha wants more; namely, forward, backward, side to side, and most importantly in-between. Wendt agrees, stating that "[f]or me the *post* in post-colonial does not just mean after; it also means around, through, out of, alongside, and against" (3). To Bhabha, the terms or categories *colonial literature* and *postcolonial literature* provide only a beginning and an ending, two overly simple distinctions. Moreover, they are generally presented as part of a binary opposition used by literary critics that parallels Bhabha's reference to "master and slave" or "mercantilist or Marxist."

In order for a literary text to move beyond, it must resist the fixity of binary oppositions. It cannot see "the colonial and the indigenous as in irreconcilable opposition, the colonial as the evil destroyer" (Wendt 4). It cannot merely portray the colonizers as the oppressor and the colonized as the oppressed or portray these groups as the victimizer and the victimized. Neither can a literary text move beyond if it merely reverses these roles so that the once-colonized are now the oppressors. Instead, postcolonial literature must avoid these types of categorizations. Rather, it must redefine old stereotypes, and in the process eliminate the stereotypes and create something new, something that is, in Bhabha's words, neither the one nor the other.

Of course, Bhabha's book *The Location of Culture* in substance is merely a theory and at times the idea of imagining the hypothesis as a reality can seem both overwhelming and frustrating. Bill Manhire, however, one of the most popular and well-respected New Zealand authors of the twentieth century, provides not discourse, but example. Manhire is perhaps best known for his poetry and his interactive Internet text *The Brain of Katherine Mansfield.* However, he is also the author of numerous short stories, including a little known work called "Cannibals," a seventeen-page short story in four parts. "Cannibals" appears to put into practice what Bhabha advocates in theory.

Through character, setting, and plot, Bill Manhire manages not only to create a postcolonial text that indicates that once-colonized people "have indigenised much that was colonial or foreign to suit ourselves, creating new blends and forms" (Wendt 3), but has also created a text that puts into practice Homi K. Bhabha's theory of "moving beyond." More specifically, "Cannibals" is a text that takes place somewhere in the South Pacific and despite the somewhat familiar setting there is unfamiliarity, a sense of uncertainty like Alice in Wonderland. The narrator, a nameless soul for most of the story, is partly a colonizer and partly a captive and yet at the same time he is neither. And of course, there are the cannibals themselves. If the title of this story does not immediately bring to mind Joseph Conrad's *Heart of Darkness,* a reading or rereading of the story will. Manhire does not reinvent or retell *Heart of Darkness,* but he uses it in such a way as to trivialize the power of the traditional, imperial, colonial text.

Manhire begins to make "Cannibals" move beyond through setting, in terms of both time and place. The story begins with a rather ambiguous reference to place: "We were sailing in the Pacific" (Manhire 105). Later, we find it is the

South Pacific. The precise location this story takes place in is further complicated by the vague references to time periods. The inclusion of a jigsaw puzzle, a Monopoly game, a cruise ship and submarine all suggest that the story takes place no earlier than the late twentieth century; but a reference to uncharted waters contradicts this idea. In the beginning of the story, the narrator states "If the charts are hard to read, that is because of the wild, uncharted waters we are venturing into" (Manhire 105), a statement that seems much more in tune with Victorian fiction.

Further complicating the idea of time is a brief break in the story in which the ship and the sea hold a conversation. After a brief discussion of their love for each other, the sea asks the ship "But who are these on your deck, oh ship, who make such clamour?" The ship replies, "They are rough diamonds—sailors, explorers, missionaries. One or two stowaways. The occasional mutineer," to which the sea replies, "Oh well … nothing new there, very much the usual stuff" (Manhire 105–06). This brief interlude between the ship and the sea does not suggest a specific time as much as it suggests the repetition of time. It presents the ship and the sea as eternal objects and the crew of the ship as little more than a temporary insertion into the sea's permanence. This encounter between the ship and the sea also seems to suggest an in-betweenness or a newness. As Bhabha states:

> The borderline work of culture demands an encounter with "newness" that is not part of the continuum of past and present. It creates a sense of the new as an insurgent act of cultural translation. Such art does not merely recall the past as a social cause or aesthetic precedent; it renews the past, refiguring it as a contingent "in-between" space, that innovates and interrupts the performance of the present. (7)

The ship and the sea work perfectly to accomplish this goal of newness and in-betweeness not only because of their timelessness but also because the ships and the seas are seldom thought of as characters. By bringing them in as characters, Manhire establishes a slightly new perspective. Moreover, this brief dialogue between the ship and the sea serves as a literal interruption because it momentarily halts the plot of the story. As the only part of the story not narrated by the main character, the passage interrupts the narrator's story and provides a very subtle interruption because it allows a momentary shift in power. Readers may want to believe that the humans are in control, but this brief passage makes it clear they are secondary to the sea.

Not only are the time and place left purposely ambiguous, but the story lacks a precise beginning and ending. Because it is a short story, obviously there is a place where the words begin and the words end, but it is only in this sense, words beginning and ending, that this story has a beginning or an ending. Written almost as a journal, the audience enters this story midway through the action. The ship and the crew have already been traveling throughout the South Pacific when the story opens. How long they have been at sea is unclear. Perhaps more importantly, though, when the words stop, there is the implication that the story continues. The narrator has been living on an island, but has decided he must leave, that this island cannot become his home. He builds a raft and as he prepares to set sail, he dreams of a possible ending to his story. The words end, but it is clear that the narrator's story continues. He has become almost a migrant figure. He has no location, no home, no culture.

His namelessness throughout the first part of this story does not defy categorization; instead, he seems to slip from one category to the next until the end of the story where the category of *migrant* appears to be the only fitting choice. In the beginning of the story he is a colonizer, although not what one might consider a stereotypical colonizer. While the line concerning his treatment of a foreign castaway, "I read to her from the Bible, I touch her private parts," does seem to boil a great number of the stereotypes concerning colonizers down to two sentences, it is also one of the few passages that suggests that any of the conventional definitions of colonizer are applicable to this character. Our narrator is a rather inept colonizer partially because he only wishes to colonize unoccupied islands. He looks forward to landing on these islands where "men will row ashore for coconuts and just generally try to see what they can see. The rest of us might swim a bit, or maybe sketch the extinct volcano" (Manhire 106). Occupied islands, on the other hand, appear to frighten him. Despite the fact that their "weaponry [was] very much superior to anything [they] might meet" (Manhire 105), natives "shak[ing] their fists above their heads" cause him to cry "[b]reak our more sail! Away! Away! While yet there is breath in our bodies!" (Manhire 106). But perhaps our narrator's finest moment is when he is describing his leadership skills to his crew. Of course, while our narrator is explaining his qualifications, the cannibals draw near and the passage ends: "[t]hen rough hands seized me and I knew that the savages had crept up on us even as we talked" (Manhire 113).

Manhire's initial depictions of the narrator both confirm and contradict his presence as a colonizing entity. He is a colonizer, at least on the surface, because he admits to "[s]eeking out new lands: savages and treasure, sex and mineral rights" (Manhire 105). However, his attitude and personality go against the traditional colonizer depicted in either fictitious or historical accounts of colonization. He is certainly no Robinson Crusoe or Christopher Marlow. Neither is he a William Jones, Benjamin Kidd, or Rudyard Kipling. By allowing the category of colonizer but changing the stereotypical definition of colonizer, Manhire is finding the in-between space of which Bhabha is so desirous. Manhire continues placing the character of the narrator in-between after his crew has mutinied and left him and several others on a supposedly deserted island.

Once the narrator has been deserted by part of the crew of his boat, his name is revealed. It is curious that his name is only made known not only when he is no longer a colonizer in any sense of the word, but also when he is facing colonization. Shortly after it is revealed that his name is William, he is captured by the cannibals occupying the island, though he escapes death by befriending them. The series of plot twists that follow depict, in addition to his displaced condition, the revisiting and perhaps trivializing of major themes found in several colonial texts.

First, William's capture serves to indicate his precarious placement in society. While his friends and shipmates are being eaten, he befriends the cannibals. Initially he is "resolved to find some way of teaching these people Christian precepts" (Manhire 112), but he soon finds that teaching them the game of Monopoly better suits the cannibals' needs, provided, of course, that he always loses. In addition, William finds it easy to mimic the cannibals' way of life. He states "[i]t is surprisingly easy to get into the habit. Jules Verne is most impressed by my behavior" (Manhire 116). But while Jules Verne and other important members of the cannibal group may find his behavior impressive, it is still merely that—a behavior—and William has become little more than a trained seal who performs tricks in the hopes of staying alive. What William appears to be illustrating is the "ambivalence of mimicry," a state of being that is "almost the same, *but not quite*" (Bhabha 86). According to Bhabha, this state of mimicry was not uncommon among colonized peoples; it was a strategy used in "normalizing" the colonial Other. In this case, however, two unusual things occur, in that William began the story as part of the colonizing culture, though his mimicry symbolizes his changing condition, and also, the behaviors to which William must adapt in order to become "normal" are traditionally thought of as the behaviors of the Other, not the dominant culture.

In addition, the insertion of the game of Monopoly does more than simply indicate William's precarious condition as a captive. The positioning of this game also provides an opportunity to mock certain colonial tenets. As previously stated, William had hoped to teach these cannibals about Christianity, but they seemed more interested in the games William had stored away. William explains why he has a Monopoly game along with a jigsaw puzzle, stating, "I managed to smuggle away a few things like that, things that would be good for trading. They have certainly come in handy" (Manhire 113). Manhire's point is clear—colonization may have been about religion ideally or theoretically, but in reality it was more about money and capitalism. Moreover, his juxtaposition of the Monopoly game and the cannibalism takes this point even further. Manhire dedicates almost two pages of this seventeen-page story to the Monopoly game, more time than is given to any other single object in the text. What is truly interesting, however, is how the game is interspersed with a conversation about the preparation of the heads, which the cannibals preserve. The passage begins "[w]e are at the Monopoly board." This statement is then followed by a brief paragraph about separating the head from the neck. "Jules Verne passes Go" and the next paragraph describes the treatment of the eyes. "Jules Verne puts a hotel on Mayfair" after which a paragraph depicts the removal of the brain (Manhire 116–17).

This passage, with its longer paragraphs on mounting and preserving the head, which are briefly separated by one-line paragraphs describing the action of the Monopoly game, bring about two cultural settings that are often if not always diametrically opposed in colonial literature. Capitalism has been combined with cannibalism. This passage is not only humorous but *familiar,* and this familiarity is important. As Elleke Boemher states in her book *Colonial and Postcolonial Literature,* "postcolonial theorists refer to the colonized as the colonial other, or simply the *Other.* The concept of the Other, which is built on the thought of Hegel and Sartre, signifies that which is unfamiliar and extraneous to a dominant subjectivity, the opposite or negative against which an authority is defined" (21). The cannibals, the native culture, are supposed to maintain unfamiliarity, and in many ways they do. However, when Manhire combines the capitalism of Monopoly with a discussion on preserving a human head, he blurs the line between the familiar and the unfamiliar. In doing so, he continues to move beyond because he refuses to allow the creation of the stereotypical binary oppositions found in so much colonial and postcolonial literature. In doing so, Manhire establishes what Bhabha terms "cultural difference" and defines a system that allows for "[t]he very possibility of cultural contestation, the ability to shift the ground of knowledges, or to engage in the 'war of position,' ... the establishment of new forms of meaning and strategies of identification" (162). Bhabha explains his idea further, stressing the idea of interdisciplinarity in relation to cultural differences when he claims that "[entering] into the interdisciplinarity of cultural texts means that we cannot contextualize the emergent cultural form by locating in terms of some pregiven discursive causality of origin" (163).

The cannibals create this form of Bhabhaian cultural difference in several ways, but primarily through their newness. These are not Joseph Conrad's cannibals, with their filed teeth and rotten hippo meat. Manhire's cannibals marinate their food. They not only play Monopoly but appear to have an "instinctive understanding of the game" (Manhire 113). One of Manhire's cannibals would never be described as "a dog in a parody of breeches and a feather hat, walking on his hind legs" (Conrad 51). The darkness, the savagery, the howling and dancing, the inhumanity of Conrad's cannibals has been replaced by lightness, by gourmet meals, and by game playing. What Manhire has done through the creation of his cannibals is to create a new form of cannibal that helps to defy the stereotype presented in much colonial literature, including *Heart of Darkness.* In doing so, Manhire creates cultural knowledge because his cannibals "add to" the colonial definition or categorization of cannibals. Because they "add to," these cannibals are the "enemy of implicit generalization of knowledge or the implicit homogenization of experience" (Bhabha 163).

It must be noted, however, that Manhire does not try to change completely the preexisting stereotype of the cannibal. His cannibals do eat people. Moreover, they play drums, worship a strange god called the Zodiac, and sing somewhat frightening songs that include the lyrics "Strip ze skin! Quarter ze body! Skin head, hands, feet and bowels" (Manhire 113). These "savage" elements of the cannibals are important because without them all Manhire would have accomplished would have been the movement of the cannibals from one polarized, fixed, binary opposite to another. By retaining some of the original stereotypical elements and adding new, non-stereotypical elements, Manhire succeeds in creating a culture of cannibals that is neither the one nor the other.

While the cannibals, along with William's character, help Manhire break down fixed binary oppositions and find Bhabha's in-between space, the cannibals play another important role because, as previously mentioned, they bring to mind Conrad's *Heart of Darkness,* to which there are numerous parallels. Both texts contain journeys made on ships, a powerful female character, and both end with the suggestion of future journeys. There are certainly enough parallels to suggest that Manhire was in some way using *Heart of Darkness,* but the differences between the two stories are the cumulative point of Manhire's work.

Heart of Darkness is, both literally and figuratively, a dark narrative, while "Cannibals" is light. The setting, with its silver and blue waters and golden sands, is light; the content is perhaps even lighter, with its bumbling but likeable narrator, humor, and irony. All this lightness, particularly when foiled by *Heart of Darkness,* suggests an effort at trivialization; not a trivializing of the colonial experience, but a trivializing of the colonial *literary* experience.

The idea that Manhire is belittling colonial literature in general and *Heart of Darkness* specifically is most apparent in his story's one real descent into darkness. At the end of Part the Second it appears that a new group has taken control of the island on which William has been living with the cannibals. Part the Third begins: "It has been a time of pain and dark confusion, and I have lost all sense of time. I seem to be alone" (Manhire 118). Part the Third, which at two pages is the shortest of the four parts, continues with dark imagery along with passages suggesting despair and loneliness. Toward the end of the third part, William is moved to a new location. In this cavern is a queen, who is no doubt meant to parallel the nameless woman who appears out of the jungle toward the end of *Heart of Darkness.* The queen in "Cannibals" receives a similar reaction from William as did the woman from the crew in *Heart of Darkness.* William is both mesmerized and afraid, but only for a moment. William's terror and horror had all been a bad dream brought about by a sudden fever. In a strange turn of events, the queen of the island is one of William's shipmate's former lovers. Her name is Mrs. Llewellyn Davies, and she is fifty. She is certainly not "savage and superb, wild-eyed and magnificent, ... ominous and stately" as is the woman from *Heart of Darkness* (Conrad 76). "The horror, the horror" in "Cannibals" is nothing more than a delirious set of feverous dreams, most likely caused by drinking too much cannibal wine. Once again, Manhire appears to be mocking the themes set out in *Heart of Darkness.* In William's mind, just as in Marlow's, the darkness was real. William, however, comes to the realization that this darkness, this evil, is only in his mind, a conclusion hedged entirely by Marlow. By trivializing the darkness found in *Heart of Darkness,* Manhire shifts the balance of power and turns *Heart of Darkness* into what it is: one man's perception rather than a universal truth. And in so doing, Manhire continues to critique colonial literature, chipping away at the traditional literary hierarchy.

As Boehmer tells us, in many ways imperialism was all about writing and literature. She states that "the nineteenth-century novel contributed to the imagination of the status quo ... important signifiers for imperial values were laid down in the novel's representation of space" where "social hierarchy ... was symbolized geographically" (25). The colonized areas could be represented in several ways: "the Empire could signify far realms of possibility and fantasy, and wish-fulfillment, where identities and fortunes might be transformed," but it could also show the colonies as "places of banishment, unlawful practice, oppression, and social disgrace, dark lands where worthy citizens might not wish to stray" (Boehmer 26). Perhaps it goes without saying, but most of these representations were not accurate. Edward Said elaborates on the British perceptions of many colonized states in *Orientalism*. He claims that Europe formed a textual attitude toward colonized nations and that one of the outcomes of this textual attitude was the "idea ... that people, places, and experiences can always be described by a book, so much so that the book (or text) acquires a greater authority, and use than the actuality it describes" (Said 93).

Considering both the content and the attitudes reflected in much colonial literature, Manhire's use of an infamous nineteenth-century text appears to be an attempt to shift the balance of power but more importantly an addition to not only the kind of knowledge literature provides but also the type. Once again, he is adding to the base of knowledge and providing information that is greater than the sum of its parts. However, Manhire does not constrain his critiques of the colonial culture to colonial literature; he also examines the idea of mapping, a very important part of imperialism and colonization.

As our narrator is seeking out new lands, he and his crew are also mapping. Mapping, of course, was an important part of the colonial process. As J. Hillis Miller states in his book *Topographies:* "The power of the conventions of mapping and of the projection of place names on the place are so great that we see the landscape as though it were already a map complete with the place names and the names of geographical features. The place names seem to be intrinsic to the places they name. The names are motivated. By a species of Cratylism they tell what the places are like" (Miller 4). He continues, claiming, "[g]eneral names and proper names, however seem to be so much a part of the topography of a given region that it is difficult to think of the region without them. What would Key West be without its name?" (Miller 3). During the time of colonization, then, the ability to map and name was a great power for its practitioners. Appropriately, Manhire trivializes this situation. The narrator reports: "This island is probably uninhabited, so we will be able to give it a name, that's always a pleasurable thing to do" (Manhire 106). The list of possible names for the island include Llandudno Junction, Seattle, Pontypridd, and Crofts of Dipple, all of which appear to be foolish names created by foolish people. Some islands are named after former girlfriends: Sharon, Yvonne, and Llewellyn Davies. These names, however, do not appear to accomplish what Miller suggests mapping traditionally does. The inclusion of the name Seattle, for example, which conjures up images of rain, coffeehouses, and grunge music for most, none of which seem to be appropriate attributes for an island in the South Seas. Moreover, Seattle and, more explicitly, Crofts of Dipple, do not seem to be the kinds of places that would generally be located in similar geographical areas. Most importantly, these ridiculous names probably only seem ridiculous because they are not already geographical locations in the South Seas. To the people in the United Kingdom who live in Llandudno Junction, Pontypridd, and Crofts of Dipple, these names probably sound perfectly reasonable. However, it would stand to reason that the names the British, French, and Germans gave to countries, cities, and towns probably sounded just as ridiculous to the indigenous cultures as Manhire's names sound to twentieth-century audiences.

"It is the trope of our times to locate the question of culture in the realm of the beyond" says Homi Bhabha (1), and this is what Bill Manhire has done. The island names, the setting, the characters, and the plot all combine to provide a story that moves beyond. It is a short story with serious ideas; it is a short story with humor and laughter. William is a colonizer who becomes colonized. The cannibals both eat humans and participate in the capitalist system. It is partially a revisioning of *Heart of Darkness,* and in other ways, not about *Heart of Darkness* at all. It is a story filled with contradictions and surprises. It is a short story that moves beyond.

WORKS CITED

Bhabha, Homi. *The Location of Culture.* London: Routledge, 1994.

Boehmer, Elleke. *Colonial and Postcolonial Literature.* Oxford: Oxford University Press, 1995.

Conrad, Joseph. *Heart of Darkness.* Ed. Ross C. Murfin. New York: St. Martin's Press, 1989.

Manhire, Bill. "Cannibals." *Faber Book of Contemporary South Pacific Short Stories.* Ed. C. K. Stead. London: Faber, 1994. 105–22.

Miller, J. Hillis. *Topographies.* Eds. Werner Hamacher and David E. Wellbery. Stanford, Calif.: Stanford University Press, 1995.

Said, Edward. *Orientalism.* New York: Vintage Books, 1979.

Wendt, Albert. "Introduction." *Nuanua: Pacific Writing in English Since 1980.* Ed. Vilsoni Hereniko. Honolulu: University of Hawaii Press, 1995. 1–8.

Part III

Encountering Issues of Gender and Sexuality

As we've seen in the previous section dealing with culture and diversity, communities form new and changing identities to create new order, or to preserve the remnants of a vanishing cultural identity.

Not only is it useful to explore cultures in the process of establishing these paradigms, it is also useful to cast a critical eye on the norms of established cultures in order to question, and in some cases subvert, dominant paradigms, and in so doing offer a new definition of oneself. That the terms *postmodernism* and *feminism* both feature constantly shifting definitions makes the former a natural fit for further study of the latter. The chapters featured in the following section present new ways of exploring gender and sexuality issues in the short story.

Edith Wharton's "complex sexual politics of wartime" during World War I are explored in a chapter by Mary Carney. Three Wharton stories featuring French, British, and American female protagonists, respectively, bring to light the "bittersweet paradox" of war as a liberating force in the lives of women. Arguing against "the canon of war literature" which "has long disdained women's voices," Carney insists that "women's work was essential to the war effort," and is therefore more than worthy of literary study.

Adrienne Gavin explores how fantasy in British short stories is an essential element in asserting a female identity. Interestingly, Gavin focuses not on obviously fantastical short stories, but on how more traditionally "realistic" writers—Katherine Mansfield, Elizabeth Bowen, Radclyffe Hall, Elizabeth Taylor, and Jean Rhys—exploit the disconnection between reality and the more "real" fantasy lives constructed by their characters, worlds which better reflect the characters' true selves.

Rounding out the section is Patrick Meanor's study of what he terms the "Fourierist Parables" of Guy Davenport, highly structured worlds ruled not by traditional methods of power, but by sensual, frequently erotic, pleasure seeking. According to Meanor, these worlds exclude the traditional "hero" found in typical fiction, offering instead a more postmodern notion, a hero of "passionate attraction."

10

Wharton's Short Fiction of War: The Politics of "Coming Home"

Mary Carney

On the afternoon of August 1, 1914, mobilization notices were posted in France, and *la belle époque* began to give way to the ravages of World War I. Living in Paris throughout the conflict, Edith Wharton observed the war's effects on the home front. She often kept a grueling schedule: writing in the mornings and administering her myriad civilian philanthropies for the remainder of the day. She published extensively about wartime life, including two books of nonfiction about France (*Fighting France* in 1915 and *French Ways and Their Meaning* in 1919), three short stories ("Coming Home" in 1915, "The Refugees" in 1919, and "Writing a War Story" in 1919), and two novels (*The Marne* in 1918 and *A Son at the Front* in 1923).[1] The interrelationship between home and warfare informs all of these texts, yet only in her short stories does Wharton focus on women's status and experiences, specifically exploring the gender politics of wartime.[2] While only the first story explicitly describes a homecoming, the other stories depict women who have the opportunity to "come home" to their dreams. All of the tales, however, illuminate the bittersweet paradox underlying each situation while making a case for women's contributions to the war. Wharton elucidates the home front's contribution to the war effort and the ironic realities of what she termed the "strange war-world of the rear" (*Backward Glance* 369).

In 1912, after a half-dozen years of migrating between America and Paris, Wharton made her home in the French capital, becoming a fixture in Parisian salon life. From the turn of the century until 1914, France enjoyed a period of remarkable stability during which the arts flourished. As R.W.B. Lewis notes, *la belle époque* provided Wharton "a perfect combination of privacy and easy access to the social and intellectual life" (176). While she was establishing herself in Paris, her marriage was coming to an end. Edward (Teddy) Wharton's mental instability, fiscal recklessness, and infidelities had become pronounced, leading to their divorce on April 16, 1913. Thereafter, according to Lewis, Wharton gained a "new sense of herself as both a liberated and a divorced woman.... She was determined, she told [Bernard] Berenson, to eat the world 'leaf by leaf'—almost as if she foresaw the fact that the historical world she had known had not long to endure, and she was launched upon a prewar tour of it" (339). The tour abruptly ended in August 1914. It is poignant that the war intervened when Wharton had finally settled in a stimulating community and extricated herself from her difficult marriage.

Despite multiple fiction and nonfiction works, this portion of Wharton's oeuvre has rarely been the subject of scholarly interest. Most critics have dismissed her war works because their readings found little more than political platitudes and warmongering.[3] Advocating for American intervention, Wharton argues that the war was necessary to prevent Germans from invading and destroying French culture. Wharton argues in *French Ways and Their Meaning* that this nation is the bedrock of Western civilization and that Americans should "read [France's] history, study her art, follow up on the current of her ideas; then look about you, and you will see the whole world is full of her spilt glory" (149). Wharton was an advocate for France and, as Peter Buitenhuis argues, both she and Henry James "were influential catalysts of American opinion" (xvii). To regard her war writings as mere propaganda, however, is to miss the complexity and subtlety with which she renders this conflict, particularly life among noncombatants.

The accusations of jingoism only partially elucidate why these works were marginalized. Another crucial factor is that the canon of war literature has long disdained women's voices.[4] Shari Benstock argues that this oversight concerning "such a significant category of Wharton's canon resulted not from an absence of interest in the broader range of her writing but from the larger problems of categorizing women's contributions to war literature" ("Introduction" x). This genre has been considered a bastion of men, particularly those who have had battlefront experience; however, some of the best war writing has been done by those who have never been in battle. One thinks of Stephen Crane's *The Red Badge of Courage*, for example. Some of the most famous war literature is set in hospitals and on the home front both during and after wartime. Walt Whitman's "Drum-Taps" treats his experiences nursing soldiers during the Civil War, and Ernest Hemingway's *The Sun Also Rises* portrays expatriates in France and Spain after the Great War.

Scholars have begun to reconsider what constitutes war literature, particularly women's contributions.[5] Wharton's are exemplary of an expanded definition of this genre, such as that offered by Claire Tylee:

> Most studies of so-called "war-literature," in poetry or prose, have been primarily concerned with descriptions of battlefront. They seem to be covertly devoted to the vicari-

ous thrills of danger and the erotic myth of the fellowship of warriors. Women's literary responses to war, however, tend to be much wider and more subtle in scope than battle-tales, since they are interested in the social context of belligerence and its connection with personal relations and the quality of ordinary life. (*Great War* 13–14)

Interest in a more inclusive war canon emerges, in part, from a recognition that between 1914 and 1918 women's work was essential to the war effort, and their new responsibilities helped to liberate them from outmoded social restrictions. During the war, women drove ambulances, manufactured munitions, nursed the wounded, reported on frontline and rear actions, protected their homes against the enemy, agitated both for and against the war, and mourned their fathers, sons, and brothers.

In Paris, the presence of refugees and the uncertainty of living only hours from the front created a sense of the nearness of the battles and the potential for occupation. The long-range gun Big Bertha demolished buildings in Wharton's neighborhood. She notes in *A Backward Glance* that "the rue de Varenne was close to the Chamber of Deputies, to the Ministries of War and of the Interior, and to other important government offices, and bombs had rained about us and upon us since 1914; and as we were on Big Bertha's deathly trajectory her evil roar was also a well-known sound" (1047–48).

World War I was notable for its effects on civilian life. In his study entitled *The Home Fronts: Britain, France, and Germany 1914–1919*, John Williams asserts that the "changes to the civilian scene [were] unprecedented in any previous conflict. War was no longer a matter almost exclusively for the fighting man, an isolated affair of clashing armies on some distant battlefield. The wearing of a uniform ceased to be virtually the sole criterion of service, privation or suffering. It was now, indeed, that the phrase 'Home Front' was first coined" (1). Wharton alerts readers to the fact that the war zone is found not only in the trenches but also in these homes behind enemy lines.

Like much of the literature arising out of World War I, Wharton's contributions often explore the paradoxes of wartime. In *The Great War and Modern Memory*, Paul Fussell argues that

every war is ironic because every war is worse than expected. Every war constitutes an irony of situation because its means are so melodramatically disproportionate to its presumed ends. In the Great War eight million people were destroyed because two persons, the Archduke Francis Ferdinand and his Consort, had been shot.... [T]he Great War was more ironic than any before or since. It was a hideous embarrassment to the prevailing Meliorist myth which had dominated the public consciousness for a century. It reversed the Idea of Progress. (7–8)

While not included in Fussell's work, Wharton's war stories subtly reveal such conflicts and contradictions of wartime, which can show with particular bittersweetness the resulting absurdities and agony, as well as heroism and self-sacrifice.

Wharton's first war short story, "Coming Home," depicts the violation of home and family. Structured within a frame narrative, the tale has been told to the narrator by an American ambulance driver, H. Macy Greer. This device creates the illusion of authenticity and authority created by a man's story of war. Greer befriends Jean de Réchamp, who was wounded in battle and now serves as a military chauffeur. His family's village is located on the Western Front and was for a time occupied by the German army. When the two have the opportunity to drive out to the area of the Réchamp village, they are amazed to find that his village was unscathed, despite the devastation in surrounding areas. Réchamp's fiancée, Yvonne Malo, is credited with saving the village by her remarkable feat of charming Oberst Graf Benno von Scharlach, an infamously brutal German general.

Despite this accomplishment, Malo refuses to discuss the specifics of these events. The mystery of Malo's remarkable power over Scharlach draws attention to her. Malo, rather than the soldier, becomes the most intriguing figure. The young woman, who is likened to the mythical, chaste huntress Diana, gives up her purity to defend her fiancée's home and family. Instead of a story focusing primarily on a young man going off to war, it is about the war coming home to a young woman. The brave warrior who saves the home is not the soldier but the woman who loves him.

As an example of home-front heroism, Malo is a figure of ambiguous character, perhaps even morally compromised. Orphaned as a child, Malo lives near the Réchamp family and is raised by a single, male guardian, the Marquis de Corvenaire. As an adult, Malo moves to Paris, lives alone, and "comes and goes as she pleases, reads what she likes, has opinions about what she reads[; she] talks, looks, behaves with the independence of a married woman—and yet has kept the Diana-freshness" (237). When Jean meets her in Paris, he falls in love; however, his family rejects his request to marry her because they believe her to be immoral. In the months leading up to the war, young Réchamp confronts the prejudices that his family harbors against Malo and fights to gain consent to marry her. The Réchamps' disapproval derives, in part, from rumors begun by a servant who was dismissed by Corvenaire. This disgruntled woman has hinted that Malo and her guardian had an incestuous relationship. When Jean learns this, he "hunted up the servant's record, proved her a liar and dishonest, cast grave doubts on the discretion of the curé's housekeeper, and poured such a flood of ridicule over the whole flimsy fable, and those who had believed in it, that in sheer shamefacedness at having based her objection on such grounds, his grandmother gave way, and brought his parents toppling down with her" (239). After the engagement is approved, Malo visits the Réchamp home, but his family is less than welcoming. Before Malo returns to Paris, the war begins, and Jean is mobilized. While Jean is convinced of her purity, the story never conclusively affirms her prewar sexual innocence.

The family persists in regarding her as an undesirable addition to their clan until the war renders her particular skills of value. Malo, like Lily Bart in *The*

House of Mirth and so many of Wharton's heroines, becomes a commodity in the sexual economy of human relationships. Malo's independent life matures her socially and intellectually; as a result, she knows how to prevent Scharlach from destroying the Réchamp village. Afterward, the grandmother admits that "there is something to be said for the new way of bringing up girls. My poor daughter-in-law, at Yvonne's age, was a bleating baby: she is so still, at times. The convent doesn't develop character. I'm glad Yvonne was not brought up in a convent" (246). A cloistered education develops little understanding of the opposite sex. In the circumstances created by the war, knowledge derived from interaction with men is invaluable and proves essential to Malo's successful defense of the Réchamp home. With dark irony, Wharton suggests that before the war the family must be convinced of Malo's purity, then after the German occupation they applaud her savvy handling of the general, turning a blind eye to the nature of her sacrifice and embracing her to save themselves and their possessions.

Malo's sexual skill functions as weaponry to defend the household, yet her silence and alienation from her fiancé are signs that this sexual encounter constitutes a hidden, unspeakable war wound. For a woman to tell her tale of direct contact with the enemy is problematized by "stereotypes of a gendered battlefield" (Higonnet, "Not So Quiet" 207). Furthermore, the words Malo must use to convey the story are ones an unmarried woman should not utter. Just as trenches have linguistic taboos, Malo on the home front feels the taboo against an honest account of her encounter with the enemy. Fussell writes that this war's "presumed inadequacy of language" is not really failure: "The problem was less one of 'language' than of geniality and optimism; it was less a problem of 'linguistics' than of rhetoric.... [W]e have made unspeakable mean *indescribable:* it really means *nasty*" (170). Malo's experience undermines "geniality and optimism," but it is also unspeakable in that it transgresses verbal proprieties that even the liberated Malo follows. Her dilemma derives, in part, from the reluctance to tell her fiancé of sexual intimacies with another man. What is also "unspeakable" is the knowledge that this soldier's "Coming Home" reveals the failure of the patriarchal military to protect this young woman from this "unspeakable" war atrocity. While the sexual relationship may have been technically consensual, it was a form of sexual blackmail; more precisely, if she did not seduce the general, then her future family's home would be destroyed.

The story concludes with a reassertion of male agency: Réchamp avenges his fiancée by killing the general, who lies wounded in the ambulance. The German occupation of his home reveals the failure of the French military and by extension of Réchamp himself. Killing the general supplies a violent (if morally suspect) episode that reestablishes the soldier as warrior and reinscribes the male war narrative. Yet the story also illustrates the compromises of victory on the home front. Private homes become battlefields with their own warriors and weapons, including the complex sexual politics of warfare.

Wharton entitles her second war story "The Refugees," seemingly for those left homeless by the conflict, yet this story illustrates the effects of war on the English home front and more precisely on women of the aristocracy. While ostensibly following the experiences of Charlie Durand, a professor of Romance Languages from the western United States, the narrative actually centers on the transformation of Audrey Rushworth, a spinster born to a genteel British family. She succumbs to what might be termed the home-front war machine.

In the story we find evidence that relates directly to Wharton's own experience. In 1914, she spent a month in the English countryside and London where she witnessed the initial response to the influx of Belgian refugees. According to Alan Price, she contemplated converting the home she was renting from Mrs. Humphrey Ward into "a hospital for refugees and the wounded" (19). When she returned to France, she continued her work organizing charities, delivering supplies to the front, raising funds to meet the refugees' needs, and using her social contacts and fame to garner support for France in America. The war had shut down numerous businesses, and many women found themselves unemployed. Wharton created and administered the Children of Flanders Rescue Committee and American Hostels for Refugees, which provided such necessities as food, clothing, and lodging. Many of the Belgian refugees were sick from hunger, trauma, and exhaustion, so Wharton organized a free clinic and dispensary. She helped create a means by which these women, children, and elderly people might support themselves, receive education and training, and enjoy a safe place to sleep. In essence, her time was devoted to working with those who had lost their homes and had been wrenched from their communities. Her efforts were acknowledged by the French and Belgian governments with the Legion of Honor and Queen Elizabeth's medal, respectively. Her extraordinary dedication to her adopted country was apparent in her remarkable philanthropic efforts on behalf of those affected by the war's violent displacements.

"The Refugees" has a curious structure, both satiric and serious. In two parts, the first segment is set only three weeks after the invasion of Belgium. In the opening scene, the Belgian and French exiles are vividly rendered from the perspective of Charlie Durand, who has a spare family life. Never married, he keeps "a mother and two sisters above want" (570). Taking a frugal sabbatical trip abroad, he is caught in Belgium when war erupts, so he escapes along with the fleeing refugees to London. At first he perceives them as "an indistinguishable animal welter" that is suffering "unanimous seasickness" on board the steamer to England; then, on the ride from the coast to London, he recognizes their humanity. Young mothers with children sit stoically, and a wealthy woman moans about her furs. Durand is struck by "a motionless old man in a frayed suit of professorial black" who represents Durand's own class and profession. Thus, the refugees seem less foreign.

When they arrive in London, Durand is mistaken for a refugee by Rushworth. She is a forgotten spinster trying to get the attention of family and friends by bringing home a refugee. Among women of her social class, war charity has become a status symbol, but she is so incompetent that she brings home the American instead. Rushworth cries at the sight of these exiles and is so forlorn herself that Charlie Durand mistakes her for a refugee, too. Through a series of polite misunderstandings, this daughter of British aristocracy takes him home to her family estate. This lively spinster's bumbling and self-serving attempts to contribute to the war effort are endearing. Rushworth explains to Durand her pressing desire for a refugee and the fear that she will not get one: "You see, I'd so completely lost hope—so completely—I thought no one would ever want me.... They all told me at home that no one would—my nieces did, and everybody. They taunted me with it" (576). While she may be self-absorbed, she also seems sympathetic because she cares about Durand and even begins to cry at his imagined plight. Furthermore, Rushworth elicits compassion because, lacking a husband or a home of her own, she is marginalized. Though she lives on the family estate, she finds herself hardly a part of the clan: "nothing much ever happened to the unmarried women of her time. Most of them were just put away in cottages covered with clematis and forgotten" (589).

The second segment of the story, which conveys the sombre tension generated by the stress of years at war, is set in April 1918 and contrasts with the sometimes comic earlier scenes. When the American professor Durand returns to London as a YMCA worker, he has changed little, but the spinster is radically altered and has become the officious Colonel Audrey Rushworth. No longer the one who is forgotten, she is the one who forgets. And, indeed, Rushworth does not recognize Durand. Her transformation is a testament to the liberation of women during World War I, yet also a criticism of the era's ability to deaden the emotions. For Rushworth, the social upheaval has given her a chance to move out of the cottage into London, find a husband, and establish her own home. She takes full advantage of the opportunity to throw off the strictures of old social conventions. Sandra Gilbert and Susan Gubar argue that in this time of crisis in masculine identity, the war allowed women more freedom: "the war functioned in so many different ways to liberate women—offering a revolution in economic expectations, a release of passionate energies, a reunion of previously fragmented sisters, and a revision of social and aesthetic dreams" (318). They identify Wharton as among those women war writers who expresses enthusiastic enjoyment of this new liberation.

Rushworth exemplifies the adventures open to women and the opportunities for new roles in society. For Wharton, this transformation, although empowering, is tinged with the sacrifice of emotional connection, as is apparent in the personality change Rushworth undergoes. She is no longer a sympathetic character. Meeting Durand, "her glance strayed carelessly over [his] congested countenance, and then dropped to the desk without a sign of recognition" (592). She brusquely answered her niece, and then she "shut her lips with a snap and her pen drove on steadily over the sheets of official letter paper" (592–93). Her callous disregard causes Durand "distinct humiliation" (593). As signaled by her emotional inaccessibility, she has become part of the war machine, albeit on the home front. Rushworth suffers the dehumanization that arises from this mechanized, bureaucratic war. This condition, as Gilbert and Gubar explain, is commonly identified as the plight of soldiers:

> World War I virtually completed the Industrial Revolution's construction of anonymous dehumanized man, that impotent cypher who is frequently thought to be the twentieth century's most characteristic citizen. Indifferent, ironic, alienated, this faceless being may or may not have gone off to the front with heroic aspirations, but the war, that dark satanic mill of death, soon taught him just what he and his aspirations were worth. (259)

The warmhearted Rushworth becomes a cog in the war machine. While Rushworth's relatively safe home in London can in no way compare with the trenches, life in the rear also changes as bureaucracy creates its unique form of alienation.

In her third tale, entitled "Writing a War Story," Wharton turns from European women's war activities to a young American woman's attempts to make a contribution and fulfill her aspirations to be a writer. This tale primarily concerns the silencing of women that occurs when their education is limited and their appearance comprises their primary social value. The focus rests on Ivy Spang who, rather than deal with a German general or become an important bureaucrat, works for several months in an Anglo-American hospital serving tea. While bitingly satiric, this distinction between American women and their European counterparts serves to illustrate the crippling effects of American society on its young women.[6]

Unlike the French and British female protagonists, Spang's attempts to contribute to the war effort are feeble because her American upbringing has poorly prepared her to participate fully in the adult world. The ineffectual education of American women is apparent, for example, in its failure to cultivate Spang's aspirations to write, much less teach her the fundamentals of this craft. While Spang dreams of being a writer, she has little training, knowledge, or encouragement from her society. She "had published a little volume of verse before the war," but her collection is generally ignored, except for some polite reviews (359). No one among her family and friends in New York has a copy of her book of verse. Her volume is reviewed only by the rector's wife in the local paper and by the editor of "*Zigzag,* the new 'Weekly Journal of Defiance.'" In the *Zigzag* review, he writes that her poems "hinted that there was more than she knew in Ivy Spang's poems, and that their esoteric significance showed that she was a vers-librist in thought as well as in technique" (359). She feels "understood," but his review is a backhanded compliment. After all, the editor suggests that Spang does not even recognize the content of her own work, which has "more than she knew." Her isolation is further emphasized: "nobody she knew read *Zigzag,* and nobody who read *Zigzag* seemed to care to know her"

(359). The aesthetic vacuousness of her world is emphasized further by the reviewer's comment that Spang's poetry "would 'gain incommensurably in meaning' when she abandoned the superannuated habit of beginning each line with a capital letter" (359). Wharton satirizes both the American literary scene and modernist innovation. Frederick Wegener has recently noted that Wharton "has much diabolical fun ... with the posturings and eccentricities of modernism" (118).

The story centers on Spang's efforts to write a piece for a new magazine entitled *The Man-at-Arms,* which will be distributed to the wounded and disabled soldiers in British hospitals. The literary value of this publication is secondary to its philanthropic aim of entertaining the soldiers. Spang has never written a short story; her frustration, therefore, grows as she tries to learn how to write a short story and produce it within three weeks. She turns to her former governess, a French woman. The dearth of aesthetic stimulation in American society is contrasted with the atmosphere that even the average French woman imbibes. French culture fosters aesthetic sensibilities, thus many have "written good short stories ... [and furthermore] were given more than three weeks to learn how" (363). This American girl lacks even the inherited, raw talent of her French governess who has recorded the stories of foot soldiers she encountered in her hospital work. The first story is based on the experiences of "Chausseur Alpin Emile Durand, wounded through the knee and left lung at the Hautes Chaumes" (364). Spang observes that the "narrative, written in a close, tremulous hand, covered each side of the page, and poured on and on without a paragraph—a good deal like life" (364). Spang uses this tale as the basis of her contributions to *The Man-at-Arms.* With her governess, she revises it into "the language that a young lady writing a composition on the Battle of Hastings would have used in Mademoiselle's school days" (364). She cannot even produce a short story that rises above schoolgirl prose. In the words of Harold Harbard, a wounded soldier on Spang's ward who is a famous author, she "mauled" the "awfully good subject" of her story (369). The raw material provided by her governess is the only thing of value in her work. In effect, Spang's only admirable contribution to the magazine turns out to be her lovely photograph.

Spang is rendered a comic figure whose impotent struggles to contribute to the war effort amount merely to serving tea and looking pretty. Her pathetic attempts to learn the craft of writing are contrasted with the soldiers' interest not in her prose but in her photograph. The irony of her situation is encapsulated by Harbard's parting comment: "You were angry just now because I didn't admire your story; and now you're angrier still because I do admire your photograph. Do you wonder that we novelists find such an inexhaustible field in Woman?" (370). Unable to appreciate her unresolvable dilemma, Harbard mocks her. As an American, she is raised to be an object of beauty, even at the expense of her own personal aesthetic and intellectual growth. Her education and the limited social interaction with men has restricted her development. Unlike Malo, she has not enjoyed the conversation of intelligent men. Ultimately,

Spang cannot fulfill her own aspirations because of this repressive gender politics.

Wharton's war writings, like those of Virginia Woolf, Katherine Mansfield, and Willa Cather, reclaim a place for women's voices in the literature of World War I. Wharton's stories reveal that wartime affords greater freedom and self-knowledge, but they also show how these benefits are tempered by the heart-wrenching sacrifices, moral conflict, and painful failures that accompany this new freedom. A greater appreciation of Wharton's war literature contributes to our knowledge about this era because, as Samuel Hynes points out, "The First World War was the great military and political event of its time; but it was also the great imaginative event. It altered the ways in which men and women thought not only about the war but also about the world, and about culture and its expressions" (ix). Wharton enriches our understanding of the gender politics of war through her stories of the home front and the women who contribute to the war effort.

NOTES

1. The stories were originally published in periodicals: Wharton, "Coming Home," *Scribner's Magazine*, December 1915; rpt. in *Xingu and Other Stories*, New York: Scribner's, 1915; "Writing a War Story," *Woman's Home Companion*, 46, September 1919; "The Refugees," *Saturday Evening Post*, 1919. They are republished in *The Collected Short Stories of Edith Wharton*, ed. R.W.B. Lewis, II, 230–256, 359–370, 570–593. Subsequent references to these stories will be to the Lewis edition and cited parenthetically in the text.

2. My reading is indebted to Clare Tylee who argues for Wharton's feminist stance in these stories ("Imagining").

3. For instance, Stanley Cooperman observes that Wharton "combined gentility with blood thirst, the manners of the social novelist with the matter of the recruiting poster" (41). In 1985, Alan Bellringer finds that Wharton's "complete emotional involvement" in the suffering apparent around her "effectively disqualifies Edith Wharton's 1914–18 experiences of France from any seriously imaginative function" (112). In 1996, Annette Larson Benert suggests that "the atrocities she witnessed and heard about, and her own commitment to what she called French ways and their meaning, seem to have catapulted her judgment into binary thinking, the all-or-nothing attitude, that this war etched onto the Western mind" (338). Yet a select few, such as Margaret Higonnet, recognize that Wharton has been "misread as a jingoist" ("Not So Quiet" 217).

4. The major critical works on literature arising out of the Great War have been almost exclusively focused on the male combatant and have shaped our understanding of this war and its literature. Standard works include Stanley Cooperman's *World War I and the American Novel* (1967), the highly influential Paul Fussell's *The Great War and Modern Memory* (1975), and Eric Leed's *No Man's Land: Combat and Identity in World War I* (1979).

5. As Shari Benstock points out: "Recent scholarship on World War I writing by British and American feminists has provided a revisionist history of women's engagement in the war, a history that challenges long held beliefs that war, like childbirth, constitutes an unbridgeable divide in men's and women's experiences" ("Introduction" x). A sampling of the scholarship revising notions of women and World War I are: Trudi Tate, *Modernism, History and the First World War* (1998); Suzanne Raitt and Trudi Tate, eds., *Women's Fiction and the Great War* (1996); Miriam Cooke and Angela Wollacott, eds., *Gendering War Talk* (1993); Lynne Hanley, *Writing War: Fiction, Gender, and Memory* (1991); Claire Tylee, *The Great War and Women's Consciousness: Images of Militarism and Womanhood in Women's Writings, 1914–1964* (1990); Helen M. Cooper, Adrienne Munich and Susan Squire, eds., *Arms and the Woman: War, Gender, and Literary Representation* (1989); and Margaret Higonnet, Jane Jenson, Sonya Michel, and Margaret Collin Weitz, eds., *Behind the Lines: Gender and the Two World Wars* (1987).

6. While this theme is extensively and persuasively advanced by Elizabeth Ammons in *Edith Wharton's Argument with America*, she does not examine this short story.

WORKS CITED

Ammons, Elizabeth. *Edith Wharton's Argument with America.* Athens: University of Georgia Press, 1980.

Bellringer, Alan W. "Edith Wharton's Use of France." *Yearbook of English Studies* 15 (1985): 109–124.

Benert, Annette Larson. "Edith Wharton at War: Civilized Space in Troubled Times." *Twentieth Century Literature* 42.3 (1996): 322–343.

Benstock, Shari. "Introduction." *A Son at the Front* by Edith Wharton. Dekalb: Northern Illinois University Press, 1995.

Buitenhuis, Peter. *The Great War of Words: British, American, and Canadian Propaganda and Fiction, 1914–1933.* Vancouver: University of British Columbia Press, 1987.

Cooke, Miriam, and Angela Wollacott, eds. *Gendering War Talk.* Princeton, N.J.: Princeton University Press, 1993.

Cooper, Helen M., Adrienne Munich, and Susan Squire, eds. *Arms and the Woman: War, Gender, and Literary Representation.* Chapel Hill: University of North Carolina Press, 1989.

Cooperman, Stanley. *World War I and the American Novel.* Baltimore: Johns Hopkins University Press, 1967.

Crane, Stephen. *The Red Badge of Courage.* 1895. Ed. Henry Biden. New York: Norton, 1982.

Fussell, Paul. *The Great War and Modern Memory.* New York: Oxford University Press, 1975.

Gilbert, Sandra M., and Susan Gubar. *Sexchanges.* Vol. 2 of *No Man's Land: The Place of the Woman Writer in the Twentieth Century.* New Haven, Conn.: Yale University Press, 1989.

Hanley, Lynn. *Writing War: Fiction, Gender, and Memory.* Amherst: University of Massachusetts Press, 1991.

Hemingway, Ernest. *The Sun Also Rises.* New York: Scribner's, 1926.

Higonnet, Margaret R. "Not So Quiet in No-Woman's Land." *Gendering War Talk.* Ed. Miriam Cooke and Angela Wollacott. Princeton, NJ: Princeton University Press, 1993. 205–226.

Higonnet, Margaret R., Jane Jenson, Sonya Michel, and Margaret Collin Weitz, eds. *Behind the Lines: Gender and the Two World Wars.* New Haven, Conn.: Yale University Press, 1987.

Hynes, Samuel. *A War Imagined: The First World War and English Culture.* London: Bodley Head, 1990.

Leed, Eric J. *No Man's Land: Combat and Identity in World War I.* Cambridge: Cambridge University Press, 1979.

Lewis, R.W.B. *Edith Wharton: A Biography.* New York: Harper & Row, 1975.

Price, Alan. *The End of the Age of Innocence: Edith Wharton and the First World War.* New York: St. Martin's, 1996.

Raitt, Suzanne, and Trudi Tate, eds. *Women's Fiction and the Great War.* Oxford: Oxford University Press, 1996.

Tate, Trudi. *Modernism, History and the First World War.* Manchester, England: Manchester University Press, 1998.

Tylee, Claire M. *The Great War and Women's Consciousness: Images of Militarism and Womanhood in Women's Writings, 1914–1964.* Iowa City: University of Iowa Press, 1990.

———. "Imagining Women at War: Feminist Strategies in Edith Wharton's War Writing." *Tulsa Studies in Women's Literature* 16.2 (1997): 327–43.

Wegener, Frederick. "Form, 'Selection,' and Ideology in Edith Wharton's Antimodernist Aesthetic." *A Forward Glance: New Essays on Edith Wharton.* Ed. Clare Colquitt, Susan Goodman, and Candace Waid. Newark: University of Delaware Press, 1999. 116–138.

Wharton, Edith. *A Backward Glance.* New York: Scribner's, 1934.

———. *The Collected Short Stories of Edith Wharton.* Ed. R.W.B. Lewis. Vol. 2. New York: Scribner's, 1968.

———. *Fighting France, from Dunkerque to Belfort.* New York: Scribner's, 1915.

———. *French Ways and Their Meaning.* New York: Appleton, 1919.

———. *The House of Mirth.* New York: Scribner's, 1905.

———. *The Marne.* New York: Appleton, 1918.

———. *A Son at the Front.* New York: Scribner's, 1923.

———. *Xingu and Other Stories.* New York: Scribner's, 1915.

Whitman, Walt. "Drum-Taps." 1865. *Leaves of Grass.* Norton Critical Edition. Ed. Sculley Bradley and Harold W. Blodgett. New York: Norton, 1973. 279–327.

Williams, John. *The Home Fronts: Britain, France and Germany 1914–1918.* London: Constable, 1972.

11

Living in a World of Make-Believe: Fantasy, Female Identity, and Modern Short Stories by Women in the British Tradition

Adrienne Gavin

In Elizabeth Taylor's short story "I Live in a World of Make-Believe" (1954), the central character, Mrs. Miller, lives part of her life in what her husband thinks is a fantasy world: "'I live in a world of make-believe,' she would laugh, boastfully, as one laughs when confessing to well-loved weaknesses" (97). This infusion of "fantasy" life into "real" life reflects a pattern common in short stories by women. Frequently in women's short stories the female protagonist is presented as having a fantasy life or a fantastic experience that is integral to her sense of female identity or to her attempt to find that identity.

This chapter is interested in the interstices of fantasy, female identity, and the short story in the work of modern women writers in the British tradition—"tradition" in that Elizabeth Bowen, Katherine Mansfield, and Jean Rhys, whose origins are not British, are included because they have undeniably both influenced and been influenced by British writing. The British tradition of women's short stories includes texts like Leonora Carrington's surrealist stories and Angela Carter's revisionings of fairy tales, both of which are overtly fantastic, but this chapter focuses on stories that infuse elements of fantasy into ostensibly realist narratives. Examination of this "infused" fantasy in Katherine Mansfield's "Bliss" (1918), Elizabeth Bowen's "The Dancing-Mistress" (1929), Radclyffe Hall's "Miss Ogilvy Finds Herself" (1934), Elizabeth Taylor's "I Live in a World of Make-Believe" (1954), and Jean Rhys's "Sleep it Off Lady" (1974) shows that female characters seek, usually unsuccessfully, to mesh their fantasy life, which contains or offers true identity, with the "real world" which disallows that identity and discredits fantasy. For female characters—and implicitly writers—the "true self" is inextricably linked with fantasy.

Hermione Lee notes of her international collection of short stories by women—fittingly entitled *The Secret Self*—that "Strangeness, fantasy, the unfamiliar, hallucination, myth, dream, memory, coexist with the verifiable world, so that in many of the stories it feels as if one can have, simultaneously, more than one life" (xii). Double lives and female experiences of fantasy are most pervasive in women's writings of the British tradition. That this is so is perhaps not surprising as there is a strong tradition of fantasy in British writing. Elizabeth Bowen suggests: "Since Poe's day, it has been the English rather than the Americans who have occupied the fantastic domain" ("The Short Story" 15). Ursula Le Guin agrees, pointing to American resistance to adult fantasy literature and to the lack of a fantasy tradition in American writing. The English, she writes, have a tradition of fantasy writing "and love it, and do it better than anyone else" ("Dragons" 32).

Le Guin is here referring to "pure" fantasy and it is important to consider what we mean by the term "fantasy." E.M. Forster states that fantasy "implies the supernatural, but need not express it" (106). Tzvetan Todorov, in his influential work on the fantastic, takes a structuralist approach, arguing that the fantastic lies in the reader's (and often character's) hesitation "between a natural and a supernatural explanation of the events described" (33). Rosemary Jackson in *Fantasy: The Literature of Subversion* fills in the gaps she sees in Todorov's analysis by also considering the cultural formation of fantasy, its social and political dimensions, and the psychoanalysis of Freud and Lacan. She stresses the importance of the unconscious to fantasy as does Le Guin who, drawing on Jung, writes that fantasy "is the language of the inner self" ("Child" 59). While this chapter will draw on ideas put forward by critics such as Jackson, "fantasy" will here be used more broadly to refer to those elements in literature which are non-realist, including "make-believe," dreams, and the imagination.

Although Forster includes fantasy as one of his "aspects of the novel," and Nancy Walker has effectively argued that fantasy is a feminist technique used by contemporary women novelists, female fantasy and the short story genre seem to be significantly linked. The short story's length mirrors traditional forms of female writing such as journal and diary entries, which are generically and culturally outside dominant forms of discourse. As Bowen has suggested, too, fantasy enters more readily into the modern short story than into the modern novel (*Mulberry Tree* 130). That this is so is perhaps because the short story's roots in folktales, fairy tales, and ghost stories mean that we are more accepting of fantastic elements within its confines. Similarly, the short story's momentariness is reflective of dreamtime and thus inherently receptive to the glimpsed fantasy world of the unconscious. Nadine Gordimer suggests that "[f]antasy in the hands of short-story writers is so much more successful than when in the hands of novelists because it is necessary for it to hold good only for the brief illumination of the situation it dominates" (265). Bowen suggests that in her own short stories, "fantasy [is] strongly represented," present as "part ... of the fabric of the actual plot, or governor of the behaviour of the characters" in a way not evident in her novels ("Preface" 130). Jackson writes of Elizabeth Gaskell's supernatural Victorian stories:

> None of Gaskell's "fantastic" tales is trapped by that ideological frame which determines the endings of her novels. Here she is able to declare her disbelief that cultural engagement might offer redemption or integration for her isolated (usually female) subjects. Unlike her novels, Gaskell's fantasies terminate in death, or are suspended upon an image of endless withdrawal from the "real." (128)

Although Jackson does not address in any detail either the short-story genre or specifically female fantasy, her comments obliquely suggest that representation of female identity through fantasy is particularly suited to the short-story form.

Writing in 1937, Bowen observes: "the general trend of the short story has been, lately, towards inward, or, as it were, applied and functional fantasy, which does not depart from life but tempers it" ("The Short Story" 16). It is this tempering of life with fantasy that is most evident in modern short stories by women; this link between female and fantasy is significant. Questions about realism's power to portray female experience have been raised. As Joanna Russ points out,

> many fine writers who are women have discovered that fantasy, fantastic elements and methods, or simply even the tone of fantasy, give them the method to handle the specifically female elements of their experience in a way that our literary tradition of realism was designed not to do. (xiii–xiv)

"The fantastic traces the unsaid and the unseen of culture: that which has been silenced, made invisible, covered over and made 'absent,'' states Jackson (4). Fantasy in short stories by women reveals the "unsaid and unseen" of female experience. The identity that female characters discover in fantasy frequently lies in opposition to culturally dominant expectations for women. It is only within fantasy that female characters find a personal identity, a female identity, which cannot be experienced by them in the "real" world of the story and which cannot be expressed by their female creators through purely realist methods.

The fantasy worlds that female characters experience in these stories vary in type: some are dream-like, others death-like, some are worlds of violence, others worlds of escape or protection which offer power, autonomy, or freedom from cultural constraints. Ironically, for some characters—often those created during periods of postwar reentrenchment of women's roles—the world of fantasy reflects perfect conformity to gender stereotypes about womanhood which "reality" then subverts. The "unrealized self" of the title character in Bowen's "The Dancing-Mistress" flickers into life as she dreams of "killing" one of her pupils. Rhys's dipsomaniac Miss Verney envisions a "fierce and dangerous" rat which threatens her, Hall's Miss Ogilvy dreams of a transgendered life in prehistoric Britain, and Taylor's Mrs. Miller appears to "live in a world of make-believe" derived from Edwardian novels. In Mansfield's "Bliss" and Woolf's "Lappin and Lapinova" fantasy, reality, and female identity inseparably intertwine.

In Elizabeth Bowen's "The Dancing-Mistress," Miss Joyce James's identity cannot fully enter "real life" because it is contained within a violent dream-fantasy of inflicting terror upon a child. Traveling the country giving dancing lessons, Miss James's life offers her little but weariness: "All day long she was just an appearance, a rhythm.... Late at night, she stopped *'seeming'* too tired to 'be'" (63–64). Her sense of herself is different from how she is perceived by others: she impresses her students, their parents, her would-be lover Lulu, her attentive pianist (and perhaps also would-be lover) Miss Peel. She is only provoked into a sense of herself by the pupil she despises, Margery Mannering, who senses the effect she has on her teacher: "She was perfectly certain Miss James hated her—Miss James did.... Margery thought, 'She'd like to kill me.' Miss James thought, 'I would like to kill her—just once'" (66). Inflicting fear upon Margery through chastising her and making her dance alone allows Miss James's identity a brief sortie into real life: "The unrealized self in her made itself felt, disturbing her calm with a little shudder of pleasure ... she thought of Lulu, she was almost a woman" (67). Noticing Margery gives Miss James "that shudder of life in her" (69). Making Margery's "eyes [stretch] with physical fear like a rabbit's" while observers think she is merely being "patient and good" with her pupil makes Miss James smile (71). Sleeping on the journey home she dreams of dancing with Margery, chanting "I'll kill you, I'll kill you" and seeing "[s]omething burst behind Margery's stretched eyes" as she faints (76). As Miss James dreams, "A new life, the self's, mould[s] her lips in a soft line" (76).

Dreaming offers her the chance to actualize the daydreams that glaze her eyes in her waking hours and to discover her "self." Her identity as "killer" in her fantasy world is at odds with the "real" world's vision of her as the silvery, melting dancer in a hyacinth dress who expands "into delicate shapes like a Japanese 'mystery' flower dropped into water" (63–64). She can only introduce her fantasy self into her "real" life if it is concealed, yet on some level Miss James wants her true identity recognized: "Did you hear me killing that Mannering child?" she asks Miss Peel (69). "Did you see me killing that child?" she asks Lulu, oblivious of his desire for her (74). Reality will not recognize her identity. When her companions do not acknowledge awareness of the violent source of her temporary exultation: "the film crept back ... she was not like a person at all" (74).

Jackson argues that fantasy "opens up, for a brief moment, on to disorder, on to illegality, on to that which lies outside the law, that which is outside dominant value systems" (4). This is the type of fantasy we see in Bowen's story. In other examples it is not so clear that the fantasy in which women find their identity does lie "outside dominant value systems." Sometimes, paradoxically, identity appears to be found in fantasy that reinforces dominant cultural stereotypes. Radclyffe Hall's "Miss Ogilvy Finds Herself" and Elizabeth Taylor's "I Live in a World of Make-Believe" were published respectively in the early 1930s and the early 1950s, periods of postwar retrenchment of women's roles. The stories' titles signal a concern with fantasy or identity and the protagonist of each story finds her identity in a fantasy of perfect conformity to a cultural stereotype. Reality, however, is not perfect and in each case disallows the conformative identity each woman discovers in fantasy.

At first glance Hall's story is an unusual one upon which to base an argument for identity that seeks conformity. Written in 1926 the story contains lesbian themes similar to those Hall soon used in her novel *The Well of Loneliness* (1928). Like Stephen Gordon, the novel's protagonist, Wilhelmina Ogilvy, is presented as a "sexual invert" who experiences a fulfilling role as part of an ambulance brigade at the Western Front during World War I. In her novel, Hall writes that female sexual inverts "found themselves" during the war: "Later on would come bitterness, disillusion, but never again would such women submit to being driven back to their holes and corners. They had *found themselves*" (*Well* 275; italics added). Extrapolating from this, we could argue that Hall's short story is about Miss Ogilvy losing herself rather than finding herself in that it traces her experience of "disillusion" after the war and ends with her death at the mouth of a cave, easily symbolic of a hole or corner. Yet the story, unlike the more realist (and, significantly, banned) novel, offers its protagonist a second chance at finding herself through fantasy. The short-story form itself offers her identity because of its readier acceptance of fantasy, and the form's "momentariness" also makes it less likely to attract the notice of censors.

The story begins in realist mode. Unable to find her identity after returning from the war to a society that does not accept her "mannish" looks and behavior and offers her only a "small" and frustrated future, Miss Ogilvy visits an island off the coast of Devon. Approaching the island she has the sense that she "remembers" a cave upon it and is profoundly affected when the hotel owner shows her an ancient "man's skull and thigh-bone" which have been dug up on the island (95). When Miss Ogilvy falls asleep, the story takes what Hall describes in her "Author's Forenote" as "a brief excursion into the realms of the fantastic" (84). In her fantasy Miss Ogilvy is transformed into a tall, strong, male member of a prehistoric tribe, dressed in pelts, who in a cave experiences physical love and finds happiness with her/his companion, a young prehistoric woman who tells her/him "all of me is for you and none other. For you this body has ripened" and calls her/him "My master" (98, 99). The story briefly returns to realism at the end when we are told that Miss Ogilvy is found dead the next morning at the mouth of the cave.

Miss Ogilvy finds her identity in a fantasy of total conformity to stereotyped, literally "caveman," extremes of gender difference; her identity is found, however, in the male role rather than the female role. Her fantasy takes her back perhaps to the very origins of cultural imposition of gender difference although in this fantasy there is an inherent case made for biological determinism. Both her modern society and her own biology will not allow Miss Ogilvy to express "male" identity in the real world; she can only achieve this in fantasy.

Miss Ogilvy's finding of herself within fantasy coincides with her death and, as Sandra Kemp argues with regard to May Sinclair's short story "Where Their Fire Is Not Quenched" and Dorothy Richardson's story "Ordeal," female characters' experience of death in feminist modernist fiction "offers terrific imaginative release" (109). At "the moment of death," Kemp notes, "the speaker registers a plurality of selves or of being" (110). "Death," she suggests, "is the moment of supreme identity with our bodies" (109). In Hall's story, death and "imaginative release," or fantasy, offer identity in even broader terms. Death is necessarily, to some degree, fantastic in literature because it is something not experienced by the writers depicting it and, as Valerie Shaw notes, is a common subject in short stories: "The boundaries between youth and adulthood, old age and death, are frequently explored within a fictional [short story] framework which evokes yet another borderland, the hazy area between fantasy and reality, dreaming and waking" (204).

Like Miss Ogilvy, Mrs. Miller in Elizabeth Taylor's "I Live in a World of Make-Believe" seeks perfect conformity to a constructed norm of behavior which reality will not let her experience. She is socially ambitious and her husband believes her fantasy life is based on "accounts of Edwardian house-parties she had read in novels" (93). "That fantasy," the narrator tells us, "was most nearly approached by the house across the road," symbolizing order, plenty and superiority, and inhabited by Lady Luna (93). Although she feels Lady Luna has slighted her with her "indifferent talk" and her casually prepared tea table when she and her son go to the Big House for tea, Mrs. Miller, chagrined at her own lack of servants, goes to enormous efforts in cooking, cleaning, creating a library, and preparing suitable phrases for Lady Luna's return visit. Poised in her own true fantasy identity as ideal hostess she waits for Lady Luna to come to tea; she is, however, unable to merge her identity into the real world. Imperfect reality refuses to allow it; first by providing an unexpected visit from the socially undesirable Auntie Flo and Little Valerie: "Her world swayed and crashed at the thought of mingling together Auntie Flo and Lady Luna," and secondly by Lady Luna's failing to turn up at all (103).

We might be tempted to read Mrs. Miller as a self-deceiving snob who overacts her household hardships into melodramas. Her husband thinks to himself "She ought to have gone on the stage" (101). He wants to tell her, "If you are always to measure your condition against other people's, let it not be forever against people who do not exist. For life will never be what you have imagined. Not for five minutes even" (97). It is also he who believes she bases her ideas of life on Edwardian novels; the only use she appears to have for books, however, is to create a room she can call a library. It is similarly implicitly his recollection that "[a]s a girl she had been affected. 'I live in a world of make-believe,' she would laugh, boastfully, as one laughs when confessing to well-loved weaknesses" (97). When considering female fantasy in short stories, it is important to look carefully at narrative perspective. Mr. Miller is imputing weakness to his wife's fantasy life, which he regards as self-deluding make-believe. In fact her fantasy life may be read as her way of creating an identity within middle-class, 1950s Britain at a time when the gender role prescribed for her was bound by domesticity and conformity. Glamorizing her role in terms of a more attractive Edwardian Big House domesticity enables her to conform to the cultural expectations of the "real" world but at the same time, through fantasy, to gain autonomy and identity by setting her own "Edwardian" rules and standards for behavior. That her attempt to introduce these perfect standards into her daily life is thwarted by the imperfections of the "real" world says more about the real world's inability to accept her than it does about "weakness" on her part.

Like Taylor's story, Jean Rhys's "Sleep it Off Lady" contains a protagonist whose fantasy life is influenced by literature and like Hall's story it involves issues of aging and death centering on that female character. Miss Verney, an alcoholic "well over seventy" (375), increasingly neglected by society and thinking about death, experiences fantasy induced both by alcohol and by fantasy contained within another short story. She imagines—or is possibly the only one to perceive—a huge rat which she fears. Looking into a corner of her "hateful shed" (376) she imagines "that a fierce and dangerous animal live[s] there and call[s] aloud: 'Come out, come out, Shredni (sic) Vashtar, the beautiful'" (376). She invokes Saki's "Sredni Vashtar," a story like this that contains a female character who is the object of a child's antagonism and who, in a narrative blurring of reality and fantasy, dies as the result—or possible result—of the appearance of a shed-dwelling animal.

Initially "rather alarmed at herself" (376) for calling out to Sredni Vashtar, Miss Verney nevertheless decides to have the shed pulled down and destroyed, but finds that builders are reluctant to tackle the job. She determines not to think about the shed in her real life but it begins to haunt her fantasy life. She dreams of it transformed into a coffin, a fantasy portent of approaching death. But just as she can persuade no one to pull down the shed, she also cannot convince anyone of the existence of a huge rat she sees crossing the shed and of which she is terribly afraid.

Influenced by alcohol, pills, loneliness, thoughts of death, and Saki's story, Miss Verney's fantasies involve visions of the "Super Rat" (386) and various dreams. She shuts herself in her house, furiously cleans so that nothing can attract the rat to her house and drinks in preference to eating; she soon physically weakens. Her fantasy life cannot amalgamate with reality as her neighbors attribute her rat sightings and her shut-in habits solely to her drinking. The real world demands, quite brutally, through the mouth of twelve-year-old Deena who does not help Miss Verney when she finds her collapsed by the dustbin that she "'[s]leep it off'" (385). Miss Verney's fantasy life brings her fear rather than happiness and leads inexorably to her ultimate meeting with identity in death.

"The short story, as I see it to be, allows for what is crazy about humanity: obstinacies, inordinate heroisms, 'immortal longings'" writes Bowen ("Preface" 130). Her reference to "immortal longings" suggests the longing for identity displayed in the fantasy worlds of women in modern stories, but her phrase "what is crazy about humanity" is also significant. The fantasy lives of female protagonists have often been implicitly or explicitly condemned or mocked, both by other characters and by critics. As we have seen in the case of Mr. Miller, those who examine female characters have been overly quick to diagnose silly or ignorant self-delusion to explain their fantasy lives. These misdiagnoses can be challenged by closer reading. The ease with which, in life as in art, madness has been imputed to women has been well established by critics such as Susan Gilbert and Sandra Gubar. As Patricia Meyer Spacks states in *The Female Imagination*, "The idea that women may find their most significant freedom through fantasy or imagination need not imply any commitment to madness" (qtd. in Walker 115).

Discrediting fantasy denies female identity, and while in stories like Taylor's and Rhys's it is other characters who belittle female fantasy, in the case of Katherine Mansfield's well-known story "Bliss," it is the critics who have been most dismissive. Mansfield's Bertha Young has frequently been regarded as immature, frigid, foolishly self-deluded, hysterical, and ignorant. Walter Anderson, for example, refers to her "dreamy self-delusion," her initial "semi-hysterical bliss," and her "hypersensibility and exaggerated manner of expression" (398, 400). Marvin Magalaner writes: "Bertha's first duty upon entering her home is to arrange the fruit tastefully, a simple task engendering an emotional reaction in her that verges on the 'hysterical'" (415). Magalaner's reading assumes "duty" instead of creative urge, "tastefulness" instead of art, "simplicity" instead of artistic endeavor, and "hysteria" instead of happiness and thus denies Bertha's identity. This type of reading imputes to Bertha a hysteria more familiarly, but again arguably incorrectly, reserved for another famous fictional Bertha—Bertha Rochester, the madwoman in the attic in *Jane Eyre*.

There is little to indicate that Bertha Young's "bliss" is immaturely delusional; moments of "absolute bliss" in anyone's life are rare enough to be noted. Her feelings may have been generated, like Mrs. Miller's, within a fantasy world of anticipating guests, particularly Pearl Fulton, but Bertha's difficulty lies in how to introduce her blissful identity into "idiotic civilisation"; "is there no way you can express [bliss] without being 'drunk and disorderly'?" she asks (92). The story's implicit answer is no. The pretentious, overly articulate, quasi-artistic set who come for dinner represent a society that will not accept anything that cannot be expressed glibly and cannot imagine the happiness of someone like Bertha. It is significant that her bliss begins exterior to her domestic life as she walks along the street alone and is only impinged upon once she enters her home and her expected role.

Critics have quite naturally been concerned with the triangle of sexual desire in the story and the symbolism of the pear tree but this concentration has led to a neglect of the central issue of female identity. The centrality of Bertha's identity is signaled immediately. Unlike the other characters thus far discussed—Miss James, Miss Ogilvy, Miss Verney, and Mrs. Miller—she is given her own full name in the first line, "Bertha Young" and is referred to as Bertha throughout rather than by an honorific which defines her in connection (or lack of connection) with a male figure.

In her initial blissful state she is "waiting for something ... divine to happen ... that she knew must happen ... infallibly" (92). Her real life, however, tends to disallow this bliss and impinges on her happiness. Watching the commandeering nurse with her baby daughter, Bertha feels "like the poor little girl in front of the rich little girl with the doll" (93), until she is allowed a brief moment with her child. She is blissful, too, when Pearl Fulton—a "find" of hers who is both beautiful and mysterious—arrives at the dinner party. She imagines a special mood existing between herself and Miss Fulton and waits for Miss Fulton to "give a sign" (101). As they stand together looking at the spring-blossomed pear tree (which has earlier reminded Bertha of her inner blissful self) as it stands under the moon (whose silvery glow reminds her of Miss Fulton), it is as if they are "understanding each other perfectly, creatures of another world ... wondering what they were to do in this one with all this blissful treasure that burned in their bosoms" (102). It is a moment of fantasy in which Bertha feels blissfully complete within her true identity. That she does not know whether Miss Fulton's murmuring "Yes. Just *that*" is real or a dream is almost unimportant, for it is true to the moment (102).

Cherry Hankin notes that "one of the most striking features which emerges from a close study of [Katherine Mansfield's] stories is the frequency with which some pattern of fantasy informs her 'sense of an ending'" (466). "Bliss" has an open ending:

> "Oh, what is going to happen now?" she cried.
> But the pear tree was as lovely as ever and as full of flower and as still. (105)

The ending is often read as indicating that Bertha's discovery of the relationship between her husband and Pearl Fulton has destroyed her happiness and her sense of self. It can, however, be read as reconfirming her identity, which has been found in fantasy, in that her focus slides back to the fantastic pear tree. Her discovery of Pearl's relationship with her husband similarly does not necessarily detract from her earlier moment of identification and connection with Pearl as they gaze, both in fantasy, at the pear tree. As Marilyn Zorn notes: "In their ideal selves there is no distinction between the two women.... What Bertha has discovered is the potential life all women possess" (146). Bertha ends as she begins, with a clear sense, in her own fantasy world, of her own identity.

Like "Bliss," Virginia Woolf's "Lappin and Lapinova" highlights the link between female identity and fantasy within the context of a marriage. The story opens immediately after the protagonist's marriage: "Rosalind had still to get used to the fact that she was Mrs. Ernest Thorburn. Perhaps she never would get used to the fact that she was Mrs. Ernest Anybody" (255). Rosalind cannot retain or find a true sense of herself within the Victorian construct of marriage that the "real" world sees her as having entered into. During the honeymoon she develops a fantasy world in which her husband joins: he becomes King Lappin, an imaginary rabbit who was "above all ... a great hunter" (256), and she becomes Lapinova, a white hare, small, with "big bright eyes" (257). Initially Ernest recognizes the real Rosalind as Lapinova: "'Is that what she's called?' said Ernest—'the real Rosalind?'" (257). They return home from their honeymoon "possessed [of] a private world" and they amuse themselves by secretly creating fantasy roles for their family and friends (257). This fantasy realm sustains Rosalind: "Without that world, how, Rosalind wondered, that winter could she have lived at all?" (257–58). She dreads the sort of future symbolized by the golden wedding celebration of her parents-in-law. An orphaned only child, she is unhappy, feeling suffocated by the large Thorburn family among whom she is "a mere drop" without separate identity (258). At the celebration dinner she feels herself "being melted; dispersed; dissolved into nothingness" (259) until she sees her husband's nose twitch, signaling their happy bond in fantasy.

After two years of marriage, however, Ernest begins to withdraw from the fantasy world in which Rosalind has found her true married identity: "It took him five minutes at least to change from Ernest Thorburn to King Lappin" (260). Implicitly he starts to find her fantasy world silly and one day as she sits imagining herself as Lapinova she hears "the crack of a gun.... It was only Ernest, turning his key in the door" (262). When she cries out to him that she has lost Lapinova, he agrees: "'Yes,' he said at length. 'Poor Lapinova.... Caught in a trap ... killed,' and sat down and read the newspaper" (262). "So that was the end of that marriage" the story concludes (262). Rosalind is not able to retain a sense of her female identity within marriage because her husband is unwilling to sustain recognition of the "real" self she has found in fantasy as Lapinova. Her future, unless she develops a new fantasy for herself alone, is bleakly signaled as being culturally enforced, represented by the houses she sees along the Cromwell Road with their "steel engravings, with thick yellow lace curtains, and mahogany sideboards" (261).

The examples discussed here are illustrative of the preponderance of fantasy in short stories by women in the British tradition. What this chapter suggests is that the short story is a form particularly receptive to fantasy and that for female characters—and inherently writers—identity can often only be found or expressed within fantasy. Female characters who attempt to mesh their fantasy life, which contains their true identity, with reality find that the "real" world rejects their attempts. Reality will either not allow expression of their identity, for example, if it is violent or mannish or in other ways not culturally conformative; or, the real world will discredit fantasy itself and label such female characters silly, ignorant, or living in a self-deluding world of make-believe.

WORKS CITED

Anderson, Walter E. "The Hidden Love Triangle in Mansfield's 'Bliss.'" *Twentieth Century Literature* 28 (4) (Winter 1982): 397–404.

Bowen, Elizabeth. "The Short Story." *The Faber Book of Modern Stories.* London: Faber, 1937. 7–19

———. "The Dancing-Mistress." 1929. *Joining Charles and Other Stories.* London: Jonathan Cape, 1952. 62–76.

———. "Preface." *Stories by Elizabeth Bowen.* 1959. Rpt. in *The Mulberry Tree: Writings of Elizabeth Bowen.* Ed. Hermione Lee. London: Virago, 1986. 126–30.

Forster, E. M. *Aspects of the Novel.* 1927. Ed. Oliver Stallybrass. 1974. London: Penguin, 1990.

Gilbert, Sandra and Susan Gubar. *The Madwoman in the Attic: The Woman Writer and the Nineteenth-Century Literary Imagination.* 1979. New Haven and London: Yale University Press, 1984.

Gordimer, Nadine. "The Flash of Fireflies." 1968. Rpt. in *The New Short Story Theories.* Ed. Charles E. May. Athens: Ohio University Press, 1994. 263–67.

Hall, Radclyffe. "Miss Ogilvy Finds Herself." 1934. *The Penguin Book of Lesbian Short Stories.* Ed. Margaret Reynolds. London: Penguin, 1994. 84–103.

———. *The Well of Loneliness.* 1928. Ed. Alison Hennegan. London: Virago, 1982.

Hankin, Cherry. "Fantasy and the Sense of an Ending in the Work of Katherine Mansfield." *Modern Fiction Studies* 24 (3) (Autumn 1978): 465–74.

Jackson, Rosemary. *Fantasy: The Literature of Subversion.* 1981. London: Routledge, 1988.

Kemp, Sandra. "'But How Describe a World Seen Without a Self?' Feminism, Fiction and Modernism." *Critical Quarterly* 32 (1) (Spring 1990): 99–118.

Le Guin, Ursula. "The Child and the Shadow." 1974. Rpt. in Ursula K. Le Guin.*The Language of the Night: Essays on Fantasy and Science Fiction.* Rev. ed. Ed. Ursula K. Le Guin. London: The Women's Press, 1989. 49–59.

———. "Why Are Americans Afraid of Dragons?" 1974. Rpt. in Ursula K. Le Guin. *The Language of the Night: Essays on Fantasy and Science Fiction.* Rev. ed. Ed. Ursula K. Le Guin. London: The Women's Press, 1989. 31–36.

Lee, Hermione. "Introduction." *The Secret Self 2: Short Stories by Women.* 1987. London: Everyman, 1995. ix–xvi.

Magalaner, Marvin. "Traces of her 'Self' in Katherine Mansfield's 'Bliss.'" *Modern Fiction Studies* 24 (3) (Autumn 1978): 413–22.

Mansfield, Katherine. "Bliss." 1918. *The Complete Stories of Katherine Mansfield.* Auckland: Golden Press, 1978. 91–105.

Rhys, Jean. "Sleep it Off Lady." 1974. *The Collected Short Stories.* New York: Norton, 1987. 375–86.

Russ, Joanna. Introduction. *The Penguin Book of Modern Fantasy by Women.* Eds. Susan A. Williams and Richard Glyn Jones. London: Viking, 1995. xii–xiv.

Shaw, Valerie. *The Short Story: A Critical Introduction.* London: Longman, 1983.

Taylor, Elizabeth. "I Live in a World of Make-Believe." *Hester Lilly and Twelve Short Stories.* New York: Viking, 1954. 91–106.

Todorov, Tzvetan. *The Fantastic: A Structural Approach to a Literary Genre.* Trans. Richard Howard. Cleveland: The Press of Case Western Reserve University, 1973.

Walker, Nancy A. *Feminist Alternatives: Irony and Fantasy in the Contemporary Novel by Women.* Jackson: University of Mississippi Press, 1990.

Woolf, Virginia. "Lappin and Lapinova." 1939. *The Complete Shorter Fiction of Virginia Woolf.* Ed. Susan Dick. London: Hogarth Press, 1985. 255–62.

Zorn, Marilyn. "Visionary Flowers: Another Study of Katherine Mansfield's 'Bliss.'" *Studies in Short Fiction* 17 (1980). 141–47.

12

The Fourierist Parables of Guy Davenport

Patrick Meanor

Guy Davenport occupies a unique position in contemporary American letters, due not least of all to the fact that his accomplishments incorporate such a wide variety of multidisciplinary skills. Not only is he considered one of American literature's most respected short-story writers but he is also one of its most notable literary critics, translators, and book illustrators. He has published more than seventy stories, some the length of novellas, through nine collections. In the first four of these collections, he provided not only words but also illustrations for many of the stories. He has also published a collection of poems and translations entitled *Thasos and Ohio* (1985) and an early long poem, *Flowers and Leaves* (1966). In addition, he has published translations of Heraclitus, Diogenes, and the poets Sappho and Archilochus in *Seven Greeks*, as well as three critically acclaimed collections of essays: *The Geography of the Imagination* (1981), *Every Force Evolves a Form* (1987), and *The Hunter Gracchus and Other Papers on Literature and Art* (1997). These volumes contain sixty essays commenting on such challenging thinkers as James Joyce, Ezra Pound, Charles Olson, Ludwig Wittgenstein, and the late work of Samuel Beckett, to name a few. Few literary critics would quibble with the general consensus that he is one of the most highly respected critical minds now operating in both American and European literary circles even though his work is virtually impossible to classify because it is completely *sui generis*. The distinguished critic, George Steiner, states categorically: "The fact is that Guy Davenport is among the very few truly original, truly autonomous voices now audible in American letters. Name Guy Davenport and William Gass. There are not many others to set beside Borges, Raymond Queneau, and Calvino" (196).

Guy Davenport's first published works begin where only the most remarkable American writers end, if their work truly evolves, in mythopoesis. There is no evidence in any of his work of a thinly veiled autobiographical persona lamenting its role as victim in the existential void. His earliest fictions produce a variety of mythopoeic procedures that expand with each succeeding work in the most unpredictable and imaginative ways.

Most conspicuously, however, Guy Davenport is a practicing modernist in a postmodernist literary world. In many of his stories he uses standard modernist techniques. By using methods often associated with the visual art of collage, he juxtaposes images of the past with the present to illustrate the enduring presence of the archaic and how prehistoric energies can redeem mankind from mindless mechanization, his abiding enemy. Davenport's stories illustrate the fragmentation that takes place when human beings are disengaged from their geographical, cultural, and spiritual origins. He described to Jerome Klinkowitz his literary methods as "assemblages of history and necessary fictions" (225), thus combining Wallace Stevens's notion of a "supreme fiction" with Ezra Pound's and William Carlos Williams's reliance on an historical tradition grounded in a specific geography. Davenport told Klinkowitz that "my stories are lessons in history" (226).

Much of Davenport's fiction struggles to regenerate an Edenic innocence that "civilization" has destroyed by its abstract rationality, or what Goya called "The Sleep of Reason." The "Fall" into time, knowledge, and experience becomes the major theme of much of his fiction, or generates variations on this theme. His most distinctive and challenging work is the trilogy detailing the intensely intellectual and erotic adventures of a fictional Dutch philosopher, Adriaan van Hovendaal, and his ongoing attempt to create utopian communities based on the teachings of the French sociologist, Charles Fourier, Davenport's most important intellectual and spiritual influence. The work of Fourier can be read as a blueprint of this trilogy, which consists of the bulk of *Apples and Pears*, most of *The Jules Verne Steam Balloon*, and the longest story in *The Drummer of the Eleventh North Devonshire Fusiliers* called "Wo es war, soll ich werden." Many other stories, while not featuring the same characters as the trilogy, treat the theme of the damage done to the instinctual life by so-called "civilization" and its perverse need to destroy the desire for affection that human beings possess. The recurring motif of "apples and pears" throughout Davenport's work becomes an analogue of those in the mythic Garden of Eden; the apples symbolize the Fall of humanity and the pears, its redemption.

Davenport's ideas about the nature and function of the imagination inform his creative process from his earliest work to the present. He told Barry Alpert the imagination is "what mankind makes of things" and adds: "My theory of the imagination is this: that in the evolution of man this was the moment in which we became what we call human. That is, it's an amazing ability to see something with your eyes closed. Which is what imagination is" (3).

Though Davenport's essays cover an enormous range of topics, one principal thematic pattern consistently surfaces in both his essays and short stories. He analyzes this pattern in what many commentators see as his most comprehensive philosophic essay: "The Symbol of the Archaic," in his *Geography of the Imagination.* He proposed that humanity's redemption can be found in reawakening the individual's passion for the archaic. He describes that process as "a longing for something lost, for energies, values, and certainties unwisely abandoned by an industrial age (24).... We are just now seeing, amidst the fads and distractions, the strange fact that what has become most modern in our time was what was most archaic, and that the impulse to recover beginnings and primal energies grew out of a feeling that man in his alienation was drifting tragically away from what he had first made as poetry and design and as an understanding of the world" (28).

The longest story in his first collection *Tatlin!* is the concluding one entitled "The Dawn in Erewhon," which takes up half of the entire volume. Though an omniscient voice narrates most of the novella, a few pages are taken from the notebooks of a fictional Dutch philosopher, Adriaan van Hovendaal, who is modeled after Ludwig Wittgenstein. The title refers, of course, to Samuel Butler's satiric, pastoral Utopian novel, *Erewhon* (1872), an anagram of "nowhere."

Davenport admits that "The Dawn in Erewhon" is an updating of *Erewhon,* one of the most prophetic books of the nineteenth century. The story's specific title comes from a painting by Wyndham Lewis. In the *Vort* interview, Davenport explains the significance of the geography: "The story is set in Holland, because Holland is the nether land. Adriaan van Hovendaal is Ludwig Wittgenstein opened up. We know very little about Wittgenstein's sex life, but it seems to have been agonized and horrendous. And that he suffered a great deal because he could not absorb it. [Davenport's comments were made before the appearance of Ray Monk's 1991 biography of Wittgenstein, parts of which cover his guarded and guilt-laden homosexuality.] So I imagine a modern Dutchman who does express himself with his body as well as his mind and seems to me (or at least I want to suggest this) that he lands in an Erewhon" (10). Davenport further explains that van Hovendaal was a disciple of Charles Fourier, Samuel Butler, and the Greek philosopher, Epicurus. His name places him squarely within an Edenic mythic tradition since van Hovendaal means "gardener," which he is in the story. Adriaan symbolizes, then, Adam the first gardener of Eden and, like Adam, van Hovendaal constructs and maintains his own pastoral Utopian Erewhon.

Setting also plays a major role in this story in that Davenport chose the Netherlands both as a literal and mythic place: "Symbolically I meant him to be an Orpheus, descending into a new underworld (another reason for the Netherlands), trying to find something like the natural archaic spirit of man.... This myth is a very modern story" (10). The story is a modernized version of the mythic descent of Orpheus into Hades.

Davenport's "The Dawn in Erewhon" is an Edenic pastoral utopia modeled on Samuel Butler's *Erewhon* and Charles Fourier's utopian communities insofar as they both measure the damage that modern civilization inflects on the life of instinct. Butler satirizes the Victorian fear of sexuality and Christianity's privileging the intellect over the body. Consistent with Davenport's Fourierist theme, that of the fall from innocence into self-consciousness, van Hovendaal regenerates a Fourierist garden that redeems both spiritual and physical conditions. The mind of van Hovendaal always accommodates the desires of the body; his life is the opposite of the overly cerebral thinker lost in abstractions. His life demonstrates in great detail the many joyously affectionate activities that vivify his feeling life and transform it into forms of ecstatic consciousness, thus, regenerating Fourier's "New Harmony."

Major characters, Bruno and Kaatje, who surface in later works, first appear in "The Dawn in Erewhon," the opening story in a three-part Fourierist trilogy. They revel in their own and Adriaan's affectionate company as they enjoy each other's bodies without guilt or jealousy. This trio has become the first group that Davenport gathers into a social unit that Charles Fourier called "Little Hordes," a group whose primary duty is to fulfill its instinctual desires for pleasure. The group spends much time in camping trips to idyllic forests, eating, assigning duties, and, most importantly, doing whatever they wish. The day concludes with multiple erotic exercises which, while described in the most specific sexual language, become elaborate rituals of innocent affection. Since corrupting elements like control and aggression are forbidden in this highly structured society, Davenport's fictions become parables celebrating and maintaining innocence.

Charles Fourier, who predated Freud by a century, claimed that people could only be authentically happy if they were allowed to construct lives that embraced their instincts rather than rejecting them. Fourier, called the only true philosopher of happiness, published twelve volumes in which he outlined precisely how such a society might evolve. Many of Davenport's long fictions from "The Dawn" to "Wo es war, soll ich werden" (1990) can be read as instructive parables of regenerated innocence but only when characters live according to their deepest instinctual desires and follow certain Fourierist boundaries. Though the rhetoric may appear to allow sexual anarchy, nothing could be further from Davenport's intention. Sexual affection is healthy because it is practiced in a healthy society; "sexual outlaws" would never be permitted within Davenport's Fourierist democracy. All sexual activity must be organized and supervised in some fashion.

What Davenport has accomplished throughout his evolving mythos is to exclude any figure that even slightly resembles a "typical" hero; that is, a charismatic male who, by the force of his egotistic, aggressive power, becomes the leader or controller of a specific locale and group. The younger Bruno and Kaatje respect Adriaan not for his ability to control situations, but by his willing participation in their "passionate attraction," a key concept in Fourier. Most important, however, is that the society created by the mutual trust, love, and care among Adriaan, Bruno, and Kaatje validates the Fourierist concept of Harmony by embodying it. As long as they help each other enjoy the healthy desires of the body, they are creating what Fourier called "Sessions of the Court of Love," which regenerates a new Eden or the Fourierist "New Amorous World."

Davenport's third collection of short fiction, *Eclogues* (1981), continues his juxtaposition of ancient and modern Fourierist, pastoral narratives. The title of the collection comes from a literary form used by classical Greek and Roman poets such as Vergil and Theocritus and is synonymous with the term "pastoral," a form used by Spenser, Shakespeare, Marlowe, Milton, Shelley, Tennyson, and Matthew Arnold, among others. Davenport expands the use of the term to include lives lived under exemplary conditions. The "ideal" that Davenport proposed comes from the word's etymological root: idyll. His principal models are the *Idylls* of Theocritus, a third century (BC) Greek poet and inventor of the pastoral form, depicting the contented rustic lives of shepherds and farmers in Sicily. The Greek root of the word means "form or picture," which applies to Davenport's delicately sensual drawings of idealized figures of adolescent boys throughout much of the text.

There are important patterns throughout this set of stories, and a major figure found in all of them is that of a shepherd of some kind. The Latin root of the word "pastoral" comes from "pastor" meaning shepherd; and the stories, closer in many cases to parables and fables, embody the idea of the "pastoral." Adriaan van Hovendaal returns in "The Death of Picasso" as a guide or "shepherd" to the young Dionysiac Sander, who will eventually focus his considerable sexual energies into becoming a painter. Tullio, an older, domestic guide of the "little horde" in "On Some Lines of Vergil," is a shepherd working to help them establish an orderly but, nonetheless, pleasurable Fourierist community.

The longest and most complex narrative in the collection is the pastoral romance, "On Some Lines of Vergil," a title taken directly from one of Montaigne's essays. The piece is carefully structured, consisting of 135 sections of five stanzas or paragraphs each; every stanza is four lines long. The allusion to Vergil immediately reveals Davenport's interest in generating a Fourierist/Arcadian community. Indeed, Vergil's *Georgics* and *Eclogues* were presentations of such idealized settings. George Steiner calls this montage "one of the most hilarious, tenderly risque accounts of sexual awakening in all modern literature" (199).

In the pastoral romance, the setting is Bordeaux, an ancient, southwestern French city and the birthplace of such famous painters as Rosa Bonheur and Odilon Redon; and writers like Francois Mauriac, Montesquieu, and most importantly, Montaigne. The artist, Goya, though not a native of Bordeaux, painted some of his later works there. Davenport carefully points out that Rosa Bonheur's *The Horse Fair* and Goya's *The Bulls of Bordeaux* are unconscious ideogrammatic manifestations of the horses and bulls found in the Caves of

Lascaux, another instance of how the modern imagination is always grounded in the archaic. Tullio, the scholar-shepherd, exhorts his "little horde" of four that true history is actually the history of attention, and that his deepest desire is "to write a history of the imagination in our time ... . All things need to be reseen [in light of the archaic]. The new modifies everything before, and even finds a tradition for the first time" (221).

The Little Horde in this sensual Arcadia consists of four French teenagers: Jonquille, Jolivet, Michel, and the barely adolescent Victor. In the midst of their frequent affectionate games, they venture to one of the ancient caves near Bordeaux, accompanied by Tullio, a mature and responsible married adult. Davenport, though giving his adolescents great sexual freedom, always stations an older scholar nearby to direct their erotic play toward discovering "the other." Tullio, the shepherd in this eclogue and whose name obviously derives from Marcus Tullius Cicero (known throughout the ancient world as "Tully"), serves as their intellectual and spiritual guide in helping them understand the selfless nature of friendship. Cicero wrote definitive essays on friendship (*De amicitia,* 44 BC) and old age (*De senectute,* 44 BC) which became handbooks on Stoic philosophy. Youth and friendship are better understood and appreciated if viewed against the background of old age, just as the preliterate tableaux in the caves of Lascaux adumbrate the later works of Bonheur, Picasso, Klee, and Goya. Tullio, besides teaching his little horde the history of the imagination and its connection to the archaic, further expands his ongoing lesson into what constitutes "true" history: "Rings of trees, giving their age, is first mentioned as a fact by Montaigne, though suspected by Leonardo. Tullio says Montaigne learned about them from a goldsmith in Italy who, it has been recently discovered, was an apprentice in Leonardo's studio" (228). "True" history, then, is the history of attention; that is, of attending to all forms of report, particularly oral and visual folk wisdom. In short, knowledge is one, and all things are, quite literally, connected.

Most critics would agree that Guy Davenport's fourth collection of stories, *Apples and Pears and Other Stories* (1984), is his masterpiece. The 233-page novella, *Apples and Pears,* constitutes the single most elaborately constructed fiction that he has yet produced. None of his earlier work rivals its richness, diversity, and brilliance, nor documents the enormous scope of his intellectual terrain. It constitutes Davenport's ultimate mythos, strongly influenced by Butler's *Erewhon* and patterned throughout by Charles Fourier's vision of *New Harmony;* its four-part structure is Davenport's most successful adaptation of Fourier's Utopian vision.

The major consciousness throughout most of the text is the same fictional Dutch philosopher, Adamic gardener, and essayist on Butler's *Erewhon,* Adriaan van Hovendaal. New members double the Fourierist "horde" into eight participants, including Adriaan, characters from previous works, Sander, Bruno, and Kaatje, while new adolescents Jan, Hans, Saartje, and Sander's sister, Grietje, enter the emerging phalansteries.

The work is, quite simply, a Fourierist treatise. The work's four major sections follow his four-part structure of an ideal society that he called "The Harmony of the Four Movements"; he divides them up into categories of the social, the animal, the organic, and the material. The four chapters of Davenport's work generally follow the same scheme. Adriaan calls section one "An Erewhonian Sketchbook" and uses a Napoleonic rather than a Gregorian calendar redesignating the months Messidor (July), Thermidor (August), and Fructidor (September). The name changes of the months heralded the arrival of the "New Harmonious World" which, Fourier assumed, was supposed to follow the French Revolution. Critic Bruce Bawer, better than most critics, clearly uncovers the Fourierist structure upon which the work rests: "The vision in question (which Fourier spent most of his life constructing) was of a Utopia called Harmonium, where man's natural virtue (as posited by Rousseau, and believed in devoutly by Fourier) would, through the eliminations of the tensions which destroy human society, be permitted to prevail, and where, as a result, everyone would live in peace, happiness, and harmony" (242). And since, as Rousseau believed, man was born intrinsically good and sex was one of humanity's most natural impulses, a society in which the passions were permitted full expression would necessarily become a regenerated Garden of Eden, or Fourier's "New Harmonium."

Davenport translates the key line from Fourier's twelve-volume work that summarizes his entire philosophy of social happiness: "The series distributes the harmonies. The attractions are proportionate to our destinies" (200). The series, to Fourier and Davenport, are groups, or phalansteries, which operate democratically and are drawn together by mutual attractions. As long as the members of the group are permitted to act upon their mutually passionate attraction toward others, order and balance are established and Harmony reigns. These harmonious conjunctions take place continuously throughout *Apples and Pears,* as the members of the group, gently guided by Adriaan, combine in multiple sexual couplings. *Apples and Pears* has become Davenport's definitive "history of affection" as brilliantly structured and detailed as anything he ever wrote. Davenport elaborates on some of Fourier's philosophical lines with great verbal flair: "The Vestals in white tunics and cloth Mongol boots have long hair embroidered sweatband bound. The series flows from rambunctious to shy, from impatience to placidity, with the attractions distributed thus: forward scouts practiced in kissing wiggly embraces, grubby foreplay through half dozen precocious and whiffety orgasms as yet vagrom enough to surge from nape to coccyx in boys, from nipples to clitoris in girls, or chime from scalp to toes and fingers in both" (70).

Butler's Erewhonian tenets are intermingled with Fourierist principles throughout the series of parables that make up much of *Apples and Pears* since both philosophers see mechanization as the enemy: "Sweetbrier agrees, wryly, that no phalanstery anything like Fourier's is possible without an Erewhonian revolution, canceling machines.... To take happiness from money and restore it to the harmony of work and its ... reward.... To reorganize society after its disastrous dispersal by train, automobile, airplane .... All work became pandering to the reproduction of the machines" (163). In the first story in *Apples and Pears* van Hovendaal is guiding the young Sander around Paris and detailing its riches through a Proustian lens and, in keeping with his consistent interest in origins, detects Proust's subtext in one of Epicurus's most famous quotations: "I know nothing of the good except the deliciousness of food, sex, music, and the sight of beautiful bodies in graceful motion" (87). No single sentence could better express the subject matter, theme and tone of *Apples and Pears* than Epicurus's ancient quotation.

Guy Davenport's fifth volume is a collection of nine short stories entitled *The Jules Verne Steam Balloon* (1987). Four of the nine are connected within the collection since some of the same characters appear in all four, thus expanding Davenport's mythic parameters even further, and some characters appeared in *Apples and Pears.* The mythos has moved from South to North, from the Netherlands to Denmark, but youthful beauty and charm continue to dictate the action. "The Meadow," "The Bicycle Rider," "The Jules Verne Steam Balloon," and the concluding story, "The Ringdove Sign," are all parables of innocence involving the same Fourierist ritual camping trips to idyllic forests where they enjoy each other's bodies in clean, childlike erotic celebration. New adolescents join the "little horde" such as Pascal, Hugo, Franklin, Mariana, Kim, and Anders, but the purpose of their projects remain the same: the more sensually comfortable adolescents help those fearful of their impulses to feel more at home in their bodies. Only in "The Bicycle Rider" does evil, for the first time, enter the organized affection of the group. One of the most attractive young men has become a drug addict, a condition that has rendered him incapable of participating in the rich, emotional life around him. More importantly, his addiction has also made him sexually indifferent. And since the social dynamics of this Fourierist phalanstery are predicated on the passional attractions among the group, he becomes the outcast and eventually dies.

There is, in *The Jules Verne Steam Balloon,* not only a new geo-mythical setting from the sensually alluring underworld of the Netherlands to the "northern idyll" of Denmark but, as importantly, a recognition of evil strikes a new moral tone in Davenport's fictions. Indeed, some of the characters in these Fourierist stories are clearly allegorical, and may lose their human qualities by becoming types. The opposite is the case, however. Hugo Tvemunding, the major character in "The Bicycle Rider," "The Jules Verne Steam Balloon," and "The Ringdove Sign," is one of Davenport's most human characters. All three of these Fourierist parables are organized around Hugo's conflict between his calling to both the ministry and to his vocation as an artist. He is the son of a Protestant minister, a doctoral student in theology, a classics instructor at a Danish folk high school, and a budding artist. He also bears some similarity to another Dane, Soren Kierkegaard, and the modern liberal Dutch priest-theologian, Edward Schillebeeckx. Kierkegaard's agonized musings over what constitutes "good and evil" mirror Hugo's conflicts when confronted with the unambiguous evil of drug addiction and other escapist schemes such as "McTaggart's Transcendental Meditation Group." And Edward Schillebeeckx's attempt to move Roman Catholic theology away from its long-standing obsession with medieval Scholastic abstractions toward a renewed focus on the experience of a Christian consciousness within a caring community, parallels Hugo Tvemunding's project to teach his students that heightened consciousness within a loving fellowship is one of life's greatest rewards. Schillebeeckx also exhorted his fellow Catholics to shift from an exhausted patriarchal paradigm for God to a fraternal one with Jesus as the model of friend and brother. He became a kind of Christological Fourierist figure in the 1960s when he organized sixty of his students at the University of Louvain into a work-study group and functioned as both their theology professor and spiritual director. He lived with them and insisted that they authenticate their Christian values by caring for displaced persons on the East German border. Hugo Tvemunding is certainly the successor to Adriaan van Hovendaal, but with more than a little of Edward Schillebeeckx's vivid charismatic energy.

Davenport's symbols converge in the concluding story, "The Ringdove Sign," when Hugo's scriptural studies reveal the interconnectedness of seemingly disparate elements. Once he discovers that "daimons" are angelic messengers and thus, the true identity of Tumble, Quark, and Buckeye and their arrival in a pear-shaped balloon, he begins to understand the whole story: "And the daimon had, in one of the longest traditions we can trace in the Mediterranean, a bird form. A dove. More than any other folktale, Yeshua mentions the sign of Jonas. That is, the sign of the dove. Jonas means 'dove'" (140). The "light" alluded to throughout the story and resonating with Paracletean echoes symbolizes the creative light inspiring Hugo to become both an artist and a minister; it also stands for the possibility of the union of the "inner light" with the "outer" or, as Hugo's father, Pastor Tvemunding, puts it at the end of "The Ringdove Sign": "I agree with you ... about the light up here. It finds something in our souls" (149).

And, finally, all of these geometric figures are variations on "pears" which, in Davenport's mythic world, stand for redemption. In this story, the redemption is clearly an aesthetic-spiritual one as Joseph Schopp points out: "Only through art, composed and combined in a new harmony, is the chaos of life transformed and transcended" (135). In short, the imagination becomes the redemptive agent. Davenport's pear-like balloon closely resembles a figure that Wallace Stevens evokes in his definition of the imagination: "It is a violence from within that protects us from a violence without. It is the imagination pressing back against the pressure of reality" (36). Like a balloon.

The sixth volume of Davenport's, containing four stories and a novella, is entitled *The Drummer of the Eleventh North Devonshire Fusiliers* (1990). While "Colin Maillard" and "Badger" both deal with the passional attraction between preadolescent boys, the novella, "Wo es war, soll ich werden," continues the activities of the expanding Fourierist phalanstery. Davenport also informs his reader that "Wo es war" is the conclusion of a trilogy composed of *Apples and Pears* and *The Jules Verne Steam Balloon.*

Of course, the activities remain the same, as do some of the characters, but a deeper philosophical and moral note characterizes both the dialogue and general discussion of the group. Davenport explicates for the reader some of his thematic concerns through a character named Allen in the story "Badger," who explains the Fall that takes place when one enters adolescence: "What you see, you know, Allen said, you own. You take it in. Everything's an essence ... at twelve you understand everything. Afterward, you have to give it up and specialize" (21–22). Most important, however, is Hugo's explanation of the title of the novella, "Wo es war, soll ich werden," a phrase from Sigmund Freud that Jacques Lacan, the eminent French psychoanalyst, said contained "pre-Socratic eloquence." And the pre-Socratics are Davenport's philosophical heroes throughout his work. Hugo translates it as: "where it was, there must I begin to be." Holger mistakenly interprets it as another proof that "genius is a disease: Mann's paradox" (61). Thomas Mann's *Death in Venice* and *Doctor Faustus* being notable examples of German Romantic Agony. Hugo kindly corrects Holger by clarifying Freud's statement: "No, no, Hugo said. Freud meant that a wound, healing, can command the organism's whole attention, and thus become the beginning of a larger health" (61). Hugo Tvemunding comprehensively summarizes Davenport's fictive and philosophical enterprise: all of his Fourierist parables of innocence attempt to disengage the lively and erotic celebration of the body from its endemic Judeo-Christian death wish. Western civilization need not end in apocalyptic self-immolation.

In the title story of Davenport's latest collection, *The Cardiff Team* (1996), two twelve-year-old boys, Walt and Sam, are informed by their eighteen-year-old guardian/shepherd, Marc, that their walk through the Bois de Boulogne is the very same one taken by the elderly anthropologist, Claude Levy-Bruhl, and the retired Lutheran missionary and ethnographer, Pastor Maurice Leenhardt, fifty years earlier. They then discuss what this "little horde" of four youngsters are discussing today: the relationship of sexuality to the life of the spirit. Pastor Leenhardt had little luck in converting the natives of New Caledonia: "rather, he was converted by them ... . He changed Levy-Bruhl's ideas about the savage mind. They were great friends, and had long walks in the Bois practically every afternoon, two wonderful old men who recognized each other's humanity" (164–165).

Marc, in his capacity as tutor/shepherd of Walt, Sam, and now the even younger Cyril, recognizes that their "little horde" of four occupy not only the same physical space previously traveled by Levy-Bruhl and Pastor Leenhardt fifty years earlier, but are learning similar spiritual lessons—the function of parables. Marc finds the archaic once again surfacing in the present: "One of the things I learned at your age was that finding about what's in books and the world and feeling great in my pants were cooperative. I thought it was just me, the way I was. Mind and body are alive together. And here we are with ants, midges, and ground spiders. The sun is delicious. A warmth with kindness in it" (163).

Guy Davenport reveres Charles Fourier for the same reasons that Andre Breton, the founder of Surrealism, honored him with an ode. All three artists regenerate forms of prelapsarian innocence and see the world with a childlike sense of the marvelous; they celebrate life in all of its ecstatic physicality. Davenport's mythic procedures a la Fourier revivify the endless capacities of the imagination, with pleasure as the primary purpose, to eradicate the entropic deadness of mechanization, to replace the Narcissistic "Demon self" with the "Daimon light" of "the other"; and to celebrate, at all times, the renaissance of the archaic.

Bruce Bawer, in *Diminishing Fictions,* once again extols his work for its clear excellence: "And make no mistake about it, Davenport's contribution is considerable. At a time in history when the prime criterion of excellence in American short fiction seems to be a sort of mindless, impersonal monotonousness, Guy Davenport's inimitable adventures in the realms of philosophy, language, and literary form are to be treasured. Davenport at his best reminds us of how exciting and valuable literary innovation can be. And he does something else that is even more important: he reminds us of our humanity, and ... of the importance of affection" (244).

Here is one of the finest examples, from *Apples and Pears,* of Davenport's ability to combine philosophical comment with some of the most exquisitely crafted prose in American literature. The passage, better than most, embodies the ecstatic vision of Charles Fourier's wish that life is always celebration:

> Rilkean angels, complex essences in a wind of light, fibrous with articulate memories, accidental events enriched into significance, a cherished smile, a long afternoon, a concupiscent dream, disappointments salvaged by courage, are the quiring that Fourier saw as a destiny of attractions. They are harmonies of essences. They are kin to us. They are messengers in that the composite knows how to appropriate the random, knows what to do with lost time, with the found moment, with a memory of apples on an autumn afternoon, of pears eaten at a kitchen table, longing in our eyes (178).

WORKS CITED

Alpert, Barry. "Interview with Guy Davenport." *Vort,* 3, No. 3, 1976: 3–17.

Bawer, Bruce. *Diminishing Fictions.* Saint Paul, Minn.: Graywolf Press: 1988.

Davenport, Guy. *Apples and Pears and Other Stories.* San Francisco: North Point Press, 1984.

———. *The Cardiff Team.* New York: New Directions Press, 1996.

———. *The Drummer of the Eleventh North Devonshire Fusiliers.* San Francisco: North Point Press, 1990.

———. *Eclogues.* San Francisco: North Point Press, 1981.

———. *The Geography of the Imagination.* New York: Pantheon, 1992.

———. *The Jules Verne Steam Balloon.* San Francisco: North Point Press, 1987.

Klinkowitz, Jerome. "Guy Davenport." *Contemporary Novelists.* Chicago: St. James Press (1991): 224–226.

Schopp, Joseph. "'Perfect Landscape with Pastoral Figures': Guy Davenport's Danish Eclogue a la Fourier." *Facing Texts,* ed. Heide Ziegler (Durham & London: Duke University Press: 1988): 128–139.

Steiner, George. "Rare Bird." *The New Yorker,* November 30, 1981: 196, 199–202, 204.

Stevens, Wallace. *The Necessary Angel.* New York: Random House, 1951.

Selected Bibliography

Allen, Walter. *The Short Story in English.* New York: Oxford University Press, 1981.

Anderson, Sherwood. *A Story Teller's Story.* New York: Huebsch, 1924.

Baldeshwiler, Eileen. "The Lyric Short Story: The Sketch of a History." *Studies in Short Fiction* 6 (1969).

Bayley, John. *The Short Story: Henry James to Elizabeth Bowen.* Brighton, UK: Harvester Press, 1988.

Birbalsingh, Frank, ed. *Frontiers of Caribbean Literature in English.* New York: St. Martin's, 1996.

Bonheim, Helmut. *The Narrative Modes: Techniques of the Short Story.* Cambridge, U.K.: D. S. Brewer, 1982.

Brown, Suzanne Hunter. "'Tess' and *Tess:* An Experiment in Genre." *Modern Fiction Studies* 28.1 (Spring 1982).

Conde, Mary, and Thorunn Lonsdale, eds. *Caribbean Women Writers: Fiction in English.* New York: St. Martin's, 1999.

Crowley, Donald. *The American Short Story, 1850–1900.* Boston: Twayne, 1989.

Current-Garcia, E. *The American Short Story before 1850.* Boston: Twayne, 1985.

Dance, Daryl Cumber. *New World Adams: Conversations with Contemporary West Indian Writers.* Leeds, Yorkshire: Peepal Tree, 1992.

Dunn, Maggie, and Ann Morris. *The Composite Novel: The Short Story Cycle in Transition.* Boston: Twayne, 1995.

Exjenbaum, Boris. "O. Henry and the Theory of the Short Story." *Reading in Russian Poetics.* Ed. L. Matejka and K. Pomorska. Trans. I. R. Titunik. Cambridge, Mass.: MIT Press, 1971.

Ferguson, Suzanne. "Defining the Short Story: Impressionism and Form." *Modern Fiction Studies* 28.1 (Spring 1982).

Fusco, Richard. *Maupassant and the American Short Story.* University Park: Pennsylvania State University Press, 1994.

Gerlach, John. *Toward the End: Closure and Structure in the American Short Story.* Tuscaloosa: University of Alabama Press, 1985.

Gordimer, Nadine. *Writing and Being.* Cambridge, Mass.: Harvard University Press, 1995.

Gullason, Thomas. "Revelation and Evolution: A Neglected Dimension of the Short Story." *Studies in Short Fiction* 10 (1973).

———. "The Short Story: An Underrated Art." *Studies in Short Fiction* 1 (1964).

———. "The Short Story: Revision and Renewal." *Studies in Short Fiction* 19 (1982).

Hanson, Clare, ed. *Re-editing the Short Story.* New York: St. Martin's, 1989.

———. *Short Stories and Short Fictions, 1880–1980.* London: Macmillan, 1985.

Head, Dominic. *The Modernist Short Story.* Cambridge, England: Cambridge University Press, 1992.

Hemingway, Ernest. *Death in the Afternoon.* New York: Scribner's, 1932.

Iftekharrudin, Farhat, Mary Rohrberger, and Maurice Lee, eds. *Speaking of the Short Story.* Jackson: University Press of Mississippi, 1997.

Ingram, Forrest. *Representative Short Story Cycles of the Twentieth Century: Studies in a Literary Genre.* The Hague: Mouton, 1971.

James, Louis. *Caribbean Literature in English.* New York: Longman, 1999.

King, Bruce. *The New English Literatures: Cultural Nationalism in a Changing World.* New York: St. Martin's, 1980.

———, Ed. *New National and Post-colonial Literatures: An Introduction.* Oxford: Clarendon Press, 1996.

———. *West Indian Literature.* Hamden, Conn.: Archon Books, 1979.

Lane, Dorothy F. *The Island as Site of Resistance: An Examination of Caribbean and New Zealand Texts.* New York: Lang, 1995.

Levy, Andrew. *The Culture and Commerce of the American Short Story.* Cambridge, England: Cambridge University Press, 1993.

Lohafer, Susan. *Coming to Terms with the Short Story.* Baton Rouge: Louisiana State University Press, 1983.

Lohafer, Susan, and J. E. Clarey, eds. *Short Story Theory at a Crossroads.* Baton Rouge: Louisiana State University Press, 1989.

Lounsberry, Barbara, Susan Lohafer, Mary Rohrberger, Stephen Pett, and R. C. Feddersen, eds. *The Tales We Tell: Perspectives on the Short Story.* Westport, Conn.: Greenwood, 1998.

Mann, Susan Garland. *The Short Story Cycle: A Genre Companion and Reference Guide.* New York: Greenwood, 1989.

Mansfield, Katherine. *Journal of Katherine Mansfield.* Ed. J. Middleton Murry. New York: Knopf, 1946.

Markham, E. A. "Introduction." *The Penguin Book of Caribbean Short Stories.* Ed. E. A. Markham. London: Penguin, 1996.

Matthews, Brander. *Philosophy of the Short-Story.* New York: Longmans, 1901.

May, Charles E. *Edgar Allan Poe: A Study of the Short Fiction.* Boston: Twayne, 1991.

———. "The Nature of Knowledge in Short Fiction." *Studies in Short Fiction* 21 (1984).

———. ed. *The New Short Story Theories.* Athens: Ohio University Press, 1976.

———. ed. *Short Story Theories.* Athens: Ohio University Press, 1976.

———. *The Short Story: The Reality of Artifice.* Boston: Twayne, 1995.

———. *Twentieth Century European Short Story: An Annotated Bibliography.* Pasadena, Calif.: Salem, 1989.

McClave, Heather, ed. *Women Writers of the Short Story.* Englewood Cliffs, N.J.: Prentice-Hall, 1980.

Nagel, James. *The Contemporary American Short-Story Cycle: The Ethnic Resonance of Genre.* Baton Rouge: Louisiana State University Press, 2001.

O'Connor, Frank. *The Lonely Voice.* London: Macmillan, 1963.

Pascoe, Allan H. "On Defining Short Stories." *New Literary History* 22.2 (Spring 1991).

Pattee, Fred Lewis. *The Development of the American Short Story.* New York: Biblo & Tannen, 1970.

Poe, Edgar A. *The Complete Works of Edgar Allan Poe.* Ed. J. A. Harrison. New York: AMS, 1965.

Reid, Ian. *The Short Story.* London: Methuen, 1977.

Rohrberger, Mary. *Hawthorne and the Modern Short Story.* The Hague: Mouton, 1966.

Rohrberger, Mary, and Dan Burns. "Short Fiction and the Numinous Realm: Another Attempt at Definition." *Modern Fiction Studies* 28.1 (1982).

Shaw, Valerie. *The Short Story: A Critical Introduction.* London: Longman, 1983.

Shklovsky, Viktor. *Theory of Prose.* Trans. Benjamin Sher. Elmwood Park, Ill.: Dalkey Press, 1990.

Smitten, Jeffrey R., and Ann Daghistany, eds. *Spatial Form in Narrative.* Ithaca, N.Y.: Cornell University Press, 1981.

Tallack, Douglas. *The Nineteenth-Century American Short Story.* London: Routledge, 1993.

Voss, Arthur. *The American Short Story: A Critical Survey.* Norman: University of Oklahoma Press, 1973.

Welty, Eudora. "The Reading and Writing of Short Stories," *Atlantic Monthly.* February 1949: 54–58; March 1949: 46–49.

Wright, Austin. *The American Short Story in the Twenties.* Chicago: University of Chicago Press, 1961.

Index

About the Editors and Contributors

JOSEPH BOYDEN was born and raised in Ontario, Canada. He received his undergraduate degree in Humanities and Creative Writing from York University in Toronto and his M.F.A. from the University of New Orleans. His first collection of stories, *Born with a Tooth,* was published by Cormorant Books in the spring of 2001.

ARTHUR A. BROWN has published essays on Edgar Allan Poe, Henry James, William Faulkner, and Raymond Carver in *Nineteenth-Century Literature, Mississippi Quarterly, Studies in Short Fiction, American Literary Realism, Colby Quarterly,* and *Critique.* He is a contributor to *A William Faulkner Encyclopedia* (1999). His one-act play "Augustina" was selected by Horton Foote as the winner of the 1999 Arts & Letters Drama Prize and published in *Arts & Letters* (Spring 2000), and his poem "Premonition" was a finalist in the 2001 Howard Nemerov Sonnet Award, sponsored by *The Formalist.* He is an Associate Professor of English at the University of Evansville, Indiana, where he teaches American literature and creative writing.

MARY CARNEY is a Marion L. Brittain Teaching Fellow at Georgia Institute of Technology. She is a Ph.D. candidate at the University of Georgia and will complete her dissertation entitled "Edith Wharton and the Incongruities of War" in the spring of 2002. She has published articles on Emily Dickinson and Lewis Nordan.

DONNA J. DAVIS works as a professional/technical writer for a private, nonprofit organization. After completing double Master's in American Studies and

Speech at the University of Michigan at the beginning of her career, she taught college speech, English, and humanities. In 2001 she completed a Master's degree in English at the University of Northern Iowa with an emphasis in multicultural literature, a field in which her research, writing, and teaching interests converge.

SUZANNE FERGUSON is the Samuel B. and Virginia C. Knight Professor of Humanities Emerita from Case Western Reserve University in Cleveland, Ohio. Her theoretical and historical essays on the short story have appeared in *James Joyce Quarterly, Modern Fiction Studies, Studies in Short Fiction,* and *Studies in the Short Story in English,* as well as the collections *Short Story Theory at a Crossroads, The New Short Story Theories,* and *Creative and Critical Approaches to the Short Story*. Her current work concerns what she calls "anti-sequences," groups of stories that subvert traditional ideas of "the short story cycle." She has also written on Randall Jarrell, poems about paintings, and recent Native American fiction.

ADRIENNE GAVIN is a Principal Lecturer in English at Canterbury Christ Church University College, United Kingdom, where she is course director for Victorian Literature and Children's Literature. She has wide-ranging research interests in the fields of Children's Literature, Victorian Literature, the Short Story, and Women's Writing, and is interested in links between literature, law, and crime. She has published on Elizabeth Gaskell, D.H. Lawrence, Anna Sewell, and Charles Dickens, and is coeditor of the collection of critical essays *Mystery in Children's Literature: From the Rational to the Supernatural.* She is currently writing a literary biography of Anna Sewell.

ANDREA O'REILLY HERRERA is the Director of the Ethnic Studies Program, as well as a professor of literature at the University of Colorado at Colorado Springs. In addition to being a published poet and creative writer, she is the author of a number of critical essays on a host of writers ranging from Charlotte Brontë and Harriet Jacobs to Cristina García and Sandra Cisneros. Her most recent publications include a collection of testimonial expressions drawn from the Cuban exile community and their children residing in the United States, *Remembering Cuba: Legacy of a Diaspora* (2001) and a novel *The Pearl of the Antilles* (2001), which chronicles the lives of four generations of Cuban and Cuban American women.

FARHAT IFTEKHARRUDIN is Associate Professor of English and Dean of the College of Liberal Arts and Sciences at the University of Texas at Brownsville. He is the editor of the literary journal *Short Story.* His research interests include postmodernism, minimalism, magic realism, and feminist issues in contemporary literature. He has published articles and papers on such authors as Salman Rushdie, Isabelle Allende, Bharati Mukherjee, and Rudolfo Anaya.

DONNA JARRELL was a mother and homemaker for sixteen years. She began writing novels and short stories while her three sons were in elementary school. At age 34 she applied to Case Western Reserve University where she earned a B.A. in English and Psychology in 1999. She is grateful to her mentors at CWRU, in particular, Dr. Suzanne Ferguson and Miss Mary Grimm. In June 2002, Donna will earn an M.F.A. from Ohio State University.

JOSEPH LONGO is an Instructor of English at the University of New Orleans. He received a B.A. in English from Rhode Island College and an M.F.A. from the University of New Orleans. His short fiction has been published in *PRISM: International* and in the anthology *French Quarter Fiction.* He has reviewed books for *Gambit Weekly* and films for *Where Y'at* magazine. Currently, he is working on *S.I.N.*, a novel.

PATRICK MEANOR was recently appointed to the rank of Distinguished Teaching Professor of English, the highest honor the State University of New York can bestow. He has taught at the State University of New York College at Oneonta for twenty-eight years, where he teaches courses in James Joyce, the Beat Generation, and the American Short Story. He has published *John Cheever Revisited* (1995) and *Bruce Chatwin* (1997). He edited Volume 130 of the *Dictionary of Literary Biography: American Short-Story Writers Since WWII* and coedited Volumes 218, 234, and 244. He has also published three previous essays on the short stories of Guy Davenport. He has served as Chair of the Graduate Program in English and as Chair of the English Department.

DONALD PETESCH is on the faculty of the Department of English at the University of Pittsburgh where he teaches American Literature and Afro-American Literature. His awards include a National Endowment for the Humanities postdoctoral research grant in Afro-American Studies and a Fulbright teaching grant to Mexico. His *A Spy in the Enemy's Country: The Emergence of Modern Black Literature* has been named an outstanding book on the subject of human rights in the United States by the Gustavus Myers Center.

CATHERINE RAMSDELL received her Ph.D. in English Literature from Auburn University in 2000. She is currently a Professor of Liberal Arts at the Savannah College of Art and Design.

MARY ROHRBERGER, Adjunct Professor of English at the University of New Orleans, received her Ph.D. from Tulane University with a dissertation on the short story called *Hawthorne and the Modern Literary Short Story.* A book with the same title was published in 1968. Since then she has published or has currently in press more than a dozen books and some 350 articles. She has received both teaching and research awards and was recently honored with a Festschrift presented to her by her colleagues in the field of the short story.

During her career she has been both teacher and administrator. She is the Executive Editor of the journal *Short Story,* Director of the Society for the Study of the Short Story, and Founder and Executive Director of a series of international conferences on the short story in English.

RIVANNE SANDLER was born and currently resides in Toronto, Canada, where she teaches in the Department of Near & Middle Eastern Civilization at the University of Toronto. Her writings deal with aspects of modern Iranian literary culture and include articles on writers and censorship in Iran during the 1960s–1970s, modern Iranian poetry, Iranian women's poetry in the first half of the twentieth century, literary developments in Iran prior to the 1978 revolution, stories and poetry by expatriate Iranians, and the changing concept of the individual in Middle Eastern society. She was the literary editor for a book of short stories and poems by an Iranian writer published in Toronto.

DAVID SHERIDAN is a Lecturer III at the University of Michigan's Sweetland Writing Center, where he helps to develop programs related to writing and technology. Recent articles include "Digital Detroit and the Frail Particulars of Everyday Life" in *Literacy and Technology* and "Making Sense of Detroit" in the *Michigan Quarterly Review*. His fiction and poetry have been published in journals like *Dispatch Detroit* and the *Beloit Poetry Journal.*